VOICES

FOR

ANIMAL

LIBERATION

INSPIRATIONAL ACCOUNTS BY ANIMAL RIGHTS ACTIVISTS

BRITTANY MICHELSON

FOREWORD BY INGRID NEWKIRK

Skyhorse Publishing

Skyhorse Publishing books may be purchased in bulk at special discounts for sales promotion, corporate gifts, fund-raising, or educational purposes. Special editions can also be created to specifications. For details, contact the Special Sales Department, Skyhorse Publishing, 307 West 36th Street, 11th Floor, New York, NY 10018 or info@skyhorsepublishing.com.

Skyhorse® and Skyhorse Publishing® are registered trademarks of Skyhorse Publishing, Inc.®, a Delaware corporation.

Visit our website at www.skyhorsepublishing.com.

10 9 8 7 6 5 4 3 2 1

Library of Congress Cataloging-in-Publication Data is available on file.

Cover design by Daniel Brount
Cover illustrations by Corey J. Rowland

Print ISBN: 978-1-5107-5126-2
Ebook ISBN: 978-1-5107-5128-6

Printed in China

*This book is dedicated to all of the exploited animals,
whose liberation is my greatest dream, and to the humans
who are working hard to make this dream a reality.*

TABLE OF CONTENTS

Foreword
Ingrid Newkirk, founder and president of PETA
xi

Introduction
xv

I. Seasoned Warriors: Inspiring & Transforming
1

How I Became a "Poultry" Rights Activist Who Started
an Organization Some Said Would Never Fly
Karen Davis, founder of United Poultry Concerns
3

Documenting Invisible Animals: Photography
as a Tool for Change
Jo-Anne McArthur, photographer and founder of We Animals Media
12

The Spectrum of Life: Not the Same but Equal
Shaun Monson, documentary filmmaker
18

Ending Bear Bile Farming: A Clarion Call
Jill Robinson, founder and CEO of Animals Asia
26

Liberating Animals and Ourselves
Will Tuttle, visionary author and speaker
32

II. Connecting the Dots: Perspectives on Animal Rights
41

Copy-and-Paste Activism Does Not Work: Perspectives from a POC
Gwenna Hunter, event coordinator for Vegan Outreach
and founder of Vegans of LA
43

Living in Alignment with My Values: My Path
to Animal Rights Activism
Brittany Michelson, teacher and writer
51

How I Made the Connection: Gay Rights,
Feminism, and Animal Liberation
Dani Rukin, citizen journalist for *JaneUnchained News*
62

The Girl I Finally Let In: How Personal Narrative Sets the
Stage for Powerful Animal Rights Activism
Jasmin Singer, cofounder of Our Hen House and Senior
Features Editor for *VegNews*
71

The Evolution: From Animal-Loving Child to Intersectional
Vegan Activist
Gillian Meghan Walters, founder of *Animal Voices Vancouver*
79

III. Overcoming Personal Challenge: Opening the Door to Activism
89

Through Empathic Eyes: A Survivor's Story
Jasmine Afshar, army veteran
91

From Addiction to Healing to Activism: An Olympic
Medalist's Journey
Dotsie Bausch, Olympic medalist and founder of Switch4Good
100

Giving My Struggle Purpose:
Overcoming Depression through Animal Advocacy
Matthew Braun, former investigator of farms and slaughterhouses
106

Activism as a Fast Track to Growth: My Spiritual Awakening
Zafir Molina, truth seeker and movement artist
114

How Veganism Transformed My Relationship with Food
Alexandra Paul, actress and cohost of *Switch4Good*
120

IV. Campaigns & Outreach: Anchors of Change
127

How to Speak about Animal Rights: What I Learned
from Working in Corporate Sales
Alex Bez, founder and director of Amazing Vegan Outreach
129

Lost Souls: Fighting the Harms of Animal
Experimentation and beyond
Cory Mac a'Ghobhainn, organizer with Progress for Science
139

The Least We Can Do: Communicating the Animal Rights Message
Natasha & Luca, "That Vegan Couple," social media influencers
150

Saving Joe and Legal Wins for Captive Animals
Brittany Peet, Director of Captive Animal Law Enforcement for PETA
157

V. Bearing Witness, Civil Disobedience &
Open Rescue: A Movement Rising
167

The Power of Protest: Learning from Nonviolent
Social Justice Movements
Chase Avior, actor and filmmaker
169

Bearing Witness to Babies before and after Motherhood
Amy Jean Davis, founder of Los Angeles Animal Save
178

Turning Repression into Liberation
Wayne Hsiung, cofounder of Direct Action Everywhere (DxE)
182

The Power and Duty of Bearing Witness
Anita Krajnc, founder of the Save Movement
187

The Urgency of Animal Liberation: A Teenage Activist's Perspective
Zoe Rosenberg, founder of Happy Hen Animal Sanctuary
198

VI. The Sanctuary Life: To Heaven from Hell
209

Farm Sanctuaries: Healing Animals, the Planet, and Ourselves
Gene Baur, founder of Farm Sanctuary
211

In the Steps of Giants: Saving Elephants in Southeast Asia
Saengduean Lek Chailert, founder of Save Elephant Foundation
217

Our Partners, the Animals: The Power of Personal Connection
Kathy Stevens, founder of Catskill Animal Sanctuary
222

Nonstop Loving: An Ode to Activists
Sean Hill, award-winning multidisciplinary artist and humanitarian
227

Closing
235

About the Author
239

About the Contributors
241

Acknowledgments
253

Resources
255

Index
261

FOREWORD

If you are wondering whether to read this book, it must mean you are curious about animal liberation: You aren't exactly sure what it means, perhaps, or you are moved by the plight of animals and wish to explore further. I'm certain you will find a lot in here that will impact and motivate you, such as the reasons why those of us who advocate for animals' rights see the link to other movements as absolute and undeniable. For anyone who is already an activist or who has decided to become one, you are sure to find inspiration, thoughts that might not have occurred to you before, ideas that you can adopt or adapt, and words to cherish.

Brittany Michelson has collected a splendid set of narratives from people who, for myriad reasons, found themselves, often unexpectedly, embracing the idea of animal liberation. It dawned on each of them at some point in their lives that the concept of injustice couldn't rightly, logically, or reasonably be limited to the human animal. They realized that injustice occurs when we fail to connect the dots between ourselves and those who were not born in exactly the same physical form as ours.

The writers' ethical evolutions often began with a question. Alexandra Paul found herself wondering at the "absurdity" of ranking kittens over hamsters, and hamsters over frogs, and asked herself why this was any different from assigning degrees of value to human beings who are often considered "lower on the societal rung."

Brittany Peet loved "Smokey," a bear she often visited at a roadside zoo as a child. Later, she pondered how, back then, she could have been so oblivious to his loneliness and the desolation of his confinement to a barren cage. Jasmine Afshar questioned how people could empathize with the torment she experienced when she was sexually violated, yet dismiss the torment inherent in the routine assault of female animals whose bodies are exploited for meat and milk. Dani Rukin "came out" for animals, casting aside her leather jacket, long after coming out as a lesbian because, after initially mocking vegans, she began to wonder how diversity could rightly be limited to a single species.

Sometimes the animals themselves asked the questions, simply by being present or with an expression. Karen Davis's beloved parrot, Jasmin Singer's waifish cat, the monkey spotted by Jo-Anne McArthur chained to a windowsill high in the Andes—all seemed to nudge them in the direction of animal liberation. Was it recognizing the universal look of despair or hope or sadness in the face of a desperately thirsty pig, seen through the metal slats of a truck in the blistering heat, that changed Anita Krajnc's life? Or was that suffering pig, one among many, who was about to pass through the slaughterhouse gates, someone—and I mean some*one*—she already understood? After all, she was trying to live, and teach her students to live, as Tolstoy advised: "When the suffering of another creature causes you to feel pain, do not submit to the initial desire to flee from the suffering one, but on the contrary, come closer, as close as you can to he who suffers, and try to help him." Anita was charged with criminal mischief for rushing to that pig and offering water, but from her compassionate action, many others came to see that animal liberation is something to work for.

Some writers, like Kathy Stevens and Gene Baur, started sanctuaries, taking in animals with nowhere else to find safety and comfort. Wayne Hsiung left his legal career to start a group that challenges the lack of legal protections for other-than-human beings. Shaun Monson became a filmmaker, whose epic film *Earthlings* has opened more eyes and minds and hearts to the reality of animal exploitation than perhaps any other.

At the end of this book, the individual writers' experiences seem to be summed up in a verse from Sean Hill's poem:

> As alone as you may feel sometimes
> you are never alone
> we are all in this together
> the vision to transform the world,
> elevate everyone's innate potential
> by teaching sacred respect for all life forms

Please read this book. Pass it on to others. And take its lessons to heart, because the Golden Rule requires each of us to do unto others as we would have them do unto us. And that is the message of animal liberation.

Ingrid Newkirk
founder and president of PETA

INTRODUCTION

Animal rights: the rights of animals, claimed on ethical grounds, to the same humane treatment and protection from exploitation and abuse that are accorded to humans

Activism: the use of direct and noticeable action to achieve a result, usually a political or social one

> "Animal rights are not a gift we give to animals. They are a birthright we have taken from them."
>
> —Ryan Phillips

> "Animals have qualities we find important to the legal rights of humans—like self-awareness, the need for sovereignty, and the capacity for suffering, love, and empathy. We will never fully dismantle the injustices humans suffer without deconstructing the same problems that lead to animal suffering."
>
> —Marc Bekoff

As an animal rights activist, it is common to hear remarks such as:

"What about human rights?"
"Don't you care about humans?"
"There are so many human problems in the world; let's solve those first."

There's a widespread view that our own issues should be solved before animal issues are addressed, as if we need to demonstrate loyalty to our own species before advocating on behalf of others. This promotes the ideology of human superiority and reinforces a disconnect between humans and nonhumans. What we should be acknowledging is our interconnectedness: the fact that all beings have the capacity for love, joy, pain, and fear. Animal rights and human rights are inextricably connected. For example, there are multiple human and environmental issues that stem from animal issues. If we want to create a peaceful world, we must pay close attention to the ways in which human and nonhuman issues are related and honor the interdependence between our species and others.

Societal conditioning has taught us that certain animals are to love and other animals are to eat, wear, and use. Speciesism is the assumption of human superiority and involves the designation of values or special consideration solely on the basis of species classification. Speciesism is what underlies the notion that a dog is a beloved member of the family, while the purpose of a chicken is to be eaten. Civil rights, women's rights, gay rights, and other social justice causes have people who fight for their own rights, the rights of their loved ones, and those of their fellow citizens. Human rights movements operate from the ability of humans to use words and actions to stand up for their cause. The animal rights movement is the sole exception: nonhuman beings do not have the benefit of being able to speak for themselves or organize a protest, although they do resist being harmed, as is evident by their struggle, their vocalizations, and their attempts at escape. These are their forms of protest. Yet animals are disregarded because of their inability to communicate in our language, which makes them entirely dependent upon humans to prevent their exploitation. We hold the unique position of being both their greatest threat and their only hope.

In today's world, there is greater reason than ever to consider the plight of animals and the impact of animal agriculture on the planet. More and more environmentalists are advocating for a plant-based diet, considering that animal agriculture is a leading cause of greenhouse gas emissions, ocean dead zones, water pollution, deforestation, and species extinction. The planet simply cannot sustain itself with the present mass-industrialized system. Add this to the increasing number of health issues related to the consumption of animal products, and it becomes undoubtedly clear that it behooves humanity to work together to end animal farming.

Some people's commitment to plant-based eating is due solely to environmental concerns, or health reasons—to reverse ailments, heal disease, or prevent health issues from occurring. Then there are those of us who do not consume, wear, or use animal products because we believe that animals' lives are their right and that harming them for any purpose is unjust.

This is a time in history when the stories of the marginalized have risen to the surface. As a species that has the ability to advocate for others, we have a moral imperative to protect the most innocent and vulnerable among us and to inspire others to take action. Animal rights activism is an obligation for living on a planet where humanity dominates and uses nonhumans in every conceivable way—for food, fashion, experimentation, and entertainment. The multifaceted objective of the animal rights movement is to denormalize violence against animals, change the deeply rooted mentality of speciesism, honor that nonhuman animals are individuals, establish rights on their behalf, and liberate them from suffering.

Australian philosophy professor Peter Singer's book *Animal Liberation* (1975) is widely considered to have set the modern animal rights movement in motion. Today, it is one of the fastest-growing social justice movements in society, and the imprint it is making on humanity is notable. Many prominent people from various fields—scholars, scientists, philosophers, and physicians, among others—have either joined the movement, support the movement, or at least acknowledge it as a necessary part of the equation of social justice. Intersectionality— the interconnected nature of social categorizations such as race, class, and gender—has become more widely honored and understood, and activists across other social justice movements are recognizing the importance of animal rights.

The liberation of nonhuman beings is vital to the whole of the planet's success and is necessary for peace on earth. The activists who are featured in this collection believe that being vegan is the least we can do, and that engaging in activism is necessary. Vegan chef, wellness coach, and writer Tracey Narayani Glover said "Fundamentally, vegans advocate for the values that all social justice movements uphold. They focus on the nonhumans, but what they are really advocating for is a society in which no sentient being is used as a means to another's end. They are fighting for the elimination of all forms of prejudice and oppression."

It is a profound decision to commit ourselves to living vegan, which enables us individually to diminish animal suffering and concurrently reduce our carbon footprint. Yet it's a decision on another level to stand up boldly for what one believes in, which often requires putting our comfort levels aside—and in some cases our freedom on the line—to make our cause heard. Being an activist is necessary for the message we seek to convey to the public: that animals are individuals with their own sense of purpose and that they deserve the right to their lives. There is a growing unit on the front line of this rising movement, armed with compassion and a strong belief in justice for all beings. As animal rights activists, we are committed to standing up for those who are viewed by society at large as products, as commodities to be used; those who, through tradition and conditioning, are deemed unworthy of rights.

This collection spotlights diverse voices in the animal rights movement with the intention of inspiring those who are sparked by the vision of a more ethical world. From attending protests and marches, engaging in public outreach, spearheading campaigns, bearing witness, doing open rescue, holding demonstrations, and establishing sanctuaries, animal rights activism takes on multiple forms. In the following pages, activists from different backgrounds reveal their perspectives on animal rights, their experiences taking action for animals, the challenges they've faced, and the meaning of activism in their lives.

I am honored to be part of the animal rights community—to be among a passionate, dedicated group of humans devoted to taking action for those who cannot take action for themselves. Anyone—from any walk of life—can join a movement and become an activist. It is my hope that these stories will inspire and empower you to take action for a cause that you greatly value.

Let our voices be heard and our actions be bold.

©Jo-Anne McArthur

I
Seasoned Warriors:
Inspiring & Transforming

How I Became a "Poultry" Rights Activist Who Started an Organization Some Said Would Never Fly

Karen Davis, founder of United Poultry Concerns

People often ask how I started as an academic and ended up an animal rights activist rescuing and defending the rights of chickens and turkeys. Other than glimpses, I did not know these birds until I was in my forties. In the 1980s, I was teaching English at the University of Maryland-College Park and pursuing a PhD in Victorian Literature. I expected to teach literature for the rest of my life. But caring about animals was in my blood as was my lifelong revulsion at seeing them suffer. My feelings nurtured a profession that had not been foreseen but that now seems inevitable.

Growing up in Altoona, Pennsylvania, I knew cocker spaniels and terriers as family pets and beagles as hunting dogs. In grade school I had a parakeet named Wiffenpoof whom I loved. One day I came home and he was gone. Unforgivably, my mother had given him away. When a baby robin fell out of its nest in our yard in the spring, I was so upset I couldn't sleep. I sobbed inconsolably on the sofa when our neighbor's white duck was killed by a car in front of our house. One year, my parents brought home two yellow chicks at Easter, and then they were gone. Later we visited a farm with a dark barn filled with young white chickens, and my mother pointed to two of them and said they were our Easter chicks. Long after it happened, a memory emerged into consciousness of my best friend Betsy's father pulling a brown hen out of a shed under their house. He laid her on a stump and chopped her head off with a hatchet. Her head lay clucking on the ground and her body ran around the yard. This memory fits with other recollections I have of insouciant animal abuse as a child, like my father beating bats to death in the attic. My father, a lawyer, affected an unsentimental attitude. He hunted rabbits, squirrels, and pen-raised pheasants for sport. He said "Everything hunts the rabbit," so shooting them wasn't an issue for him. As a child, I had a hand-carved wooden ring-necked pheasant I colored with crayons. Later I understood that ring-necked pheasants were raised solely to be shot. Occasionally a wounded pheasant would hit the windshield of a car on a country road.

For thirty years I was a meat eater. I didn't connect meat, milk, or eggs with animals in a way that involved experiences or feelings. My brothers and I would fight over who got the first slice of roast beef on Sundays. At home, I would eat leftover meat off other people's plates, a habit I continued as a waitress at restaurants. I ate so much steak one summer in the 1960s that the landlady of the boardinghouse where I was staying in Norwalk, Connecticut bought me a steak knife. In Baltimore in the early 1970s, I'd run to the Lexington Market after graduate school classes and buy a barbecued chicken, which I took to my room and devoured on the floor.

While working as a juvenile probation officer in Baltimore, I bought a blue-fronted Amazon parrot whose loneliness in a cage obsessed me to the point where I could not rest until I rescued her one night after work. My beloved parrot Tikhon lived with me for twenty-two years until she died in 1994. It was during that time, in the early 1970s, that I read an essay by Leo Tolstoy called "The First Step." He argued that vegetarianism is a necessary first step to living nonviolently—an effort he made late in his life when he renounced foxhunting and other cruel pleasures that had plagued him for years with guilt and remorse. Tolstoy's description of cows and lambs in the Moscow slaughterhouse he visited caused me to stop eating animals. I agreed conceptually with Tolstoy and later with Peter Singer's argument in *Animal Liberation*, but in both cases it was the searing evocation of animals and their misery that converted me. I had never "supported" eating animals to begin with but had merely done what I was brought up to do, so I didn't need to be persuaded to change my opinion on the subject. I regretted my thoughtless animal abuse and did not miss eating meat.

In 1974, I moved to San Francisco, where I worked briefly at a deplorable "no-kill" dog and cat shelter before returning to the East Coast and graduate school. One day I saw an ad for World Laboratory Animals Day in Lafayette Park near the White House. Despite fearing the images I would see there, I decided to go anyway. As I looked at the faces and bodies of animals tortured in laboratory experiments, I vowed never again to forsake animals to this same fate, because I could not bear their suffering. From that day forward I was an animal rights activist. Throughout the 1980s I volunteered for everything happening for animals in the Washington, DC, area. I read about the plight of animals past and present while participating in PETA-sponsored rodeo demonstrations, rallies to free the Silver Spring monkeys from the National Institutes of Health, trips to Hegins, Pennsylvania, to protest the Labor Day pigeon shoots, and much more. When a PETA van drove a bunch of us to Salisbury, Maryland, one day to protest in front of the Perdue chicken slaughter plant on the main highway across from a McDonald's restaurant, I saw truckloads of chickens for the first time, and tears poured out of my eyes at the sight of them.

In 1989 I founded the Animal Rights Club at the University of Maryland. We campaigned to get the administration to approve alternatives to dissection and provide vegetarian options in the dining hall. Our biggest campaign, reported on by the *New York Times* and *Time* magazine, was to get the University of Maryland to remove chicken slaughter mogul Frank Perdue from the Board of Regents, to which he'd been appointed by Maryland's governor. Perdue served out his two years, but during that time our crusade dominated the opinion pages of the student newspaper, *The Diamondback*, and we followed Perdue and his bodyguards to every Regents meeting across the state with our placards, disruptions, and shouts of "Cluck You, Frank Perdue!"

Gradually I knew I was going to focus my activism on farmed animals. Working as a summer intern at Farm Sanctuary in Avondale, Pennsylvania, in 1987, I fell for all of the animals but especially the chickens and turkeys, for whom I felt a particular affinity. Together these birds represent 98 percent of land animals raised and slaughtered for food in the United States. The overwhelming majority, in the billions, are chickens. By then I had met the hen my husband named Viva who, more than any other single factor, precipitated my decision to found United Poultry Concerns in 1990. She'd been abandoned in a wooden shed, where she had been raised with a small flock of chickens by our landlady for slaughter. Probably she was left behind because she was crippled and thus overlooked under the shelf, where she crouched in the dirt before I lifted her out of there and took loving care of her in our home until she died. My story of "Viva, the Chicken Hen," first published in *Between the Species: A Journal of Ethics* in 1990, has caused many people by their own account to stop eating chickens and to see all chickens in a new and deeply sensitized light.

Who was it that said, "I'm so low down I declare I'm looking up at down?" That's rather how it was when I decided to start an advocacy group for chickens and turkeys in the late 1980s and was told by some that if I was going to "do" farm animals, I had better do pigs, because people weren't "ready" for chickens. However, the whole point of activism is to find ways to get people ready. I remember hearing a demonstrator tell a newspaper reporter at a chicken slaughter protest, "I'm sure Perdue thinks we're all a bunch of kooks for caring about chickens, but . . ." My question is: What difference does it make what the Tysons and Perdues of the world think? Imagine one of their CEOs standing in front of the camera, pleading "I know the animal rights people think I'm a kook, but . . ."

Notice came that my organization United Poultry Concerns was officially a 501(c)(3) nonprofit in October 1990. We promote the compassionate and respectful treatment of domestic fowl and address the treatment of these birds in food production, science, education, entertainment, and human companionship situations. Our work includes a sanctuary for chickens, turkeys, and ducks and the promotion of an animal-free diet. We published the first issue of our quarterly magazine *Poultry Press*, which began as a four-page newsletter, in 1991. In the 1990s, United Poultry Concerns led two major campaigns: a fight for legislation that would include birds under the federal Humane Methods of Slaughter Act (from which they are still excluded), and a fight to expose and eliminate the US egg industry practice of starving hens for days and weeks at a time, the practice known as forced molting, to manipulate the economics of egg production. I discuss both of these complicated, high-profile campaigns in my book *Prisoned Chickens, Poisoned Eggs: An Inside Look at the Modern Poultry Industry*.

Before moving from the Washington, DC, area to rural Virginia in 1998 to accommodate our sanctuary, I spent hours at the National Agricultural Library in Beltsville, Maryland and in the halls of Congress lobbying for poultry slaughter legislation. Among the volumes of poultry science publications at the library was a book by avian specialist Lesley J. Rogers called *The Development of Brain and Behaviour in the Chicken* (1995). Years earlier, I had sat on the floor of a room in Baltimore devouring a barbecued chicken. Then I sat on the floor of the Beltsville agricultural library devouring a book that said "It is now clear that birds have cognitive capacities equivalent to those of mammals, even primates," and "With increased knowledge of the behaviour and cognitive abilities of the chicken has come the realization that the chicken is not an inferior species to be treated merely as a food source." Along with much else, Rogers wrote of the battery cages in which the majority of egg-industry hens have been confined since the 1960s: "In no way can these living conditions meet the demands of a complex nervous system designed to form a multitude of memories and to make complex decisions." I wished then, as I do now, that I could inscribe these words in the hearts and minds of every human being and generation to come. What I *did* do immediately was rush to inform my colleagues working on farmed animal issues about this book and its strong statements that could be quoted without piecing together the usual equivocations of industry-based "science."

Soon after, I decided to write a book about turkeys, and in 2001 *More Than a Meal: The Turkey in History, Myth, Ritual, and Reality* was published. Through my sanctuary work I came to know turkeys as individuals with distinct personalities, sensitivities, and intelligence.

As with chickens, I was struck by the discrepancy between the actual birds and the demeaning stereotypes. Each November, the run-up to Thanksgiving was filled with media stories satirizing turkeys in contrast to the sentimental piety bestowed on Plymouth Rock and the Puritans. As part of my research, I visited the history museum Plymouth Plantation in Plymouth, Massachusetts. I spent a day on the floor of the gift shop reading everything I could find about the place of turkeys in Native American cultures and the continental landscape encountered by the Europeans. I walked out that night with an armload of books. In *More Than a Meal*, I wrote: "While it is fair to say that turkeys were not treated particularly well by Native Americans, a worse fate awaited them under the European invaders and their descendants, who conducted a full-scale assault upon the species." I have much to say about turkeys in my book reflecting my own experiences along with illuminating reports by others going back centuries.

Some animal advocates consider farmed animal sanctuaries a waste of resources better spent on "bigger" things, but I disagree. A good sanctuary provides an educational opportunity for visitors, staff, and volunteers as well as rescuing animals from a life of misery and oblivion. Thanks to the Internet, people who cannot physically visit a sanctuary can visit one online. Our sanctuary birds are an invaluable source of information that has enabled me to challenge false claims by cockfighters, farmers, and agribusiness interests (and yes, the sanctuary birds' essential nature and activities are intact despite the debilitating breeding that has weakened their bodies and the horrible living conditions they endured before they were rescued).

In September 2000, United Poultry Concerns organized the first national forum in the United States on the Role of Farmed Animal Sanctuaries in the Animal Advocacy Movement. Our forum focused on the concept and ethical obligations of the farmed animal sanctuary by addressing issues such as:

- Is rescuing and giving a permanent shelter to farmed animals "enough?"

- Does the physical labor and veterinary care the sanctuary demands use resources that could be better spent on other projects to help farmed animals?
- How does the farmed animal sanctuary deal with the deluge of animals at the door?
- Is purchasing farmed animals to save them from abuse and slaughter a morally legitimate form of rescue?
- Is it right or wrong to rescue farmed animals illegally?
- How do farmed animal sanctuaries get funding?

The previous year United Poultry Concerns presented the first conference in the United States (or anywhere else to my knowledge) on Direct Action and Open Rescues. On June 26–27, 1999, nine months after moving our headquarters and sanctuary to Machipongo, Virginia, on the Eastern Shore, I conceived and organized this historic conference, inspired in part by animal rights philosopher Tom Regan, who wrote in his book *The Struggle for Animal Rights* that instead of wearing masks and concealing their identity, "right strategy and right psychology is for the people who liberate animals to come forth and identify themselves as the people who did it." Regan was challenging the Animal Liberation Front practice of concealing rescuers behind masks, versus disclosure of personal identity as a strategy for achieving animal liberation through appeals to public perception and conscience. Back then, attention to the plight of animals raised for food was still relatively new in the United States. In 1987, when the first ALF action at the Beltsville Maryland Agricultural Research Center was carried out, even ALF activists who used the term "animal rights," according to Ingrid Newkirk in *Free the Animals*, "had not yet incorporated the systemized abuse of 'farm animals' into their agendas, couldn't 'see' an attack on the farm industry at all." One reason they couldn't envision such an attack was that they didn't yet "see" the billions of chickens and other animals locked out of sight in the industrial compounds to which they were relegated in the mid-1950s.

In keeping with Tom Regan's perspective, I was drawn to the strategy developed by prominent Australian activist Patty Mark of what she called the Open Rescue, in which undercover investigators show their faces and admit to rescuing animals and documenting the conditions of their abuse instead of liberating animals behind a mask. I invited Patty to speak at our conference. Her presentation, including video footage of her Action Animal Rescue Team's rescue of chickens and pigs from factory farms, created the revolution in farmed animal rescue strategy in the United States.

By chance, our conference coincided with a televised ALF raid at the University of Minnesota showing rescuers clad from head to toe in black. All rescues were shot at long-distance angles, making it difficult to be sure in some cases what kinds of animals were being pulled out of laboratory cages. The focus was on the rescuers, whose manner expressed no empathy for the animals for viewers to identify with. By contrast, Patty Mark's video of a well-planned rescue of several hens from a battery-cage facility focused attention on the agonized hens being carefully extricated from unimaginable filth, and on the compassionate gentleness and firmness of the rescue team, who, as part of their operation, contacted the police, got arrested, and explained their mission with the intention of putting battery-hen farming visibly on trial before the public and in the courtroom. As I describe in my article "Open Rescues" in *Terrorists or Freedom Fighters*, our conference on Direct Action inspired three highly publicized undercover investigations of battery-caged hen facilities in the United States in 2001. To this day, Patty Mark's Open Rescue is the model for farmed animal investigative and rescue operations in North America, even though most contemporary activists are unlikely to know the history.

Unlike some other kinds of animals, rescued farmed animals cannot be set free in a forest or field. For one thing, many chickens, turkeys, and ducks bred for the poultry and egg industries are white and unable to camouflage themselves in the natural world. Birds, pigs, sheep, and others bred specifically for meat suffer from congenital lameness and other infirmities that only years of regeneration could eliminate from their gene pool. Most farmed animals have endured some form of bodily mutilation at birth, such as debeaking or tail docking, weakening their chance of survival on their own. Thus, a successful farmed animal rescue necessarily involves sanctuary for the animals who are rescued. Investigation, rescue, and sanctuary care are all forms of direct action for animals.

Farmed animal sanctuaries are places where the public has a chance to see farmed animals as individuals in the light of being treated with respect and reciprocating the experience of love and interspecies companionship. A sanctuary puts faces on the countless billions of invisible beings whose only true rescue can come by being rescued from dinner plates and the vocabulary of belittlement and food. This form of rescue must be the ultimate goal of farmed animal sanctuaries and implicit in all forms of animal activism at every level from individual to organizational. Rescuing Viva the chicken hen in 1985 and getting to know her helped foster my decision to found an organization dedicated to liberating all chickens for a life worth living, and by extension enabling all animals to fulfill their lives.

Documenting Invisible Animals: Photography as a Tool for Change

Jo-Anne McArthur, photographer
and founder of We Animals Media

My path as a photojournalist has taken me to over fifty countries on six continents, where I have encountered animals who have endured unimaginable pain and suffering, and others fortunate enough to be cared for, or living freely. Because my work focuses on our complex relationship with animals, people assume that I'm driven by a deep love for animals, but that's only part of the story. I do this work because I'm deeply concerned about what we've done to the animal kingdom, and its effects on the planet and humanity.

Years ago, I learned something that empowered me to do this intense, yet rewarding work. As a photographer, I had a powerful tool in my hands—one that could change the course of history; one that could change hearts and minds about how we treat animals; one that could show us hope and a way forward. I've been taking pictures for twenty years now, going to the ends of the earth in order to tell the stories of animals who so desperately need our help. This became my life's mission, and there is no turning back. Despite its drawbacks, I wouldn't exchange this life of travel and photography for any other.

Dreamers like me need mentors, and they have never been in short supply. As a young woman, I watched with great fascination the life and career of Dr. Jane Goodall. Emboldened, I recognized that if people like her could live adventurous lives, blaze new trails, and fight for animals, I could do the same. During my geographic and literary studies at university, I took an elective black-and-white printing course, and my love affair with photography thus began. An encouraging friend taped a note to my locker, with Goethe's famous words written on it:

Boldness has genius, power and magic in it . . . BEGIN IT NOW.

To this day, I have kept that tattered note on the wall in my office as inspiration. In 1998 I was backpacking with friends in the Andean mountains of Ecuador, when we came across a monkey chained to a windowsill. He seemed to have been trained to pick the pockets of passersby. Tourists crowded around to take pictures. I elbowed my way into the crowd to take pictures as well, but for an entirely different reason. I wasn't amused, but appalled that this wild animal was held captive for human use. I knew that what I was witnessing was wrong. Through another lens, this monkey was viewed more or less as an object. Through my own, I wanted to show a form of slavery, perpetrated upon a complex, sentient being.

My long-term body of work is called *We Animals*. We are *all* animals, after all, but we humans forget. Our anthropocentric hierarchy is so entrenched, it's invisible. *We Animals* examines our relationships with other animals around the globe by highlighting this hierarchy. It became a book in 2013, the same year that Liz Marshall's award-winning documentary film *The Ghosts in Our Machine* was released, which followed me as I did animal investigative work in Europe and North America. Recently, I published a second book, *Captive*, which is my contribution to the growing conversation about the ethics of captivity. I spent years thinking about the issue and months planning and shooting the work, observing us with my camera as we observe them. *Captive* shows that we often fail to really *see* the individuals who are right before our eyes. Instead, we might see an object for our entertainment, or the ambassador for a species. Do we really continue to believe that the complex emotions and behaviors they exhibit, such as despondency, loneliness, and despair, which are stereotypic of captive animals, offer no true insight into their experiences?

As I grew into this career in photojournalism, I realized there was something doubly wonderful about the act of taking pictures. The camera always felt like a passport for me, or an all-access pass into the lives of others. Taking photographs helped to satisfy my curiosity about who we are and why we do the things we do. And how wonderful to realize that I could *give* by *taking* photographs. That, whether human or animal, I could help the subjects I was photographing by showing the world what I was seeing; that I could bear witness to the wrongs in this world in order to help start a conversation about how things need to change.

I have sailed through the luminous Antarctic Ocean to document brave activists intercepting whale poachers, and spent months in the fecund forests of Uganda and Cameroon documenting efforts to end the bushmeat trade. I've posed as a buyer of macaque monkeys in Asia to expose the cruelty of the wildlife trade, and I've snuck into bear bile farms, to film how Asiatic moon bears live in the miserable confines of cages barely larger than their own bodies. In some cases, the footage I've obtained has helped close farms, and in all cases, this work has helped to raise public awareness about the cruelty animals endure at our hands.

For conflict photographers, our job is to do our best to capture the moments that tell the story of those who are at ground zero. It's in these moments that photographs can galvanize, enrage, and inspire. It's here that still images move. A vital part of creating change is documenting, gathering visual proof, and bearing witness to what is and what should never again be. Photography helps create history; it makes visible what should be, and will be, in the history books.

It seems that anywhere I choose to travel, there's an animal story that needs to be told. Part of being a photojournalist is that you have your eyes wide open to the important issues of our time. The stories of animals are incredibly underreported. By and large, we simply want to see images of wildlife's majestic beauty or cute, cuddly images of puppies and kittens. Anything else is too painful. I understand. It *is* painful. I'm thankful that now, we are more willing than ever to turn our collective gaze to their plight. From the ivory trade to hunting, from the cultural practices that harm animals to those whom we eat and wear, we *must* look, and we must not turn away. Seeing is a key ingredient to transformation, and it's something we all can do.

Everyone asks how I can handle bearing witness to so much violence. It is undoubtedly brutal, but I find catharsis in action, and momentum surges through people who choose to not turn away. We're amid a global rise of engagement in animal journalism, a collective seeing. Photographs and stories can foster change, and this is what keeps me grounded.

Because the stories of these individuals need to be seen as far and wide as humanly possible, I have made over twelve thousand of my animal images available for free, via our We Animals Archive, to any person or organization helping animals. Since its launch in March 2017, we have fulfilled more than 1,500 requests for images in support of animal advocacy and conservation worldwide. We Animals—once a solo project—has now grown into a small but mighty international media agency. We Animals Media is a team of seven staff and almost a dozen creative contributors, focusing on photography, filmmaking, and journalism, with the goal of illuminating important but untold stories of animals worldwide and galvanizing people to be part of the change.

As frequent travelers in an increasingly accessible world, we have even more opportunities to revere animals and to live alongside instead of against them. We can enjoy and learn from their natural behaviors by observing them in the wild, rather than paying money to see them swimming circles in a tank, or circumnavigating well-worn grooves into the dirt of small, uninteresting enclosures. We must avoid buying their body parts as trinkets or as folk medicine. I've seen young primates on chains in the markets, because their families were poached so that we might sample some chimpanzee meat or buy a gorilla-hand ashtray. We can avoid tourist traps like elephant riding, as well as circuses, rodeos and bullfight. Elephants are taken from their families and subjected to the practice of Phajaan, a horrific breaking of the spirit, before we can climb on their backs, for example. We can visit and support reputable wildlife centers and sanctuaries, and we can aim our telephoto lenses, instead of guns, at animals. Of this I am certain: exploitation and domination of other animals have no place in an enlightened society.

One of my greatest joys is combining my big loves: photography, travel, and volunteerism at animal sanctuaries and rescue centers. My three all-time favorite trips have been to Elephant Nature Park in Thailand, Ape Action Africa in Cameroon, and recurrent trips to Farm Sanctuary in the United States. At Elephant Nature Park, rescue and rehabilitation efforts provide a safe haven for abused elephants and challenge the traditions of tourism by helping trekking camps transition to an ethical model where elephants are no longer exploited. Ape Action Africa is home to over 350 primates rescued from the bushmeat and pet trades in western Africa. The great apes are on the verge of extinction, and we need all hands on deck in order to save these species. Since its beginnings, Farm Sanctuary has rescued tens of thousands of animals used for food, while educating people about animal sentience and the horrors of industrialized farming. (My first Farm Sanctuary visit in 2003 inspired me to become vegan.) The women at the helm of these organizations, Saengduean "Lek" Chailert, Rachel Hogan, and the Farm's National Shelter Director Susie Coston are featured in my photo project *Unbound* about women on the front lines of animal advocacy worldwide.

There are still many stories to tell, and thankfully a growing number of journalists are seeking out and sharing the stories of animals who need our help. As I've traveled the world, I have observed that women greatly outnumber men in animal advocacy work. In fact, women make up 60–80 percent of animal advocates in the Western world. I felt that this was a fact worth uplifting and celebrating. *The Unbound Project* gives visibility to the trailblazing work of women and their organizations. These women are leaders in conservation, sanctuary work, law, science, the arts, philosophy, and journalism.

This leads me to the most important message that I can share. Every single one of us, in all of our actions, can make a difference for animals. No act of compassion is too small. Just as I've found my voice for animals through photography, so too can you find your voice for those who need our help. Figure out what you love to do and what you are most skilled at doing, and use those skills to make the world a better place. What is happening to animals is an emergency. Just as I have, tape these words on your wall, or in your notebook, as a reminder:

BEGIN IT NOW!

The Spectrum of Life:
Not the Same but Equal

Shaun Monson, documentary filmmaker

Several years after I made the documentary *Earthlings*, activists began hosting private screenings of "the scariest movie you will ever see." The screenings were free of charge, held in movie theaters, and some event planners even budgeted to pay viewers $5 each if they sat all the way through it. This was intriguing to moviegoers, particularly in October. In fact, the closer to Halloween, the better. Hollywood has always had a perennial interest in the genre of horror. People the world over have strong appetites for gory imagery, from gladiators killing each other in the arenas of ancient Rome to ultimate fighting championships today. Violence in movies, television shows, and video games is no different.

From a conscious perspective, however, it's sad to think of a documentary as a horror film. In Hollywood terms, this suggests mixing genres, except for one notable difference. The nonfiction film is not a fantasy. Documentary horror means that humankind commits such acts in reality. Sadder still is the realization that such acts are considered normal. This brings to mind a lecture by Joseph Campbell about the cycles of the world through the origin of myth. The principal image was that of the ages of gold, silver, bronze, and iron. In India these ages are of the four, the three, the two, and the one. In the age of the four, the golden age, a sacred cow, representing the Goddess of Virtue, stands on all four legs. In this period of time, according to the myth, you didn't have to look for your soul's companion. Lovers were born together. The rivers ran with wine, the trees rippled beautiful melodies, and the whole world, even the soil itself, was sweet as sugar to eat. The houses had no doors, for there was nothing to keep out. People were very happy in those days, and they didn't have to think about what they should do because they automatically acted virtuously. Then came the age of silver, or the third age, when the symbol of a cow representing the Goddess of Virtue suddenly appeared standing on three legs. This time people were not quite so virtuous. They had to pause to consider what should be done and how they should behave, but they would act virtuously even so. And though they were not as tall or as beautiful as those from the golden age, from our point of view today they were still divine. Then comes the age of bronze, or the second age (counting backward), when the cow of virtue appears standing on only two legs. Of course, a cow can't stand on two legs, so at this time a "prop" is brought into being. This began the period of scriptures and of little writings that would tell people how to behave. It represents the period of the coming of religion into the world. Religion was unnecessary before, because people acted righteously and correctly of their own accord. No promptings, no spiritual preceptors, no temples or rituals were required. But by the bronze age they had drifted or forgotten and stood corrected. When I heard this lecture, I figured this was our age, but Campbell took the myth a step further. It is into the age of iron, our unfortunate time, where the sacred cow appears standing on only one leg, teetering, really, because at this point nobody knows their own true nature anymore. The worst of it, according to Campbell, is that people wouldn't even read scriptures, or holy writings, and when they did, they didn't understand them, and came into collision with one another over what they should or shouldn't mean.

It was Oswald Spengler in *The Decline of the West* who suggested that when creativity turns to violence it has lost its Art. That book was written in 1918, just over a century ago. No doubt, many a Hollywood filmmaker would beg to differ, convinced their violent forms of entertainment are, in fact, Art. *Earthlings* is a violent documentary film, without question, but the horror is not intended to be creative or artistic, or even to frighten or entertain. Instead, the imagery in the film has a very prominent morality attached to it. This is because the words we use for human pain and suffering can't begin to touch what is witnessed among the animals. But if I had to choose words, then "torture" and "murder" would be the most accurate, and the word "slave." After all, a slave is anyone over whose life, liberty, and property someone else has absolute control. When it comes to animals raised for food, and those used for clothing, entertainment, breeding, and for medical and scientific research, I can't think of a better definition than slave. Like so many issues involving humankind's use of animals, it is simply a case of judicial murder. Yet we prefer not to call it murder ("harvesting" or "processing" are the industry terms), because we believe these beings are separate from ourselves.

In *Earthlings*, despite all of its horror, brutality, and darkness, the overall message (unlike a horror film), is one of empathy, mercy, and compassion. The film seeks to illuminate viewers (human earthlings) about the treatment of animals (nonhuman earthlings.) None of us who are more intelligent, more powerful, more famous, or wealthier can take away the fact that those who have none of those qualities still exist. In this we are all equal. In fact, "not the same but equal" is the entire message of my follow-up film, called *Unity*, which is the sequel to *Earthlings*.

The true horror of documentaries like *Earthlings* and *Unity* is how harshly they shine a light on choices we make every day, specifically choices that impact the lives of others, and to their detriment. I call this "radical truth." People often say "this is my truth," which is a glorified way of saying they have perceptions or opinions. Everyone views the world through the prism of their own reality, a reality influenced by society and their environment. However, when people argue in a court of law, both telling their sides of the story, it then falls to a judge and jury to deduce whose truth is more believable. Radical truth is when we take an all-encompassing view, not just our own, but one that is absolute. Environmentalists might say this is what it means to have a biocentric mind-set. In *Earthlings* I used this approach to go beyond the human point of view (as it pertains to animals), and presented the pet's point of view, the farmed animal's point of view, and the point of view of animals used for clothing, for entertainment, for medical research, etc., to highlight types of animal exploitation. In our Age of Iron, such radical truth may be the only truth that penetrates an otherwise disinterested and indifferent state of mind.

Some viewers complain that *Earthlings* has a negative connotation to it, that it is depressing and doesn't focus on positive change. This got me thinking about what is positive and negative when it comes to the welfare of animals raised for human purposes. Take a plate of food, for example, prepared with loving care and exquisitely presented on a beautiful platter with garnishes all around. It could be filet mignon or foie gras, roast duck or lobster. Out of a few raw materials, a cook may concoct any number of dishes, each with a different and unique taste, but basically all from identical materials; namely animals, spices, vegetation, herbs, oil, and water. Depending on one's preference, this food not only smells enticing but is delicious to eat. Afterward, however, we usually don't think of it again. And not only that, but all of this delicious, exquisite food disappears as waste within the span of a day. Our favorite delicacies go from alluring to appalling in less than twenty-four hours. That's the overall essence of food—preference, taste, waste—but if we go back and look at how that very same meal was produced, one discovers it is quite unpalatable. This raises the question: Which component of the meal is positive or negative—the beginning, the middle, or the end? A picture of a perfect meal is enticing. The cooking of the meal is rather interesting and can be fun; the preparing of the meal prior to cooking is less mouthwatering; the shopping for all the proper ingredients beforehand can be a bit of a chore, and so on. Each step backward becomes less gratifying. And if we go all the way back to the source, particularly when it comes to animals raised for food, suddenly it's quite ghastly and repulsive. No one even wants to look at it. In fact, there are laws in this country called "ag gag" (i.e., agricultural gag laws) that forbid such imagery from being seen. Is the origin of a meal a negative thought? No, it's a fact. Why close our eyes to it? It's because people want to watch something happy, entertaining, and hopeful. This makes us feel good, and there's nothing wrong with that. But the problem is, when it comes to food, so much of what we interpret as happy on the surface (such as celebrations, traditions, holidays, feasts), is based on a great deal of suffering and misery. Subsequently, the backdrop of that which is joyful for so many of us is unendurable pain (literally un-endurable because it is pain unto death), for them.

It makes one wonder how the human earthling, with all its potentiality and grandeur, has somehow evolved to a state of such wanton cruelty and indifference toward other earthlings. We're not just talking about animals now, but other humans and the environment. In this sense, it's as if we haven't evolved at all and are still Neanderthals, right out of the cave, clubbing to death anyone that looks, acts, or believes differently from us. That's the mentality of the Age of Iron. The chest-thumping caveman has been replaced by chest-thumping technology or intelligence. One wonders when civilization will evolve into that recognition and affirmation of Absolute Existence, of no more separation based on form, or shape, or sex, or accent, or pigment, or belief, or preference, or boundaries . . . but of the entire spectrum of earthlings, this absolute spectrum of life.

We have to abandon this idea of separateness. By imagining ourselves as different and separate from other beings, we create a gap. To rediscover the common factor, we simply have to abandon any egocentric need for distinction. Equally true is how we see nature. Rapidly growing climate change reveals that we have somehow imagined "nature" as a distinct and separate state, even though it's all around us and all-encompassing. Nature is not an individual tree or rock or insect or river or animal. Nature is not an entity of separate selves—all of these are what we consider "nature."

Somewhere, way back when, a division occurred. We hear stories of a Garden of Eden, where all beings lived in harmony with one another—not the same, but equal, like the age of gold Campbell talked about. But then something happened, a shift occurred, and all the beings were divided. At times, these beings have observed toward each other very friendly relations, to be sure, but generally speaking they (meaning we) have been opposed ever since, always warring with each other, suspicious, fearful, wary. This fact is instanced by the following: Mankind has been at war for 95 percent of recorded civilization. It's as if only by separateness and opposition can either side maintain a distinguishing status. And there it is again—that need for distinction. What all this really means is that our "reality" is distorted by the perceptual apparatus of the ego. The Age of Iron is all about ego. And there's only one way to return to a state of harmony—stop separating the inseparable.

Why is it taking so long for human beings (the inventors, explorers, thinkers, and framers) to fully comprehend and embrace that nature is, and always was, a spectrum, of which we are merely a part? Despite our extraordinary evolution from the cave or the tree, humans are still spectacularly barbaric to one another, even to this day. If that's how we treat ourselves, then it's easy to see how merciless we are to animals. Taken further, this is why humans have little to no empathy for the insect kingdom, who too are earthlings and also a part of this vast spectrum of life, with their wings and mandibles and stingers and multiple legs. Is this why our conscience doesn't flinch when it comes to killing insects or "harvesting" them for their silk or their honey, or chemically exterminating them en masse? Statistically speaking, you're never more than three feet from a spider. But all too often, a spider in the house is an uninvited and unacceptable guest, warranting swift execution, the undue consequence for simply existing in this immense spectrum of life.

This is the personification of "separation based on form," which is the basis of *Unity*. I should mention that *Earthlings* was always meant to be part of a trilogy, which is hinted at in the poster beneath the title where it says: Nature, Animals, Humankind: Make the Connection. The goal was one film about nature (called *Beings*, which is in development); one film about animals, which is *Earthlings*; and one film about humankind, which is *Unity*. Only fourteen minutes of animal footage is featured in *Unity*. A large portion of the film focuses on our preoccupation with war. Like *Earthlings*, it is divided into five chapters, but in essence, *Unity* is a film about duality, about why we can't seem to get along with each other after thousands and thousands of years.

Isn't it ironic that the word *earthling* encompasses such an enormous spectrum of life-forms, but that we human earthlings feel the need, or rather the right (and some argue a God-given right), to police, mandate, or utilize whichever life-forms are useful to us and eradicate, exterminate, or eliminate those who are not? It's as if other beings have no real worth (apart from some utility that serves us), or no intrinsic value of their own, which permits them the right to be left alone. After all, aren't all the forms and movements of the world, in all their depths, an ensemble picture, inclusive of everything? The so-called Ocean of Life contains all, not only humans. And just like the term "nature," are not all beings the very picture of life? That is what it means to have a biocentric mind-set. Why then do we have this ongoing, selective, preferential treatment of some beings over others (white/black, gay/ straight, rich/poor, human/animal, etc.)?

We are living in an Age of Iron, even though it isn't sustainable. The sacred cow from Joseph Campbell's myth is falling. Not to sound like a wannabe guru, but at some point, we have to stop giving in to mere biologic drives at the price of higher love or understanding. A biocentric mind-set is a good place to start. Moral progress has always been inconvenient to a stubborn mind. Abolishing slavery was inconvenient to the world economy. The female right to vote was inconvenient to the male-dominated society. Civil rights are inconvenient to a white-dominated society. Animal rights are inconvenient to a carnivorous society. And so on. But most people are so entrenched, so deeply caught up, in the authority of mass agreement that they fail to step back and recognize how we are all part of a spectrum. We must save ourselves from the ongoing calamities of separate existence. We are all earthlings, universalings. Global warming will certainly, and most radically, change all that. If our destruction of the natural world, the animals, and each other persists, then obviously we are dealing with a very unsympathetic entity—ourselves. Is our ignorance really so invincible? Is mutual existence really so difficult to see, even as a possibility?

As Carl Sagan famously stated "If you want to bake an apple pie, you must first have a universe." There is no apple without a tree; no tree without a seed; no seed without soil, no soil without an environment; no environment without a firmament; no firmament without an atmosphere; no atmosphere without air; no air without a sphere;

no sphere without a planet; no life on a planet without light; no light without a star; no stars without a galaxy and a universe. Can't we see how abundantly evident and blatantly obvious it is that everything is interconnected? All that happens is the cause of all that happens, because every cause is universal. Living universally is to understand this and love whatever contacts you. That's a tall order for most of us, even though humanity has always revered those throughout history who lived life doing that very thing. This is universal life, the harmony of being. In the vast spectrum of life, we're not the same, but equal. To put it another way, the universe contributes incessantly to the existence of all, including "us" but not excluding "them." Let's not mistake ignorance for perspective. And let's not mistake perspective for absolute reality. The hard truth is that the world goes on spinning regardless of what we think of it. In fact, maybe we should spend less time thinking and overthinking. Maybe a bit more emotional intelligence is required. To quote historians Will and Ariel Durant, "Perhaps within these limits we can learn to bear reality patiently, and to respect one another's delusions." We live on a biosphere where compassion is the first step back to the Age of Gold.

Ending Bear Bile Farming:
A Clarion Call

Jill Robinson, founder and CEO of Animals Asia

"We all receive messages we can choose to listen to, or ignore. The decision we make can both shape our lives and change the lives of others." This is the advice I've given to students in schools and universities the world over since receiving a message from a caged moon bear in China, a bear who changed my life and so many others, after we met for the one and only time in 1993. It was spring and I was on a bus traveling through the countryside of southern China. All around me were the excited voices of Japanese and Taiwanese tourists, but my emotions were very different. Instead of being excited about where we were going, I was deeply pensive and troubled by what I might find. At the time, I was working undercover to investigate a disturbing report that the bus tours were stopping at a farm selling bear bile, a form of traditional Asian medicine. I had never been on a bear bile farm—very few people had—and frankly, I was afraid that the horror stories I'd heard might turn out to be true. What I found was even worse than I could have imagined.

When we stepped off the bus, the farmer and his wife were quick to hustle us into an area overlooking a concrete pit. Below were the breeding bears. With beaming faces, the owners gave us crude fishing lines on which we could hook apples and hold them over obviously hungry bears, who stood on their back feet and reached up, desperately grabbing at thin air. This was the first mortifying experience, seeing the tourists encouraged to tease the animals, flicking the line upward when the bears were just inches away from the fruit. Fights were breaking out in the pit, as the starving bears tried to grab each apple that fell to the floor. Once the tourists were convinced that real live animals were held on the farm, they were more interested in seeing the bear bile products for sale, and the farmer wasted no time in ushering us all into his shop. The products ranged from bear bile wine, tea, and eye cream to "fresh" crystallized and liquid bile in tiny glass vials that were selling for several US dollars each.

While the tourists were immersed in their decision of what to buy, I sensed the opportunity to find out more and crept quietly out of the shop. I quickly found steps to a basement, where we had been told the caged bile-extraction bears were held. The steps led down into darkness, and it was the smell which hit me first, a horrible stench I will never forget. As I opened a door, the overwhelming presence of urine, feces, and infection filled my senses. Soon I made out thirty-two tiny cages, each holding an Asiatic black bear. The silence was broken only by the clank of metal as the bears weaved back and forth and by strange popping sounds that grew louder the closer I approached each cage. I realized with sad disbelief that this was the sound of bears frightened by my presence, not able to tell the difference between a person who felt such deep sympathy for their plight and someone who would do them harm. Looking closer, I saw each bear had metal rods protruding from bleeding, infected holes in their abdomens. The ends of these metal pipes oozed a yellowish liquid as the bears' bile seeped out of permanent wounds in their skeletal bodies. What gruesome acts had the farmer done?

Walking around in silent shock, surrounded on all sides by animals in deep pain and anguish, I backed too close to one of the cages, felt something brush my shoulder and turned around in fright, convinced I was going to be attacked. Instead, there was a female moon bear with her arm stretched out through the bars looking directly at me. Common sense left me, and I reached back to her. I felt her long claws curl around my fingers, gently squeezing them as we looked into each other's eyes. Many seconds passed in that moment, as time really did stand still, and the bear I later called Hong sent the most profound message I have ever heard. As I walked out of the basement back into the light, I had a feeling I would never see her again, and I never did. But Hong left an indelible footprint on my heart. She sent me on a journey to end the industry that caused her and so many other bears such unimaginable suffering.

I have always hoped that Hong is dead. And now, over twenty-six years later, perhaps she is. I will forever be haunted by the fact that I couldn't save her, but death is a peaceful place away from pain and torture, and I earnestly hope that she is no longer suffering.

The weeks and months following that day in April 1993 saw a learning curve that couldn't have been more vertical. I began searching for as much information I could find about the industry that was causing such unimaginable misery. I learned that bear bile actually is an effective medicine for certain conditions and that its active ingredient, ursodeoxycholic acid, is artificially synthesized for use in medicine all across the world. I consulted the traditional medicine community and was told that the Chinese pharmacopeia identified more than fifty herbal alternatives to bear bile. It quickly became clear that not one single person was suffering because of a lack of bear bile. While it was painful to know the suffering of Hong and other bears was completely in vain, this fact also gave me the realization that this cruelty could end.

I learned which government departments regulated the farms, I met officials, and I consulted lawyers on the laws. I continued to expose farms across the country and, in 1995, was elated when the Ministry of Forestry in Guangdong Province shut down a farm that I had exposed for operating illegally. This was a breakthrough that led to a huge realization. The closing of the farm left nine horrifically sick bears in need of health care and sanctuary. Thankfully, the International Fund for Animal Welfare, where I was working, was able to give them sanctuary. But if more farms were to close, and I yearned dearly to close them all, where would the bears go? This was when I knew that I had a big decision to make. Clearly an organization dedicated to the care of these animals was needed, but how to even begin setting up such an organization? How would it be funded? What if it failed?

In my heart, Hong was urging me to do everything I could to help the bears, but my head was telling me all the obstacles. I've long admired the actress and founder of Born Free Foundation, Virginia McKenna and, knowing that she had faced a similar decision, I turned to her for advice. She was unequivocal. There was only one possible decision to make, and she helped me when she said "just do it." In 1998, Animals Asia was legally founded with a mission to end bear bile farming, and permission from the authorities in Chengdu Province to build a bear sanctuary capable of rescuing hundreds of bears. Launching Animals Asia and committing to working permanently on the ground in Chengdu was a strategic move recognizing that the movement against bear bile farming couldn't just come from outside. I knew we had to work from within. Taking on board the words of one Chinese government official who advised us to "start the debate in China," we began building a core team of people who shared similar principles—passionate, professional, compassionate people—to represent the bears, to tell their story, and to work with the authorities and local communities to end bear bile farming. Later, a second sanctuary in Tam Dao National Park, Vietnam, was born.

Looking back, I sometimes wonder how I had the temerity to drive such a campaign. Perhaps if I'd known how difficult it would be, I wouldn't have dared try. But in truth, it was empathy for Hong that drove me on, as well as the thought that she'd chosen to tell me what was being done to her and so many other bears. I couldn't ignore the message; I had to carry it and tell everyone I could.

Over twenty years later, the lives of over six hundred bears have been saved because of Hong. Animals Asia's sanctuaries in China and Vietnam are bursting with previously broken bears who are walking into spring and loving the lives and choices we have been able to return to them. Bears like Kevin, who smile, very deliberately turning their mouths upward in joy, as they swim in cool pools or play with their friends. Chubby Nicole, who has the baldest bottom and the most beautiful face, forages for hours. Crazy Tuffy, whose thirst for life delighted millions around the world as cameras caught him splashing with sheer delight the first time he waded into a large sanctuary pool. Each bear's special, individual character demands the respect of everyone who sees them. They play, they make friendships, they empathize. They are living, breathing, thinking personalities with their own little quirks, and not a single one deserves to suffer on a bile farm. As each rescued bear, broken by years of cruelty and neglect, is mended again, so they become the bearers of Hong's message. The damage the industry causes is evident on their bodies and minds. Their beautiful personalities emerging prove that it doesn't have to be this way; that it should never be this way.

So many years later, Hong's message is still being heard as bears continue to be saved from her fate. In Vietnam, we are on the very edge of achieving our ultimate goal. The government, convinced by everything they have heard and seen, wants the industry to be completely shut down and has signed an exclusive partnership contract with Animals Asia that will close every farm and send every bear to sanctuary by 2022. I know that this success is because we worked from within. We spoke to every party, engaged every audience, and made bear bile farming an issue in the places where it was happening. It's not enough to attack and criticize and vent rage and frustrations from the outside. You have to offer solutions and work together until your goal becomes the shared goal. That's where this approach has taken us in Vietnam. Now everybody is working together to end bear bile farming. It's not just Animals Asia—it's the Traditional Medicine Association, the government, the public, and the media; sometimes it is even the farmers themselves.

When creating change, you have to expect pushback. There will always be vested interests resisting, but if one approach doesn't work, you try another. If that fails, you go to plan C. The key is being versatile, being creative, never closing a door or burning a bridge—and never, ever giving up.

For Hong, I remain full of gratitude for the message she sent all those years ago; for the journey she started; for the courage she gave me; and for the world of happiness she brought to every bear who was luckier than her. In life, we all receive messages we can choose to listen to or ignore. The decisions we make can both shape our lives and change the lives of others. Hong's message defined my life and saved the lives of so many others. I am eternally grateful that I had the courage to listen to her—hers was my message I chose to listen to, and I never looked back.

Liberating Animals and Ourselves

Will Tuttle, visionary author and speaker

It seems that at a certain point, most vegans yearn to discover the magic button that we can push that will light up the consciousness of our non-vegan friends, family members, and others, and transform them into vegans. It seems completely anti-rational, self-destructive, and untenable that people, upon hearing of the devastating effects of animal agriculture on innocent animals—as well as on ecosystems, wildlife, hungry people, and human health—nevertheless continue to take out their wallets and vote for animal-sourced foods and feed them to their unsuspecting children. We long to find the phrase, image, meme, gesture, or vocal intonation that is able to reliably pierce the armor of indoctrination and soften the hearts and open the eyes of the people with whom we share our world. The search for this magic button is like the search for the fabled fountain of youth or the mythical wish-fulfilling jewel, but the fountain of youth and the wish-fulfilling jewel are actually within ourselves, and to transform the world we must transform ourselves.

Veganism is not a static goal or state, but is instead a process of continually learning; it's an ongoing journey of refining our awareness and behavior. With continued effort and exploration, all of us are wounded by being born and raised in a herding culture that's organized at its core around enslaving, mutilating, raping, and killing billions of animals and using them as mere objects and products. As infants, we are born into this, and it wounds us on every level. Not only are our physical health, our society, and our Earth harmed, but at a deeper level we are harmed psychologically, spiritually, and morally. These wounds cry out for healing, and we can all deepen our healing, wherever we are in our journey.

Born into a culture based on relentlessly stealing the purposes as well as the physical and mental integrity of animals, we can lose touch with our purposes and our integrity and participate in and cocreate systems of human exploitation, waste, and injustice that are destroying the web of life and our basic cultural sanity. Living in a culture that's been organized around herding animals for ten thousand years now, we see the tragic environmental devastation, war, and inequity that the herding mentality creates and intensifies with its underlying attitudes and its technology and cultural systems, which enable and promote exploitation and oppression.

Through a vegan journey of awakening, we come to understand that the conflict and disease that we experience as humans is both a direct and secondary result of the abuse that we perpetrate on animals. Animal agriculture, with its relentless inefficiency and toxicity, directly harms the health of our ecosystems, our culture, and our physical health. It secondarily implants the attitudinal, emotional, and ethical disconnectedness and numbing that harm us and reduce our capacities to effectively address our problems. The animals and our violence toward them are made invisible by our herding culture's established traditions, language, institutions, and assumptions. We are collectively wounded by indoctrination and blinded to the devastating consequences of our daily actions.

As vegans, we are helping to heal these physical, psychological, and moral wounds both in ourselves and in our world. Veganism is the one philosophy and practice that targets the core of our interconnected problems and addresses the underlying cause of the disease our culture experiences and inflicts relentlessly. Our task is to nurture and deepen this healing in ourselves and also to heal other people who have been similarly wounded and are still trapped in the cages of conformism into which they were born. To the degree that we are authentically healing our inner wounds and opening to the light of inner truth, we are able to help others heal and awaken from the dark trance of violence that is the essence of our culture, violence embodied by animal agriculture in all its forms. Liberating animals is the direct path to human liberation, peace, and justice.

The truth that all of us, vegans or not, know in our bones is that animals suffer as we do. We also understand that our lives and our welfare are interconnected, and that all life is interdependent. The ancient Sanskrit word for truth is *satya*, and *graha* means insistence or force. Satyagraha, or truth-force, was a central tenet of Gandhi's approach to social change. Satyagraha is about as close as we can get to the fabled magic button that we can discover to help transform our world. When we speak our truth with respect and kindness, we are fulfilling our mission as light-bearers and healers and as world-transformers. The hardest part is to uncover this inner truth and to articulate it clearly, without judgment and without trying to manipulate others to change.

Sometimes people ask what the most effective formulation of this underlying truth might be. For example, if we're in an elevator and only have a half-minute or so, what words could we say to convey the essence of healing truth to another person? The good news is that even though it's counterproductive to try to change others, and often prompts them to resist, defend, and fight back, we can nevertheless plant seeds of truth and positive change in others through our words, actions, creative expressions, and examples. When we deeply and fully embody vegan values of kindness and respect, our words, gestures, and actions become congruent, and we can plant these seeds with effectiveness. Congruence is the key, and with it, satyagraha, truth-force, works through us. When we express this truth, in our own words as befits the occasion, on an elevator or anywhere else, we are conveying a simple and basic set of transformative ideas, which *is* our truth. Usually it's best to say something brief, and then let go so that the seed we have planted can germinate and grow organically. Done with respect and without an underlying motivation to manipulate others, we plant a healing depth charge, as it were, a potent seed of light, truth, and awareness in the consciousness of the person. The truth-seed we plant with goodwill and respect will help them to heal as well, because that is what truth-power does. Basically, our experience is all the same growing up in this herding culture, and our personal truth is also a universal truth that resonates with all of us.

The reason any of us eats animal foods is because we're following orders, and we know this deep down. We also understand that it's not in our best interest. When we articulate and embody this fundamental, world-transforming truth, and then share how liberating and healing it is for us to be free of this indoctrination, we are essentially opening the door of the invisible cage that keeps human beings imprisoned in destructive, anti-rational behavior. We can point out that we have discovered this for ourselves. If we do this well, the seed we planted in a seemingly casual way is alive inside them, growing every day, and propelling them to awakening and freedom. It is their own wisdom and compassion that are actually growing, and when they go vegan, it will not be because they are being shamed into it or pushed, but because their own inner caring and basic intelligence have been activated. So, even though there is no outer magic button, we do have within us the capacity to be an instrument of satyagraha, and to speak our truth, which is a universal truth.

To be effective in our vegan advocacy, it's essential that we do the inner work to understand and live veganism as nonviolence and respect in all our relations, both with nonhuman animals and also with human animals, who are often much more challenging. This effort helps us to understand and embody veganism more deeply. Deep veganism transforms our awareness. We realize, for example, that our entire culture is, in many ways, modeled on a farm where we, as newborn infants, are treated like calves, as exploitable commodities in a heartless economic system. Like the calves, we are not allowed to bond with our mothers properly. Toxic foods and pharmaceuticals are forced on us, and we enter a system of intense social and economic competition where we are seen as objects. We are taught to see ourselves and other people as competitors and as instruments to be manipulated and used. We are also compelled to consume foods, attitudes, and media that embed terror, despair, and anxiety. Our natural sense of kinship with other animals (and ultimately with each other) is fractured as we dine on their misery.

Our capacity for sensitivity and intuition is repressed as we undergo the emotional numbing that herderism, the mentality of materialism, requires, and our sense of celebrating our lives in an essentially benevolent and loving atmosphere is compromised if not completely shattered. With deep veganism, we grow to understand how all of us have been psychologically wounded by being born into this herding culture's violent and materialistic way of living, and through this understanding, we reawaken our compassion not just for animals but also for other wounded people. As this happens, our tendency toward prejudice, blame, criticism, and trying to change others dissolves into a deeper yearning to help them take the journey of healing that we are in the process of taking. A new sense of respect informs our advocacy efforts, and while we are still keenly aware of the misery and abuse inflicted by animal agriculture and the actions of indoctrinated and wounded people, we are grateful for the opportunity that we have to learn more, grow, and contribute our unique gifts to bring healing to our world.

Because we are all wounded by our culture's herderism and pervasive materialistic assumptions, we can cultivate a sense of solidarity with other people and a sense of compassion and understanding for them, even though they may be acting in ways with which we disagree. We see that the perpetrators are also victims. Hurt people hurt others. We all need healing, and healing comes from love. Disrespect cannot heal disrespect; only respect and love can heal. The most effective contribution I can make is the effort to heal my consciousness, so that I am ever more authentically living the truth of veganism, which is kindness and understanding for all beings, including myself.

The movement to liberate animals is the movement to liberate ourselves. This is the liberation movement that goes to the essential root of all our many problems, injustices, and crises. It requires us to question the old dualistic way we have engaged in social campaigns—that we are right and they are wrong—and to honor the deeper truth that we share similar wounds. In healing them in ourselves, we help others to heal them in themselves. It seems that the animal liberation movement is developing and maturing based increasingly on this understanding. As we take responsibility for changing others, we create a new foundation for embodying vegan values of respect for all. As more of us question the official story of materialism and strive to embody deep veganism, we are creating an unstoppable movement that will positively transform our world. Undertaking the challenging inner work to more fully embody the presence of loving understanding, we will attract and motivate others to take the same journey.

What is this inner work? Essentially, it is the practice of cultivating mindfulness and inner listening. Just as we've been relentlessly programmed by our culture, we're called to be relentless in our effort to free ourselves from this conditioning. Through questioning inner stories and the ongoing internal dialogue, as well as cultivating receptive awareness and stillness, our consciousness is essentially free, pure, and vast, like the clear and unencumbered sky. Through this, we can see more clearly the clouds of conditioned thought and habit as they appear, and that we are not these clouds; we are the space of awareness in which they arise and to which they return and ultimately disappear. We see that we are not mere objects nor are others ever objects or instruments. When we discover the deeper truth that we are all manifestations of eternal consciousness, the blinding spell of materialism and herderism begins to dissolve. Our relationship with ourselves and with other expressions of life is transformed. The roots of speciesism, racism, judgmentalism, entitlement, and other delusions are recognized as the programming of herderism's materialist delusion. As vegans, these delusions may still inhabit our consciousness, impeding our effectiveness and awareness, but our vegan journey calls us to bring mindfulness and healing to our consciousness so that we can more fully embody the vegan ethic of respect for all.

Veganism is far more than working for the rights of other animals. It calls us to a complete social transformation through transforming our attitudes, assumptions, and relationships at the deepest level. It's the adventure of a lifetime to awaken our awareness and deeply live the truth of our interconnectedness with all life. Transforming ourselves transforms our advocacy efforts so that, in Walt Whitman's words, "I and mine do not convince by arguments. We convince by our presence." It's not so much what we say; it's how we say it and how congruent we are in manifesting the message we are conveying.

As we increase our capacity to embody veganism as kindness and respect for other human animals, our movement will become the change we'd like to see in the world, dramatically increasing our effectiveness. We will plant seeds of positive change in others with every word, intonation, and gesture, and, awakened from the dualistic materialism of herderism, others will change without our trying to change them. Authentic education is self-discovery that takes place in a context of trust and respect. Our main effort is to increasingly exemplify veganism and connect with our intuitive wisdom. From this can flow a profusion of campaigns, films, books, blogs, websites, products, music, art, and grassroots efforts that all embody the vegan message. Sharing our experiences, examples, and insights is what helps create lasting and empowering change in others, and it also frees us as advocates from burnout, anger, and despair.

The vegan (r)evolution of kindness, inclusion, and healing calls us to take the ongoing inner steps to deepen our veganism. Through this effort, we will become the people who can cocreate the fundamental social and personal transformation that our positive future is calling from us. Buckminster Fuller emphasized that the way to a positive future is not through fighting against an abusive and inefficient system or situation. Rather, it is to build an alternative that reflects the harmony, freedom, and integrity that we envision and that naturally renders the existing system obsolete. Veganism is not merely a critique of a violent and outmoded system; it is living an inner and outer alternative that is nutritious, delicious, sustainable, healing, liberating, and transformational on every level. Each of us can contribute to it with our unique abilities and insights and help heal the foundation of our relationships with other animals and the Earth and with each other.

The vegan wave is building and is irresistible, because it is our true nature calling. May our words and example instigate the benevolent revolution that liberates animals and all of us from the herding delusion of materialism so that we discover our purpose and celebrate our lives as we are intended to on this bountiful and beautiful Earth.

II
Connecting the Dots:
Perspectives on
Animal Rights

Copy-and-Paste Activism Does Not Work: Perspectives from a POC

Gwenna Hunter, event coordinator for Vegan
Outreach and founder of Vegans of LA

As the founder of Vegans of LA and the Los Angeles community events coordinator for Vegan Outreach, as well as a volunteer for various animal rights groups, I have found that when communicating with communities of color, it is best not to stand before them and say "go vegan because animals are suffering." One would assume that a community who knows what it's like to suffer would understand this as an easy conversation. However, living in a reality where you still struggle with being treated equally, along with constant news and social media showing people of color being treated unfairly and brutalized by police officers with little to no consequences, makes it emotionally painful to hear about animals having their rights fought for with such consistency, passion, and unity. This is why, when speaking with communities of color, I always start my conversations with health and self-love. Twice in my career as a community events coordinator, I made the error of starting these conversations with animals. I was basically doing what I had seen and heard in an attempt to follow the "go vegan" script, yet I was met with harsh resistance, particularly from older black men.

The first time I experienced this type of reaction I was presenting at a library in the Watts neighborhood of Los Angeles. I started talking about animals and a gentleman stood up and yelled "You're an evolutionist!" He was a large man with a face that revealed pain and stress. He began to tell me in front of a roomful of people that the Bible says it is okay to eat animals, and if it weren't true then God wouldn't have said it. Getting into a debate with anyone over the Bible typically creates more frustration and separation, and I did not want to have that conversation. I was actually terrified of this type of confrontation. It was something I hoped to never experience while giving a talk about the vegan lifestyle.

At the time I was new at giving these talks and when confronted with what I had hoped to avoid, I had to take a deep breath and remind myself to see him as a victim of the same programming I was once part of. I asked him if he felt that a loving God would want to take the life of someone who loved, gave birth to children, and felt joy and sadness. His response was: do not question God! I had no idea how to respond, but, luckily, prior to the event starting, he and I had struck up a conversation. He wasn't aware that I would be speaking, but he knew that I was the organizer of the event. He shared with me that he once worked at a carnival and was responsible for being the caregiver of several animals there. He said that to his amazement the animals would greet him every time he showed up and that he felt a bond with them and an affection that he had never expected. He was also very surprised to experience their reactions and their attachment to each other.

I was able to use that conversation to express how he may have felt if, during that bonding time, someone came and slaughtered those animals in front of him and then ate them. I said that this is how vegans feel about all animals. We believe that they are all aware and express a full range of emotions, just like us. I posed the question: "Why have anyone suffer so that we can have the experience of eating their dead bodies?" He listened and connected with his own story and then quieted down as he went for a second helping of the vegan food that we had provided.

I understand how easily people can become provoked when they feel they're being told that what they have believed their entire lives is not true, when it challenges their religion, when it raises questions about their traditional food choices, and especially when they feel that an animal's rights have priority over theirs. Or worse, when their own suffering is compared to an animal that they have been programmed to believe is here for us to do what we want to it.

Another situation where a person of color was offended by my promoting a vegan lifestyle was during an outdoor tabling event in a black community called Leimert Park. I spoke during a panel discussion about being a black vegan influencer, and I had a table with free booklets provided by Vegan Outreach. An older black gentleman approached me and asked, "Sister you're out here telling people not to eat animals, but what are you doing for our black community? Black men are being shot in the streets." I could see and feel his anger. It wasn't necessarily toward me, but toward the system he felt I was representing because he may have felt that I was in it just for the animals. I looked him in the eyes and said, "I *am* doing this for black people. I want us to stop eating dead bodies and believing that it is nourishment. I want us to wake up and eat better, because if we eat better then perhaps we can unite and make better decisions for ourselves and our communities. This is why I am here. We need to expand our consciousness and capacity to love." He looked at me and said, "Okay, my sister. Thank you for being out here."

Conversations like these let me know that people of color will often make assumptions and criticize this type of work if the activist isn't wearing a dashiki and a head wrap, or doesn't have obvious images of POC on their outreach table. Our culture is hurting. We are hurting so much that it is often hard for us to show love and empathy for nonhuman animals because of the comparisons we grew up hearing—that we are lower than animals, an eighth of human, "savages," "apes," "monkeys," and are subject to having dogs sicced on us during protests. Experiencing, watching, and reading about these experiences can cause resentment toward animals, when it seems like they are being shown more love, empathy, and kindness. It's like having a sibling who gets treated with special attention, while the other sibling is constantly being compared to the perfect sibling and never gets the same amount of attention. At some point, no matter how nice the praised sibling might be, resentment will inevitably creep in. This is why so many POC are triggered when they hear non-POC talk about animal rights and when animal exploitation is compared to human slavery. POC wonder why more white people are not out there marching, fighting, and doing the same work on our behalf. We want to know: Why does it feel like animals are more important? Why are so many outraged when an animal is hurt, but the same outrage is not expressed when a black person is brutalized by the police? What do they see in animals that they do not see in us? This at the very core breaks a piece of my heart.

When doing activism with POC it is best to start the discussion by helping people think differently about food through self-love and how to change genetics. We want to look and feel our best. Then the conversation can ease into the topic of animals. Explain how animals are fed antibiotics and how they walk around in their own filth. Prompt them to think about how we are a society that is obsessed with eating dead body parts and how eating someone's wings, thighs, and ribs is rather strange when you really think about it. Create a space for deep critical thinking and questioning. Conversing like this can often trigger a new form of awareness. Tell them how the mothers cry out for their children and how they are not able to nurture them properly. Let them know that when a cow gives birth to a boy, whom she had carried in her womb for nine months just like human mothers, he is taken for veal. Paint a picture and tell a story so that empathy has permission to flow from their hearts. But please do not say that animals have rights before assessing the energy of those you are speaking with. It is important to make a connection, gain trust, and show that you care about the community you are speaking with. If not, you will lose their trust, and if they feel that their lives are seen as less important, they will be resentful. Copy-and-paste activism only works when you are preaching to the choir. If you want to reach the congregation, you must feed people with the information that they are hungry for. It doesn't matter how they get their foot in the door, as long as they come in. Plant the vegan seed and let it grow on its own.

Activism in the White Community versus the Black Community

When I got involved in activism, I wasn't vegan yet. I was vegetarian and working toward it. I was new to LA and knew very few people, so I started creating meetups where I would host an event at a vegan restaurant and people from the area would come out to make new friends and have conversations. My meetups were mostly frequented by white people. When I began getting more active and volunteering, the white vegan community embraced me and I got involved in many events and causes. What I noticed that concerned me was the strictness of their veganism and constantly policing each other on being vegan. For example, if someone in the community did anything that was not considered vegan, such as consume honey, they would get attacked. However, I did learn about speciesism, and checking my language, and the importance of referring to an animal as "he" or "she" instead of "it." I learned more about animals' unique personalities by being invited to events where they would roam freely. I felt more connected to the innocence of animals, and I could understand how easy it is to love them and want to defend them with everything you have. I understood this powerful connection.

In the black vegan community, rarely was there conversation about animals' ability to love, communicate, and feel. The commentary I heard was mostly along the lines of "Don't eat animals because of what they are fed" and "Don't eat animals because it's not good for us." Conversations were centered on taking better care of ourselves, breaking family cycles, creating new eating habits, encouraging exercising and being active, eating raw foods, and loving yourself. I didn't hear this kind of discussion as much in the white vegan community.

I am fortunate to gain value from both sides. What is unfortunate is that the white vegan and black vegan communities are often separated. Imagine if we came together to make change; it would be a day of reckoning for the meat and dairy industries. We would be much more effective if we took the time to learn how to gain an understanding of each other and help educate one another on how to advocate for the other in ways that go beyond veganism. After all, this lifestyle is about doing no harm; no harm to any being. This is why I often include conversations about human oppression on my Vegans of LA page. I often hear white vegans say that the vegan conversation should only be focused on the animals because they are voiceless, but if we cannot interact with oppressed humans and show them that we care about them as well, people will continue to eat animals. We cannot save one species without saving the others. Forms of oppression are all connected and operate from the same methods of control, commodification, and mental programming to keep us enslaved and oppressing each other. For me, the definition of veganism has evolved to encompass a harmonious balance on earth for everyone, where danger, fear, and toxicity are replaced with compassion and love for all.

My Spiritual Awakening

My journey really began in my early teens in Cleveland, Ohio. I lived within walking distance of a mom-and-pop health-food store called Weber's. I would go there with money I earned and purchase sodas made with natural ingredients and chips made with vegetables and I would spend a lot of time reading ingredients on packages. I was curious about foods made without animals, and I understood vegetarianism, but at that point in my life I had never heard the word "vegan." One day I purchased a frozen package of veggie burgers (this was in the late eighties) and prepared one. It tasted like a tire sandwich. That was it for me . . . or so I thought.

Many years later, when I was living in Charlotte, North Carolina, a dear friend called and asked if I would do the Daniel Fast with her. This fast was based on the Bible and called for abstaining from eating animal products with the purpose of gaining clarity and getting closer to God. At that time, I still ate some meat, but had stopped eating cows and pigs because of an earlier health scare. (My body started having trouble digesting meat, and I would break out in cold sweats, vomit, and experience stabbing stomach pain and severe back pain. I was first diagnosed with kidney stones, and then a peptic ulcer. When all treatment failed to stop my symptoms, I was finally able to diagnose myself when I realized that these symptoms only occurred when I ate cow's flesh. Once I made the connection and stopped eating beef, the symptoms disappeared.) So, when my friend gave me that invitation in 2008, I figured I could do it. I felt there was something divine about the fast, and, after completing it, I felt amazing. The menstrual cycles that once wreaked havoc on my mind and body came and went with ease—no cramps, no spotting, no heavy bleeding, and I was actually pleasant. It felt like a miracle. I was convinced that eating meat was the reason I felt awful all those years during my cycle. So, I decided to stick with it and become pescatarian, and then vegetarian.

During the first few months I had one of the most profound dream experiences. I dreamed that I was in the sky overlooking a green pasture. In the pasture was a beautiful cow, and I could feel that she was aware of my presence. She looked up at me, and our eyes connected. All of a sudden, my soul and my body merged with her. I could feel and interpret her thoughts and feel her energy. I was her consciousness. I woke up from the dream crying uncontrollably because I felt her love so strongly. I have always been someone who seeks the truth and wants to learn about ways to expand my own capacity to love and see the world. In all of this, I had never considered that the animals we eat actually love. The cow's love was pure and innocent, yet powerful. I also felt a physically warm sensation on my chest over my heart when I awoke, and when I touched the spot, I was paralyzed with the most beautiful feeling of peace. I felt that this cow had given me a piece of her heart, and from that moment on I knew that cows were aware and that they were no different from us. However, I still had yet to make the connection to the dairy industry. In my mind, cows were milked by gentle hands, and they mooed, and it was a mutual agreement. It wasn't until the YouTube video *Dairy Is Scary* by Erin Janus crossed my path that I learned how cows are treated like slaves, raped, and mistreated. I saw that industrialized milking wasn't done with gentleness but with machines, and that cows are treated like their lives don't matter. Knowing that cows are not milk machines on legs with no thoughts or consciousness, I was immediately stunned that these loving, conscious beings were experiencing this type of treatment for our unnecessary pleasure. I went vegan on the spot and have never looked back.

Because I know what it is like to suffer, I don't want anyone to intentionally suffer so that I can eat them or wear their skin. I know what it is like to live on a planet where people judge and treat you differently because you don't look like them. I know how it feels to be part of a society that doesn't believe a woman can make her own decisions regarding her own body. I know what it's like to be treated lesser than because my body produces more carbon than others and therefore having darker skin is often treated as a form of punishment rather than the magic it truly and scientifically is. I know what it is like to experience physical and emotional abuse as a child and being at the mercy of another individual, and yet still having compassion and love for them. Animals are so incredibly forgiving.

Not everyone will have a dream giving them a divine connection to a cow. Most people will have to make the connection another way. I was fortunate to have this experience, as it changed my entire outlook. If you are living hand to mouth and seeing your friends and family being mistreated by the world, the last thing on your mind is animal rights. You want to enjoy pleasure any way you can, and for some people, eating is the only simple pleasure they have in life. Food is often the one thing we believe we can control. If you approach someone and tell them to stop eating animals, expect to be met with resistance, because what they are hearing you say is "I don't want you to have this pleasure." It's a matter of different perceptions and interpretations of reality.

We as vegans often speak to people from where we are and not necessarily from the psychological level of the person who is still eating animals. You don't teach someone one plus one equals two and then immediately get into trigonometry. People all over the world are hurting, and everyone wants their pain acknowledged, not just by those in the same oppressive category, but more importantly by those who are not. As for those who feel like vegans only care about animals because we acknowledge their suffering, it's important to understand that we can support and advocate for the liberation of humans *and* animals. We do not have to choose between the two. We can stand up for all. The sky is not the limit; the mind is.

Living in Alignment with My Values: My Path to Animal Rights Activism

Brittany Michelson, teacher and writer

"Living with integrity means behaving in ways that are in harmony with your personal values."

—Barbara De Angelis

Like many children, I grew up loving animals. My family had a variety of pets that we adored—dogs that slept on our beds, rats that my brother and I made climbing structures for, guinea pigs we let scurry around our bedrooms, and other furry and shelled companions. While we considered ourselves animal lovers, we would sit down at the dining room table to eat spaghetti with meat sauce, lemon chicken, and tuna melts. And there was always ice cream for dessert. We didn't think of the animals we were eating. We also thought nothing of the leather shoes and wool sweaters we wore, or the down jackets for skiing.

When I was a high school senior, my brother, who is two years younger and had recently stopped eating meat, showed me an undercover video that was my first glimpse into the animal agriculture industry. It was a PETA video from a meat-producing facility. I remember the cow that hung upside down in a warehouse-like building. I remember her face and big eyes, her degradation and defenselessness, and the angry man kicking her with a large boot. I was stunned, the air nearly sucked out of me. It was as if my cells had rearranged with this new knowledge of where meat came from. I loved animals; didn't most people? How could this be allowed? Why was nobody stopping it? The wide eyes of the gentle animal stared through the screen with a mix of fear and surrender, and I could do nothing but stare back at her suffering. There was innocence, hanging like an object.

I made it through only a minute of the video, then reached over and shut it off. I locked eyes with my brother. There was a thick sadness between us.

I could never unlearn what I had learned.

I wish I could say that the video made me instantly give up meat, but seventeen years of ingrained meat eating was more influential than the sadness I felt over that suffering cow. I tried to justify meat consumption by telling myself that humans had always eaten it, that we are omnivores, that we need meat for protein. All of my friends ate meat, and my father owned a restaurant at the time that was known for its steaks. I also told myself that the footage my brother showed me was surely an exception, that usually cows lived in fields—not in metal buildings—and that they weren't treated like that.

I shut the video out of my mind and went on with my busy teenage life, but the visual of the hanging cow in the building surfaced, creating an unsettled feeling inside of me. I found myself questioning the reality behind meat, but I didn't allow myself to do any research, because I never wanted to be subjected to images like that again. The pressures of maintaining a successful grade point average, managing a demanding varsity sports schedule, and navigating the dramas of adolescent social life were more pressing than educating myself about what I was eating. It was easier not to think about it.

Also, at the time I would do anything to avoid creating extra anxiety. I already battled a barrage of obsessive internal repetition about how I said things or how I didn't say them, how I acted, and what others were thinking about me. I couldn't shake the underlying anxious feeling that lived in my chest. I already felt different from my peers due to persistent anxiety—it seemed like *nobody* I knew experienced anxiety to the degree that I did—and I was determined not to let it define me. Though I had very good friendships and socialized at weekend parties, at school I was quite shy and felt more awkward than anything.

Shortly after my brother showed me the video of the cow, I graduated from high school, and then a few months into my freshman year of college, I decided to become vegetarian. Eating dead animals had started feeling strange to me. I also started buying plant-based milk because I no longer liked the taste of cow's milk. I was eighteen and living in the university dorms a couple of hours from my family's home in northern Arizona. The following spring, my brother, who was then sixteen, turned vegan. He didn't vocalize his reasons for changing from vegetarian to vegan, but later on, I found out that he had been inspired by his favorite band Propagandhi and an older musician friend that he greatly looked up to. My parents accepted my brother's "dietary choice" but they also figured it was something that he, as a teenager, was experimenting with. He was in a punk band and into anarchy, and at the time being vegan was an anomaly that seemed to fit right in with rejecting societal norms.

During my years of vegetarianism, there were periods where I was pescatarian, as I thought I needed the protein, and my mom told me that omega-3s from fish were very important. Also, at the time I didn't think eating fish was the same as eating animals like cows and pigs. It seemed like they didn't have as much capacity for pain and emotion as mammals do. My assumption was rooted in speciesism, and I had no idea. Speciesism involves the lack of consideration to certain animals based on species classification. Its premise underlies the notion that fish don't suffer as much as cows, or that animals classified as "pets" are worthy of love and protection while animals who are designated "food" are for human consumption.

What I didn't know back then is that the dairy and egg industries also operate from serious animal suffering. I thought that cows readily produced milk and were living in fields. I assumed that eggs were collected after hens laid them, and I figured they were pecking atop grass and dirt, certainly not crammed into cages so tightly they couldn't spread their wings. I had no idea that animals were genetically manipulated to produce much more than they naturally would.

It never crossed my mind that their production levels would go down, nor did I think about what happened to them after their production ceased. I didn't know that male calves are slaughtered for veal and that female dairy cows are eventually sent to slaughter. I also believed that the widespread "Milk Does A Body Good" and "Got Milk?" ads were informing the public about the calcium for our bones and other nutrients that we needed from milk.

An Awakening

"There are things known and there are things unknown, and in between are the doors of perception."

—Aldous Huxley

In 2014 I began dating someone who led a plant-based diet for health. At some point he started talking about the negative health effects of dairy. Curious, I looked into it and found plenty of information online validating that dairy is acidic and causes inflammation. I also learned about the growth hormones given to cows and about the antibiotics in their feed that help control bacteria and the infections that result from being overmilked. I was disgusted. Milk cartons and company trucks show images of peaceful animals grazing in green fields, but upon discovering the disturbing reality of dairy, I went vegan. It was the first of May 2015, and it was only then, through that crucial decision, that my actions became fully aligned with the values I had always considered important to me—compassion, non-violence, peace, and justice.

In becoming vegan, I realized that something known as cognitive dissonance had been responsible for the rift between my values and my actions. Cognitive dissonance is the state of having inconsistent thoughts, beliefs, or attitudes, especially as related to behavioral decisions. Although I had always considered myself to be someone who loved and respected animals, I had been passively accepting their torture and misery by eating and wearing animal products. I also learned the concept of speciesism, which is rooted in the assumption of human superiority leading to the exploitation of animals.

Dogs are widely considered to be beloved companions, yet in some Asian countries they are slaughtered for the dog meat trade. While cows are sacred in India, they are one of the most popular "food staples" in America. Growing up, I never would have accepted the idea of eating dog meat, and had I known back then that such a thing existed, I would have been outraged and disgusted. Yet I ate hamburgers without thinking of the cows who had been killed. We have been conditioned to reject the abuse of certain animals, yet ignore the abuse of animals used for food, clothing, and testing. We are taught contradictions at a young age and have also been taught how to compartmentalize.

The philosopher Hippocrates said, "The soul is the same in all living creatures, although the body of each is different." This prompts the simple, thought-provoking question often vocalized in the animal rights movement: "Why love one, but eat the other?" A frequent chant at animal rights protests is "Humans and animals, we're all equal." This is essentially what Hippocrates's quote means. We are all made of the same energy. How could I be opposed to racism and sexism and homophobia and yet ignore the largest group of oppressed (in the trillions) and most severely abused beings on the planet?

Years prior, during my high school graduation trip to Europe, our student group visited the historical site of Dachau, a former concentration camp in Germany. Upon our arrival, we watched a video that showed emaciated human bodies put into ovens and dumped into a huge pit in the ground. Then we toured the grounds, where we saw rows of wooden barracks and buildings containing the large stone ovens that had burned the bodies. Behind the walls of farm facilities, animals—who are just as capable of love, fear, and pain as the dogs and cats we share our homes with—are confined, tortured, and killed. By the billions. The definition of holocaust is destruction or slaughter on a mass scale. A speciesist would argue that the purpose of certain animals is to be bred for human consumption. An anti-speciesist believes that humans are not superior to animals, and that animals do not exist for human use. Speciesism is responsible for society's failure to acknowledge that what happens to animals on a daily basis in the animal agriculture industry is indeed a holocaust.

Another frequent chant at animal rights protests is "One struggle one fight, human freedom animal rights." At its core, the animal rights movement is about dismantling oppression, just as any social justice movement seeks to do—whether it is oppression based on race, gender, sexual orientation, or species. I suppose that animal rights has not yet been fully accepted as a social justice movement by the mainstream public, not only because the exploitation of animals is so deeply entrenched in society but also because this oppressed group is the only one that is nonhuman. Due to the fact that speciesism is so ingrained in our human actions and behaviors, sentient beings are reduced to objects and items by consumers who purchase their packaged body parts and secretions.

How many times have I heard non-vegans say they are animal lovers? How many times did I say that as a child and an adult, all the while eating and wearing animal products? This "love of animals" is usually (and unconsciously) compartmentalized, reserved for animals known as companions like dogs and cats, or fascinating wild animals like dolphins and elephants. Yet how many people who say they love dolphins and elephants go see them at aquariums or zoos? For many, the idea of being an "animal lover" is only a constructed idea of what love is, as we wouldn't actually pay for the exploitation and confinement of anyone we love. The unfortunate truth is that not enough of the general population realizes that visiting places like these funds the exploitation of animals, as these venues promote "species conservation" and "education" messages.

Though animals are similar to us in the ways that truly matter—such as the capacity to experience pain, fear, joy, and emotional connection—they have been deemed inferior and thereby have no real rights as citizens of the earth. Albert Einstein said, "Our task must be to free ourselves by widening our circle of compassion to embrace all living creatures and the whole of nature and its beauty." Our ability to achieve planetary peace depends on our ability to stop the mentality of separation based on form, and instead honor our interconnectedness by embracing *all* beings. If we hope to evolve into a society of justice, it is crucial that we value everyone, including nonhuman animals, as deserving of rights and autonomy.

Taking a Stand for Animals

"I will not stay silent so that you can stay comfortable."

—Anonymous

Animal cruelty is like the domino effect. You hear of one form of cruelty and then another and another, forming a line of horrors that seems to collapse into itself. When I started learning about the abusive practices inherent in animal food production, I felt an acute level of anger. I found out that male chicks are ground up alive—tossed into a macerator like trash—because they are of no use to the egg industry. I learned of an industry practice called thumping, where piglets deemed too sick and weak are slammed headfirst onto concrete to kill them. I thought of cows hooked up to machines so that their milk could be extracted for humans instead of being fed to their babies. I thought of their worn-out bodies being hauled off to slaughter after they had spent several years in a cycle of impregnation and having their babies taken away. I thought about the male calves, kept in crates so small they couldn't turn around, being tenderized for veal. Thinking about the confinement, mutilation, and abuse of these animals caused me anxiety. I lost sleep at night; images of animal suffering flashed in my mind. I was overwhelmed, to say the least. How could I live in a world where this kind of sickening abuse happens to the most innocent and vulnerable beings simply because they aren't able to speak out and defend themselves?

The acute anxiety I was experiencing in regard to animal cruelty quickly led me to do more than simply be vegan. In July 2015, just a couple of months after going vegan, I attended my first animal rights protest at a grocery store. The action involved standing on the sidewalk holding signs to draw the public's attention to the awful conditions of animals bred for food, and chanting phrases like: *It's not food it's violence; Their bodies not ours; There's no excuse for animal abuse.* We proceeded to go inside the store and chant. I was intrigued and empowered by this experience, both by the act of speaking up for animals in a public space, and the immediate sense of camaraderie I felt being with a group of like-minded individuals. A number of shoppers and employees stopped what they were doing and watched us; a few took out their phones to record a video. After about five minutes inside the store, we made our way outside and continued chanting on the sidewalk.

I learned that the concept of doing a disruption is to challenge normalized violence against animals by vocalizing the message of animal rights in a public setting. Deceptive advertising leads consumers to believe that meat, dairy, and eggs come from peacefully raised animals who are somehow killed humanely. Yet from an activist's standpoint, there is no humane way to kill someone who doesn't want to die. I immediately aligned with this philosophy, and attending that protest solidified my decision to become an activist. I realized that I needed to go beyond the refusal to consume or purchase animal products. Taking action was the only way I could move forward knowing the atrocities that humanity inflicts on innocent animals on a daily basis. I decided I would do everything in my power to dismantle speciesism.

A couple of years after becoming an animal rights activist, I was presented with the unique opportunity to bring activism to the classroom. In college I majored in education, and I have taught in various capacities since then. In September 2017, I started teaching in a private K–8 program centered on inquiry with a variety of unique and creative classes. Along with various writing classes, I teach activism classes, where I encourage students to explore human, animal, and environmental causes. They each focus on a cause that's important to them during a semester-long Action Project, which involves making awareness signs and a visual display to educate other students and teachers. Most of my students have chosen animal causes, which isn't surprising given that kids naturally tend to feel compassion toward animals. In Spring 2018, my ten-year-old vegan student chose the topic of animal agriculture. She and her vegan mother met me at a few of the Los Angeles Animal Save pig vigils and she shared her experience of bearing witness with the other students. She also incorporated video footage from the vigils into her project. I added my voice to the dialogue to support her and to educate students about the effects that animal agriculture has on animals, the environment, and human health.

Since I started teaching these activism classes, I've often thought about how my life might have been different had I been exposed to the truth about what happens to animals in zoos, marine parks, and the food industry when I was growing up as an innocent and unaware animal lover. There is this idea that children should be protected, so as not to upset or traumatize them, but this fear is often what keeps the truth carefully hidden. It also enables animal-abusing industries to get away with heinous standard practices. It's often said that kids are the future, and I believe that if activism classes were taught all over the country, we would be educating a new generation of activists, which would naturally inspire great change.

Building Fundamental Connections

"Tell me, what is it you plan to do with your one wild and precious life?"

—Mary Oliver

Becoming vegan was one of the best decisions I've ever made for two significant reasons. It was from that moment that I started living in true alignment with my values—as I am against animal abuse, against the destruction of the environment, and against damaging human health. Veganism also resonates with me on a spiritual level—the idea of non-harm to fellow beings—and I realized that, energetically, I didn't want to consume torture. As someone who values feminism, I realized that I could not accept the exploitation of female bodies, regardless of species.

Second, becoming vegan led me to animal rights activism, which has gifted me with a focus and motivation that is greater than myself. It has inspired me to be of service to suffering beings and the planet, while bringing human connections into my life that are based on fundamental values. It is a challenge being vegan in a world that values convenience, tradition, and palate pleasure over sentient lives—but when I feel overwhelmed by the cruelty and frustrated with the societal conditioning that permits animal exploitation, I focus on the amazing community of animal rights activists that I am a part of. While society at large views "food" and "clothing" animals as products, we view them not as unknowns in the industry's machine, but as individuals worth fighting for with the privilege of our human voice.

Over the past several years, I have participated in all kinds of disruptions, demonstrations, protests, marches, and vigils, and I have connected with people from diverse walks of life. Some have been vegan for many years and some have recently turned vegan. Many of us feel that it is our obligation to stand up for animals by engaging in activism, to make up for the years that we were complicit in their suffering. People who are not involved in the movement often refer to animal rights activism as a passion, but in a world where innocent animals are horrifically exploited by humanity, taking action for them is a moral imperative.

As a part of the animal rights community, I feel a sense of belonging that surpasses any sense of belonging I previously felt. Regardless of age, background, experience, or any other categorical factor, there is an instant bond with fellow activists, a bond between those who believe that animals' lives are more important than taste, habit, convenience, or tradition. It is a profound experience to come together to bear witness to truckloads of animals outside a slaughter facility and to spend hours with hundreds of activists at a factory farm for a mass open rescue. While some might wonder what the point is of giving water to pigs about to die, or singing songs of liberation to chickens trapped in buildings, we know that every individual deserves to be honored and that their stories must be told.

I am dedicated to bringing justice to the victims of speciesism and planting seeds in the minds of people who have been conditioned by society (as we all have) to passively accept and fund the abhorrent treatment of sentient beings by industries that view them as dollar signs. Within my activism, I have discovered the power in my voice as I speak truth to the public through a megaphone at nonviolent protests and disruptions. I feel empowered in speaking up for silenced victims by attending actions, and also in the form of writing. I have written a number of awareness-raising articles on animal issues, which is more gratifying than any material I had previously written.

My commitments have merged—teaching, writing, and activism—and in this I have found tremendous satisfaction. As a teacher, I am in the profession of helping youth, which is certainly fulfilling, but animal rights activism is a different type of fulfillment in that it's fighting against oppression and advocating for justice. It's standing up for the most mistreated beings on the planet. I've come to realize that my definition of a life well lived is to be of service to others and the planet. It is true that a gift we give to others is a gift we give to ourselves.

Living in alignment with my values and being committed to work that inspires and fulfills me has also helped alleviate anxiety. My struggles pale in comparison to the nightmare that so many animals are constantly subjected to. Furthermore, while animal cruelty continues to upset me, it doesn't provoke the level of anxiety that it used to, because I know that I am actively part of the solution. I live for the day when animal exploitation ceases to exist and when nonhumans are valued and respected for the individuals they are. Until that day, I will continue to take action.

How I Made the Connection: Gay Rights, Feminism, and Animal Liberation

Dani Rukin, citizen journalist
for *JaneUnchained News*

"Human beings see oppression vividly when they're the victims. Otherwise, they victimize blindly and without a thought."

—Isaac Bashevis Singer

Prior to 2016, if you had told me I'd be a vegan animal rights activist, I would have said you had the wrong person. I didn't quite know what a vegan was other than an extreme version of a vegetarian, and someone who took themselves a little too seriously. Years ago, I had a vegan girlfriend while living in New York City, and I never asked her why she was vegan. All I remember was complaining to friends "She doesn't even eat honey! Honey!" And then there was the time my longtime vegetarian friend finally started eating meat again when she got pregnant. I was thrilled. No more hassle chowing down together.

In college I was an out, loud, and proud lesbian who, at eighteen, moved to San Francisco and cofounded AGLA (Alliance for Gay and Lesbian Awareness). We fought hard for, and lost, the right to meet on the University of San Francisco's Jesuit-run campus. Among many failed tactics, we held a rally with then-renowned San Francisco supervisors Carol Ruth Silver and Harry Britt, speaking out in support of our civil rights. The faculty and student council both voted to ban our group from becoming officially recognized, because, in their words, homosexuality was a sin. We argued that we weren't asking for the right to form the group to "commit the sin," we were demanding our civil rights not to be denied from forming a recovery and progress (RAP) and support group based on our sexual orientation.

Historically, the argument for justifying discrimination against any individual or group stems from the notion that those being discriminated against are, in some prejudicial way, viewed as inferior, and therefore underserving of equal treatment. Throughout past and present civilization, "different but equal" has not been an easily digestible notion for many. "Can't we all just get along?" Apparently not.

When it comes to justice for humans, the most socially, emotionally, and spiritually conscious among us are quick to defend the marginalized yet ignore the legitimate suffering of animals. Racism, sexism, homophobia, and xenophobia are all socially agreed-upon parasites of the human heart and mind, and refuting these prejudices is an acceptable indicator of an "evolved" understanding and an appreciation of diversity and inclusion. Yet, most of those very same people, when confronted with their own socially conditioned use and abuse of nonhuman animals, will defend their right to eat animals despite knowing the suffering and anguish the animals go through. Seeing ourselves as the oppressor is not so easy.

It wasn't until I came out against using animals for food, clothing, research, and entertainment that I understood the concept of speciesism—the presumption that humans are superior to animals, which conveniently justifies our exploitation of them. Isn't that the key ingredient to any rationale that allows one group to oppress another?

I spent the eighties riding motorcycles in my custom leather biker jacket, 501® jeans with the requisite chain of keys dangling from my belt loop, and sporting a rebellious "boi" haircut. I eventually left the conservative USF for progressive San Francisco State University, filling my course credits with women's studies classes—anthropology, history, literature, and politics from a woman's and WoC's perspective. I was no stranger to activism and speaking truth to power. I've always had an insatiable hunger for the truth. Fast-forward decades later, and I went from a passionate voice for gay and lesbian rights chanting "We're here. We're queer. Get used to it!" at Dyke Marches and Pride parades, to an outspoken animal rights activist shouting, "It's not food, it's violence!"

It was in fall 2015 that I was having dinner with a friend who was upset about an elephant in a zoo in Pakistan who had been chained in a dilapidated concrete shed for twenty-eight years. Like most, I was appalled but felt helpless to do anything, let alone have a clue what the "anything" would have been. She told me about an online petition circulating to free him to a sanctuary, and I agreed to sign it even though I didn't believe it would actually make a difference. Twenty-seven thousand signatures later, the zoo responded to the outside pressure by unchaining Kaavan and giving him (slightly) better care. And although the fight to free this elephant continues, it catalyzed my interest in not only the welfare of this particular captive wild animal, but in elephants in general. Like many Westerners, I didn't know much about these larger-than-life pachyderms other than they lived far away in the wild, unless they were in a zoo. I did ride an elephant twenty years ago while in Thailand, expecting it to be a "memory of a lifetime," but instead it left me feeling unexplainably melancholy. The elephants seemed downtrodden. Still, I shook it off and didn't return my thoughts to it until decades later. I became engrossed in learning everything I could about these gentle giants. It was like cramming a decade of intensive research and knowledge into one semester. I could not get enough of these majestic creatures. Not yet vegan, I testified before our city council members on behalf of the elephants confined in the local zoo, arguing that elephants are not designed to live in captivity and that there is no humane way to imprison, breed, and use other sentient beings for entertainment. In my testimony, I likened their plight to that of a slave, who can be defined as "someone who is the property of, and wholly subject to another, and entirely under the domination of some person." Elephants belong in the wild. And the remaining captive elephants belong in accredited elephant sanctuaries so they can live out the rest of their lives in peace and dignity. Our plea before the council was not for larger enclosures, but for the total abolition of capturing, buying, selling, trading, and imprisoning elephants and other wild animals for any reason.

Before the Civil War, the goal of the abolitionist movement was the immediate emancipation of those enslaved. At the time abolitionists were viewed as radicals. Any cause of great historical importance was considered extreme while in its resistance stage. As Captain Paul Watson, founder of Sea Shepherd, has said "If you want to know where you would have stood on slavery before the Civil War, don't look at where you stand on slavery today. Look at where you stand on animal rights."

Looking back, I can see how, in my testifying for the emancipation of elephants, I was building the case for my own veganism. I could not be against the abuse of elephants if I was paying for the confinement, breeding, exploitation, and killing of other animals. This was my "aha" moment. Elephants were my "gateway animal" into veganism. In my deeper dive into learning about the rampant and worldwide abuse of elephants, I came across footage and images of the abuse of other animals, including the extreme cruelty toward "food" animals and, as much as I wanted to look away, I could not. I understood the slaughtering of animals to be cruel, but considered it a necessary evil. How else were we going to get our protein? I was trying my best to eat mostly "humane meat," which in hindsight was not as often as I wanted to believe. Not to mention, how do you humanely kill someone who does not want to die? After educating myself about what was really going on in the multibillion-dollar meat, dairy, and egg industries, I could no longer justify eating anything from an animal and live with myself. Like us, they feel pain and fear, pleasure and joy, anxiety and loneliness, and want to live and love as much as we do. It's impossible to morally justify being the cause of violence and suffering toward anyone. Like any moment of truth, I stood at the turning point and chose love, justice, and truth. I went vegan.

I immediately wanted to share my life-changing epiphany with friends and everyone on social media. I was sure that once they saw the horrors of animals suffering, and learned that animal agriculture was a leading cause of climate change and that animal products are terrible for our health, they would also transition to veganism. But they didn't. In fact, no matter how I approached the conversation, I was often told I was being inappropriate or that it wasn't the right time to bring it up. As it turned out, there never seemed to be a good time or approach. Meanwhile, the animals continued to suffer . . . by the billions.

That otherwise good and kind people were unwilling to open their minds and hearts to the plight of other sentient beings was disheartening. I laid out the facts and made myself available to help anyone transition, yet they didn't want to talk about it. In fact, many people I had known for years stopped following me on social media—they said my posts were offensive and stopped inviting me to anything.

Just as coming out as a lesbian in the seventies was a radical act, so was coming out as an ethical vegan decades later. Speaking truth to power has never been easily received by the status quo. Coming out as anything that threatens whatever is considered the norm is challenging for society. When I came out decades ago, although my family was "accepting," I encountered the not-uncommon attitude that I should avoid disrupting the family system and not be so vocal about it. I was made to feel that my being gay was somehow lower in status than their "superior" heteronormative lifestyle. Years later, returning to family gatherings as an ethical vegan has been just as upsetting for them: "Here she goes again with her wacky theories and lifestyle." I'm a truth seeker, so "It's always been this way" has never been a good enough reason to accept something as just or true.

All of us should be encouraged to search within and explore what we think, feel, and believe; otherwise we are just robotically following rules that, at best, are not aligned with our values and, worse, may not be morally justifiable. We know from history that just because something is legal doesn't make it right. And just because something is illegal doesn't make it wrong. "Gay marriage" was illegal, but two people of the same sex being able to marry and create a life and family together isn't wrong.

Most don't think twice about the fact that we are inundated with and surrounded by images of heterosexuality on billboards, TV shows, movies, and in magazines and advertising—everywhere you turn, the storyline is male/female love and desire. As soon as there's a lesbian peck on the lips on a sitcom, we're accused of pushing the gay agenda. The same goes for veganism. Carnism, defined by psychologist Melanie Joy as "the invisible belief system, or ideology, that conditions people to eat certain animals" dominates our global mainstream thought system. We are surrounded by images of meat and dairy on billboards and in commercials, and fast-food restaurants line the streets of America. Yet when someone identifies as vegan, they risk being told to stop pushing their views, are often shunned, and are viewed by some as attention-seeking troublemakers. Why do we feel the need to "flaunt our lifestyle?" Why not just keep it to ourselves? I can't count how many times conversations have been cut short as soon as I bring up veganism.

Just as disheartening was the reaction I got from many longtime lesbian feminist friends when I "came out" as vegan. While at an all-gay New Year's Eve party, various women asked what I was up to, so I told them about my vegan journey, and even asked for their thoughts on it. It did not go over well. The next day my friend said to me about my veganism, "It feels a little obsessive. It has me a little worried, actually." She also happened to be a former decades-long vegetarian.

The very same women who had paid many dues for being lesbians in a homophobic world were unwilling to hear about the reality of dairy—that cows are forcibly and repeatedly impregnated, separated from their calves at birth, and hooked up to painful milk machines so that we can drink the milk that is meant for their babies. As feminists, we say rape is rape. None of these animals reproduce by choice. They are all sexually violated. It is the ultimate patriarchy.

That progressive lesbian women were not receptive to the conversation of animal agriculture being based on the exploitation of the female reproductive system shows how conditioned we are to be obedient consumers. Their response was along the lines of, "I love your passion. But can you please not talk about it?" and, "There's a fine line between passion and fanaticism." One of my friends said, "You no longer need to discuss this topic with me. This is your passion and you'll find your tribe to reach the goals you envision."

There I was at an all-lesbian party, and I felt like a gay at a Mike Pence affair where I had the audacity to assert that "all people should have the right to love and marry whomever they want" and then was told I was being aggressive. The mentality is the same: "Don't rock my perfectly constructed world with any inconvenient truths. Don't shatter my self-perception of being an evolved, compassionate person with the breaking news that killing is not compassion."

Those against slavery were called radicals, extremists, and even obsessive. They were told they were upsetting the natural order. They certainly would've ruined a dinner party if they said nobody should own another human being as property. Women who were outspoken for women's right to vote were told to go back to where they belong— the kitchen. They were accused of upsetting the natural order and disrupting cocktail parties with their ridiculous chatter. Those who claimed that being gay is a natural state of being were pathologized and classified as having a mental disorder.

Every time we try to move society forward and expand our circle of compassion to include those who are different than us and ask people to put themselves in the shoes of the exploited, there will be pushback from those unwilling to open their minds and hearts to the impact of their actions. It can be painful to look at ourselves when we are in the role of the oppressor, given how much we detest this quality in others who are oppressing those more vulnerable than themselves.

If I'm told to stay quiet about the truth of dairy with progressive feminists and lesbians, what hope do we have for humankind? I even had a feminist lesbian friend who identified as "mostly vegan" and who believed that "eating plant-based" was a personal choice for everyone, say to me on social media "What happened to you? You used to be kind?" Speaking truth to power in an oppressive society will always be considered unkind. But the pressing reality of the animals' plight and my increasing awareness of speciesism made me realize much more needs to be done to break the centuries-long belief that animals are here for us to use.

Animal rights activists are often met with arrogance and willful ignorance when trying to help others connect the dots. As most activists will tell you, the depth and breadth of animals' suffering weighs on us heavily, and we can expect to encounter many dark nights of the soul. At six months vegan, one of those dark moments got me to walk into a supermarket and, using the meat department as my platform, disrupt the status quo to speak out for the 60 billion animals who are killed every year for "food" (and that's not counting fish, which brings that number to the trillions). That "solo demo" was recorded on a phone by another activist and sparked a widespread conversation on social media from all sides. I continue to do these speak-outs, as well as film other activists doing theirs. The animals cannot wait for us to have sporadic one-on-one chats and a brochure exchange with every individual.

Going into establishments where there is violence against animals, alone or in groups, and disrupting is one of the many powerful ways to convey the message that animals' lives are their right and that killing them is violent and unjust no matter how it's done. Doing direct actions with other activists inside meat-centric gastropub that I used to frequent has been one of the many ironies of my journey. Not too long ago I would have been one of the annoyed customers who would have been thinking "get a life," which we're often told.

Early on in my activism, while at an animal rights conference, I was introduced to nationally known TV journalist Jane Velez-Mitchell, who had recently launched *JaneUnChained News Network* (JNN), a fast-growing digital media outlet producing original videos about animal rights and the vegan lifestyle. I attended her workshop on using smartphones as a way to show the world what's happening to animals. Shortly thereafter, I became a citizen journalist for *JaneUnChained* and have been traveling the globe reporting on a wide range of stories, events, organizations, and programs to spread the vegan message. We need to find it inside ourselves to care about all injustices and inequalities, no matter who is being exploited. No one should get to decide that someone is more deserving of rights than another. As for anything of moral consequence, it's never just a personal choice when there's a victim. It's not about *what* you're eating. It's about *who* you're eating.

There is much injustice in the world and many complex problems that require even more complex solutions; what's unique about veganism is that for those of us who have agency over what we eat, going vegan is the smallest thing we can do to make the greatest difference. And going vegan does not preclude anyone from working on behalf of other marginalized groups. It's not a zero-sum game. As Martin Luther King Jr. said, "Injustice anywhere is a threat to justice everywhere." We need to expand our circle of compassion to include animals. The only thing more dangerous than ignorance is indifference. Just because an atrocity is not happening to you or those close to you doesn't mean you don't have a moral obligation to do something. History shows most will not speak out until it happens to them. Is that the kind of world we want to live in?

To anyone who is curious about what it's like to align your actions with your values, to get out of your comfort zone for the purpose of something greater than yourself, to dedicate your life to alleviate the suffering of the most abused among us, on a scale and magnitude unrivaled by all other atrocities combined in human history, consider going vegan and becoming an animal rights activist. It does wonders for your soul. The cruelty that dare not speak its name is hidden in plain sight, and, until their voices are heard, more and more of us will continue to raise ours. Silence is the voice of complicity.

The Girl I Finally Let In: How Personal Narrative Sets the Stage for Powerful Animal Rights Activism

Jasmin Singer, cofounder of Our Hen House and Senior Features Editor for *VegNews*

Stella was the type of beauty you rarely see. It's possible that her jet-black hair and gold-flecked green eyes were the most captivating part of her striking look, but it was really the intensity of her expression that made curious onlookers unable to turn away. When she showed up at my door, I was startled both by her fragility and her inability to look at me. Though I'd soon start to see fierceness in this small wonder, the day she came to live with me, I almost couldn't handle how wilted she appeared. I acted unflappable anyway, even though on the inside I had no idea how on earth I would be capable of caring for someone who had been left on the streets to fend for herself. How did she wind up with me, of all people?

On that autumnal afternoon when Stella came into my life like a quiet yet unrelenting storm, the timing couldn't have been worse: I was newly separated from my spouse, and still very heartbroken—so much so that I had moved across the country in an attempt to escape my former life. The perplexing, aging-hippie beach town of Santa Cruz, California—ripe with billowing palm trees, cool ocean breezes, and a rampant homeless population—was where I somehow landed, a far cry from the bustling streets of Manhattan, where I had pounded the pavement for seventeen electric years. On a purely logistical level, it was work that took me to the easy-breezy Central California coast, but it was also that work—managing the editorial team for a thriving vegan food magazine—that I had specifically sought out as a means to starting new. Running away, it turns out, is overrated.

Maybe it was this complete reframing of reality that gave me the idea that taking in Stella would somehow be okay. I was starting fresh and acting the part, so why not act the part of someone who could let in this little lost soul? The harried representatives from the foster agency didn't realize just how small my apartment was, and when they arrived with Stella, I could tell by their expressions that they were miffed. Even Stella seemed to register a bit of disappointment, clearly not prepared for living in a studio apartment with virtually no privacy and nowhere to hide. Still, we forged on, and those first few days were painful. At night, I would regularly hear sweet Stella cry for her babies, from whom she had just been separated, mere days before arriving. Other than those after-dark weeping sessions, she barely made a noise, keeping very much to herself even when I tried to relate to her with shared activities and meals. The agency assured me this kind of behavior was normal, but it felt almost too hard to bear. What she had seen in her short life on the streets of Santa Cruz would, I'm sure, be more traumatic than I'd ever experience.

As time went on, Stella and I grew to find a friendly enough rapport. She was still extremely guarded, but she became more and more curious sitting beside me, usually in silence, each of us lost in our own vastly different worlds of heartbreak and trying as best we could to put it all back together. Though Stella had been so thin and malnourished at the time she came to me, I started to notice with secret relief that she had begun to eat more, putting on a few desperately needed pounds so she could regain her strength. The agency was thrilled, saying we were a good match for each other, after all. This sentiment moved me more than I expected, and the knot in my stomach that I'd had since she arrived loosened a little. But Stella was only meant to stay with me for a short period, so I tried my best not to get too attached to this fierce young beauty who was starting to find a home in my heart. The agency started badgering me for updated info; they needed it for her records so she could be placed in a permanent home. I found myself conveniently ignoring their emails, and later, their phone calls. Stella had made my home hers, and though I maintained the line that I was in no shape to keep this up, I seemed to refuse to let the system work, repeatedly ignoring their requests.

As the months passed, Stella was, in fact, beginning to thrive. She was engaging more, instigating contact, expressing herself when she needed something instead of bottling it inside. She no longer cried at night, though she did remain awake for much of the dark hours. Admittedly, so did I. The agency managed to track me down, and the day finally came when I was to pass her along to her next family. I needed to keep reminding myself that I was just a stop along her way. I told myself that I refused to let this goodbye be emotional, even though defiant tears would regularly form at the corner of my stoic eyes anyway, just at the thought of letting her go.

And when that inevitable day arrived—just one day before my thirty-seventh birthday—I suddenly decided to change the course of our lives, Stella and mine. With a determination so strong that I didn't have time to talk myself out of it, I picked up my phone, dialed the numbers stuck to my fridge, and immediately got Stella's caseworker on the line. "It's Jasmin," I said nervously. "I'm calling about Stella." There was silence. "I think I want to start the process of adopting her," I continued, no longer shocked by the words coming out of my mouth—realizing at once they were the realest I'd uttered since moving to this sleepy town where I didn't quite belong and absolutely never would. "Yes, I want to keep her," I repeated, more firmly this time. "I want Stella to officially be my cat, and . . . I want to be her human."

I have long thought it strange that the animal rights movement hasn't really latched on to personal narrative as a means of creating change, as readily as other social justice movements—from the LGBTQ movement to the fight against racism. By the time my memoir—*Always Too*

Much and Never Enough—was released in 2016, I had already discovered the magical powers of storytelling. I had spent my career up until then advocating for animals through a variety of means: everything from leafleting in NYC's Union Square, to organizing weekly protests against foie gras, to writing gut-punching exposés detailing egregiously cruel (yet flinchingly standard) animal agriculture practices.

Finding myself frustrated by the commonly held belief that we must wait for top-down, organizational campaigns to latch on to in order to change the world for animals, in January of 2010 I cofounding a media nonprofit, Our Hen House, with the goal of providing thoughtful podcasts and other media outlets for anyone who wanted a place to explore various ways to become activists. Our Hen House quickly evolved to become a community for people who wanted to get involved with animal rights activism, but had no idea where or how to start.

The guests that my cohost, Mariann Sullivan, and I interviewed became the portals for thousands of inroads to change-making. It took me some time, but I finally understood the reason why OHH became successful: it was not only providing ideas, but the guests themselves were telling their stories. This was my first foray into personal narrative and storytelling as a means to moving the needle. I have learned that a person's lasting impression is rarely the information they disseminate; rather, it's how that person made us feel. It's the stories people tell that become memorable, not the facts spouted out.

Nothing taught me this more acutely than the process of going on a sixty-city book tour with my book. From Tucson to Philly, San Francisco to Kansas City, I told my story of becoming vegan to auditoriums full of people who actually wanted to be there. Unlike when I was leafleting and people would hold their hands in front of their faces because they didn't want a vegan telling them why they needed to throw out all of the food in their fridge and rethink their worldview, the folks at my talks remained, for the most part, rapt. They had opted in.

I stood at the front of the room and told them about my journey with food, starting as a chubby kid following around my thin mom from weight-loss program to weight-loss program, finding solace only in a box of cheese crackers. This journey led me to a food addiction so profound that it took me decades to understand, and in many ways, I still am unpacking it.

Food took on an entirely new meaning when, at twenty-four years old, I blindly took a first date to see a documentary about animal agriculture, having my mind blown as I reexamined my feminism through the lens of the eggs and dairy I consumed during every single meal. I sat there watching the movie while my leg shook so frantically that the person next to me had to gently ask me to stop. I looked up at the screen, and in front of my eyes, families were being torn apart. I thought of my own broken home as a child, and I could barely hold myself together.

The adrenaline shot through me, and I didn't know where to put it; at one point I jolted into a standing position in sheer horror because of what I was seeing: how could I not have known? The female animals on the screen were essentially being exploited for their reproductive parts, much like I had been years prior when I was date-raped in a scene so painful that I can't linger on the memories for long, even now, twenty years later. Plus, I fancied myself a feminist, so how did this new-to-me information stack up against what I ate for lunch?

Stories like that one—and how, when I went vegan, I began to redefine food as something I stood for, no longer against—filled the pages of my book, and I filled living rooms and bookshops and universities with these stories during my colossal tour of the United States. Simply by talking about my own journey with food and veganism, I in turn emboldened people to look at their own such journeys in a new way. And time and time again, these people went vegan and did not turn back.

When I wasn't writing, I was acting. I grew up doing a lot of theater, and I found safety and comfort in the "fourth wall," theater-talk for the invisible wall that exists between actors in a play and the audience. Not only did I find safety from the fourth wall, but so did the onlookers. There is something very calming and entrancing about learning life lessons by way of characters on a stage in front of you. It has the exact opposite effect of *proselytizing*. If you're a vegan, chances are, you've heard this word before. Animal activists are often accused of lecturing to others, though many of us think we're simply sharing something deeply important about the treatment of animals behind closed doors. The inherent issue there, of course, is that most people don't want to hear the truth about animals, because associated with that truth is an implicit judgment (real or perceived) of their own behavior, so their defenses go right up. That's one of the reasons why genuine humility is such a deeply important part of advocacy and of communication in general. And yet, when you're in the audience of a play, or you're reading a book, or you're on the other end of someone who is sharing with you a vulnerable story, you are much less likely to feel lectured to. Proselytizing seems to go out the window; onlookers tend to no longer feel judged. They are witnesses, not students who didn't ask for a lesson. They are in it with you.

Personal narrative is powerful stuff. Finding our truths and telling our stories is a paramount way of eliciting change—starting with ourselves, and then extending outward to anyone who comes into contact with our words. Like theater, and much like the arts in general, telling our stories is a safe, nonjudgmental, humble way to talk about what is happening to animals and to magically and purposefully begin a revolution. Social change will not happen without our stories, and our stories cannot be fully realized without social change. The reason my book resonated with the audiences at those venues where I shared my most personal moments—knowing their interpretations of my experiences was entirely a reflection of them and not me—was because I am extremely ordinary. My story of being "always too much and never enough" is, in fact, universal. We each struggle with versions of the same demons. And we each want to do better at being ourselves. I found that as I became relentlessly discerning about my own choices and motivations, veganism was a natural evolution. Not only can personal narrative change the world, but it might actually be the only thing that can. We just have to tell our story to somebody who wants to listen, and the rest of the story will simply unfold.

As it turns out, Stella and I are indeed a perfect pair, bringing out the best in one another through roundabout ways. She's almost inevitably her neediest when I am my grumpiest, and her reliance on me for food and other necessities has brought me out of some dark moments. Though I don't speak cat, my guess is that the same could be said of her. Stella came from a traumatic past, so her inclinations toward trust are often murky, and yet I remain present and loyal, reaching out my hand only when she lets me and allowing my reassurance to extend to her with the unrelenting-yet-focused determination that only two survivors brought together against all odds would be able to understand. If you have a companion animal, my suspicion is that you know exactly what I'm talking about. That kind of quiet connection is, I think, the true definition of love, and the arbitrary separation of species is irrelevant when it comes to this kind of life-changing companionship.

Though my relationship with Stella thrives when she and I are simply keeping each other company—nowadays in our new apartment in Los Angeles (which has proven to be a phenomenal move for each of us), it is my narrative about our relationship, not the relationship itself, that is key to social change. Social change has the opportunity to take place when we give voice to the voiceless and hold space for their stories, as well as our own. It's about crafting words from a revolutionary moment that would otherwise pass by, adding tangibility to a valuable and pivotal perspective: ours. Believing ourselves, trusting our perception, and writing it down also means that we are giving others the opportunity to connect with the universal themes that oftentimes make us feel so completely alone. Writing down our stories is indeed a political act that can inform communities, allow space for marginalized groups, and ultimately elicit change.

I told Stella's story because it is one that deserves to be told. Her bravery against all odds, the intrepid ways she allowed herself to trust again, and the hope that can be gleaned by how authentically and relentlessly she moved through her grief and came out whole is something we can all stand to learn from. That, in itself, is enough inspiration for a lifetime, but add to that the value of personifying animals as a reminder of their sentience and magnificence—and the moral imperative of adopting these family members—and I know that I've done my job.

Stella does not speak for all cats, of course, but the commonality of her story can speak for many. My hope is that someone will hear it and shift, just a little bit more, toward compassion for others—the ones we too readily cast aside. The second we silence ourselves, we might actually be silencing a movement. The solution is to continue to find our truths and tell our stories.

The Evolution:
From Animal-Loving Child to
Intersectional Vegan Activist

Gillian Meghan Walters, founder
of *Animal Voices Vancouver*

For as long as I can remember I have had a spiritual connection to animals. In conversation or in silence they would listen to me, and I to them, a reciprocal unconditional love. As a child I dreamed of one day becoming a Jacques Cousteau or a Dian Fossey and living side by side with animals. This innate bond with animals allowed me, at a young age, to see through the cloud of secrecy covering their oppression.

When I was a young person, my body wanted to dance, my mind wanted to dream, and my heart wanted to love unconditionally. However, my creative expression was discouraged by verbal and physical messaging: the rolling of my mother's eyes and various boundary violations. The institutionalized educational system reinforced the suppression of my unique self by maintaining spaces that were not conducive to self-directed creative thinking or exploration. Accompany this with twelve years of social bullying, and I learned to believe that my whole body and every act of my expression was wrong. The trauma of an extinguished self later led to addiction, where I could soothe my anguish and at times feel a false sense of power. But addiction would bring sexual, physical, and emotional violence that increased my powerlessness and paralleled the objectification that I witnessed with animals.

1970s Vancouver Island, British Columbia

A few years after my birth in Vancouver, British Columbia, my father found an acre of land in a remote area of Vancouver Island. This decision to root our family of four in a rural community paved the way for my deep connection to and love of nature. I remember at the age of four I stood wide-eyed watching our fawn boxer dog Taffy give birth to eight pups in our one-room cabin. We kept Hannibal from the litter and had a steady stream of stray cats, kittens, and rabbits over the years. My dad insisted on keeping all of our animals outside, but I can remember many times pleading for him to bring them inside. Whenever he let me curl up with them in front of the woodstove, all was well in my world. I spent most of my early childhood outside playing hide-and-seek through the bushes and trees, pretending I was swimming with dolphins in the summer sea, naming worms, rescuing birds, and studying salamanders.

I, like most children of the era, was taught to believe that we needed to consume certain species of animals. We gorged ourselves on their flesh and secretions, wore their bodies for fashion, gazed at them behind metal bars, applauded for them as they swam around in tiny pools, cheered as they performed in movies and the circus, and used products that had been tested on them. The myth that humans must consume animal flesh to be healthy was perpetuated by a well-engineered system. The animal agriculture industry lobbied the government, and the educational system preserved the myth through lunch programs and the Canada Food Guide, which told us to consume three to four servings of meat and dairy products daily. What I didn't learn from family traditions or the school system was reinforced by the media, which manipulated the public into believing that eating and wearing animals was normal, glamorous, and entertaining. Saturday-morning cartoons were punctuated with TV commercials that told us "Milk does a body good" and everywhere that animals were exploited, the public saw images of kid-friendly cartoon animals. Like any young vulnerable mind, I soaked this all up like a sponge, and it became normalized.

I was raised on the typical northwestern diet in which there was a never-ending supply of milk. My sister and I would take turns standing by the open fridge door as we guzzled milk from the container. Running out of milk in our house was like running out of gas—panic ensued, and someone would have to run immediately to the store before it closed. When we occasionally got milk from our neighbor's cow, I remember watching her being milked one day, staring at the cow's teats being forcefully and rhythmically pulled and squeezed, the liquid squirting out with such force it hit the metal bucket like a drumbeat. When my neighbor turned to me and asked if I wanted to try, I believe that my hesitancy to answer and the discomfort I felt was the first sign of my consciousness rising. It did not feel or look right, and my young body knew it.

Family dinners spotlighted various animals cooked in various ways. The more expensive meat was reserved for special occasions. On these days my mother would cook all day in her apron, as if the turkey, roast beef, or ham was the reason we were celebrating. I remember never liking the smell of meat permeating the entire house. When I made the connection years later that it represented injustice, betrayal, and horror, that smell became even more unbearable. But I didn't speak about the anguish I was feeling. Instead I kept silent, shutting off a part of me that wanted to scream.

There were times when I became conflicted because of the messages I was being fed through my parents, school, and the media, and I could intuitively feel that something was not right. There were specific instances when I felt unsettled by my connection with animals and food, like my neighbor's cow, the teacher who revealed after we ate the spaghetti dinner that the sauce was made with deer meat, and the relatives we visited who made a dinner of rabbit stew. But it was the heart-wrenching screams coming from our neighbor's yard one day that broke through the surface of my social conditioning around food. I knew the neighbors across the road had a pig farm, but I never emotionally connected this to the hot dogs and pork chops I had been eating and enjoying for years. I will never forget those screams I heard that day that began my declaration to never eat meat again. But as a child I had no safe spaces to express these feelings, which led me to feel isolated in this awakening and confused as to why my friends and family were not as angry as I was. I felt completely alone.

Coming of Age and Questioning Systems

Punk rock was my savior in high school. Anarchy fit perfectly into my rebellion from school, peers, teachers, parents, and the system. For the first time my feelings that were simmering just below the surface had a place to be unleashed in the music, the fashion, and the attitude. When I was seventeen, my parents stood in the driveway, waving goodbye as I left home. With a skateboard and a red electric guitar, I headed to a big city where I met other like-minded people and experienced an array of cuisines for the first time—Japanese, Thai, Malaysian, Indonesian, Indian, African, and Caribbean. It was at that time that I became aware of PETA, and I versed myself in knowing everything I could about animal cruelty. When I saw images of tigers and elephants forced to perform in the circus, gorillas isolated behind bars, lions and bears being hunted, and monkeys in laboratories being tortured, I could resonate with the agony, the loneliness, and the aching for someone to notice. They were innocent and taken advantage of like I was. Like me, they were powerless, and no one was noticing.

The freedom I initially sought from leaving home was bittersweet. At twenty-two years old I hit rock bottom: addicted to heroin, homeless, penniless, and gravely ill. My childhood dreams of becoming a marine biologist, a veterinarian, and a dancer were gone. I entered a sixteen-week addiction-treatment program for women. While many in the house were complaining of the vegetarian menu, I was secretly jumping for joy. I believe that the vegetarian food was an important factor that allowed for my success during treatment (along with the secret access to my Prince CD that I fell asleep to at night). Knowing that I could do the most important emotional work of my life in a home that did not serve dead animals as food was incredibly important for my emotional safety. My spiritual journey in recovery allowed me to delve deep and find my true self again. The treatment program was my first introduction to feminism, self-love, and empowerment. For the first time I was learning the truth about the history and the systems perpetuating racism, sexism, and homophobia. I came to realize through my own curiosity and search for the truth that I had been fed a lie. Government-funded programs had created policies that oppressed humans and other animals, and the media was responsible for reinforcing our dissociation though language and imagery. The cultural narrative denied the horrific truth of the settler colonialism that to this day continues to oppress the indigenous peoples and the earth. The history I had been taught, even at the university level, continued to leave out people of color.

Fresh out of treatment, I came upon the work of Carol J. Adams and read her book *The Sexual Politics of Meat* like it was my bible. Her words spoke to me in a way similar to what I had experienced when reading Charlotte Kasl's writing on feminism and addiction. Each passage resonated on a personal level, and I began to see the interconnectedness in all oppressive systems. I wanted to know why some humans were privileged and others oppressed because of gender, skin color, ability, and sexual preference. I was also aching to know why certain species of animal were protected and cherished, while others were ignored and exploited. For years I viewed animal rights and human rights as two separate social justice issues until I began to take a critical look at intersectionality following the Rodney King beating in Los Angeles and became interested in studying race relations. As I prepared myself for a volunteer overseas cross-cultural work experience program, I came face-to-face with defending my veganism at a pretraining camp. I learned overseas that being vegan was easy compared to the challenge of working through layers of white privilege. I felt that educating myself on the suffering of animals and eating a plant-based diet during this time was all that I could do and all that I had time for. The thought of becoming more active in the animal rights movement rose and fell. I basically lived my veganism in isolation, attempting to find community at times, and then being disappointed when it was absent. I yearned for a deeper connection.

Motherhood, *Blackfish*, and the Liberation Pledge

The birth of my son came unexpectedly early. Nine weeks before his due date, my water broke, but I waited five days in the hospital before labor pains began. He was not breathing when he entered the world and was rushed to the ICU to be given oxygen. I remember feeling alone and powerless, with an emotional pain so great it tore me apart. Even though I was able to see my son hours after his birth, I felt the wound of having him taken from me before I could look into his eyes, feel his skin against mine, and feel his heart beat. That panic and fear the second my baby was taken away stayed with me years after his birth in the form of postpartum PTSD. I think of the baby animals who are repeatedly ripped from their mothers shortly after birth. Mother cows who have carried their babies for nine months and are then separated from them, deprived of any bonding, are often heard bellowing for them and have been known to chase after the farmer who has taken them away.

After I was able to sit up, I made my way to a small room and sat alone trying to figure out how to attach the metal machine and suction cups to my swollen breasts. It felt incredibly unnatural, but I knew my baby would soon have the nourishment designed for him. The mother cow is not so lucky. After birth she is hooked up to machines that stretch and pull her, stealing her baby's nourishment and packaging it for human consumption.

Giving birth and raising my son as a single mother had me reflecting on my own childhood. I wanted to provide my son with what I never had: the space to learn the truth and the opportunities to question everything. I wanted to empower him to lead by curiosity and to be guided by his inner wisdom. Raising him vegan was natural; living without a vegan community, family acceptance, and resources was difficult. When my son was young, I noticed a lack of vegan children's books and a further lack of books that reflected his image, that of a little boy with big curly hair and brown skin. The absence of racial representation and veganism in children's literature drove me to write and illustrate two children's books. My intent was to document and share Kingston's compassionate work, to celebrate his voice, and to normalize the words "vegan" and "activist."

As a white vegan single mother raising a vegan mixed-race child, I was prepared to have ongoing conversations about inclusion and race. Four years in the public-school system amplified the need for safe spaces, and so I made the decision to take my power back through home learning, where I designed a curriculum grounded in peaceful communication, empathy, black history and indigenous history, social justice, veganism, art, spirituality, and movement.

Blackfish aired on CNN in 2013. I watched it over and over and sobbed uncontrollably at the shame I felt as a human being. I knew the story of Tilikum—when I was nine my parents had taken my sister and I to see him at Sealand of the Pacific in British Columbia. I remember watching the thin young woman in her wetsuit joyously directing the whale to splash the crowd. My body felt a combination of excitement and fear. He was so big, and the little pool could barely contain him. But the thoughts passed quickly as I succumbed to the energy of the cheering crowd.

Watching *Blackfish*, I was subjected to real-life footage of Tilikum being kidnapped from his mother. Her screams as she chased the kidnappers' boat trying to get her son back was unbearable. A rage inside me grew that I could no longer ignore. I grabbed a piece of paper and wrote with tears falling onto the paper. "Every moment from this day forward I will use my voice and my body to do whatever it takes to stop this injustice." I felt the anguish in Tilikum's mother's screams. Watching humans take her baby away while she tried desperately to get him back was almost too much to bear. I could have sat with this shame and anguish as I had in the past, but for some reason this moment moved me to take action. For the next two years I worked alongside other activists to push for a ban on holding cetaceans in captivity both locally and countrywide. It worked, and history was made on May 16, 2017, when the Vancouver Parks Board voted 6–1 to ban the captivity of cetaceans at the Vancouver Aquarium. Then, in July 2019, Bill S-203 passed, banning cetacean captivity in Canada.

Nothing has propelled me closer to the type of activist I always wanted to be than taking the Liberation Pledge. At an activist potluck, I noticed a silver fork bracelet on a friend's wrist, and I leaned into a conversation he had already begun with another activist about the pledge. The pledge goes beyond living vegan. It is the refusal to sit where animals are being eaten. Something about what I was hearing propelled me with an urgency to immediately take the pledge. As I headed home, I was consumed with feelings of fear and anxiety. As I prepared a written statement, my body began to shake. I had for decades silenced myself around family dinner tables. Now, years of sitting in spaces where I would have to disassociate to carry on a conversation would come to an end. I took a deep breath and pressed the share button on my Facebook post. Immediately someone wrote me back—an acquaintance from middle school I had not seen or heard from for over thirty years. It became apparent why I was so scared. The pledge would disrupt the narrative that society was fixed to, and family, friends, and strangers would respond with immediate judgment, implying that I was pushing my beliefs on them.

Within the past couple of years, after standing my ground in difficult emotional conversations, I have observed my family coming around. For my fiftieth birthday, my sister made an entire vegan dinner and cake! My niece proudly stated that my birthday gift was vegan and not tested on animals. Each time I have visited they have not eaten animals in the house.

Turning Fifty

When I turned fifty, I started reflecting on my previous years and the overwhelming urge to be everywhere and do everything for the animals, even if it meant that I would suffer physically, emotionally, and financially. I asked myself how I could be the most effective and balanced animal activist. My inquiry led me to think about what gave me the greatest passion as a child—animals and my camera. With my camera fully charged, I headed toward a dairy farm. As I wandered around unnoticed, I witnessed firsthand rows of crates housing individual calves, some bellowing and others reaching their heads out. I observed their mothers one hundred yards away. My eyes connected to one calf in particular, number 3874. I bent down and he suckled on my hand. His eyes conveyed yearning for his mother—for her nourishment, comfort, and protection. His individual life flashed before my eyes. He would be murdered soon unless I took him out of that crate right there. Looking around, I saw at least fifty more crates with fifty more individual lives soon to be taken. I felt like the world was spinning, and I was physically shaking.

I gave 3874 the name "Om" and poured my feelings through my paintbrush onto a large acrylic canvas. My interaction with "Om" haunted me for weeks. I couldn't sleep, as all I could think about was how he would die if I didn't stop it. "Om" had given me my answer. I would focus my energy on exposing the truth about the dairy industry through photography, and so my new project, *MummyMOO*, was created.

There has been a great deal of progress made since I first decided to stop eating animals decades ago. But animals are still being exploited, tortured, and murdered, and the exploiters are fighting hard to keep it that way. Eating and promoting a plant-based diet is not enough. Action is needed on a massive scale to bring about animal liberation. Acknowledging the unbelievable scale of the atrocities committed against sentient beings is a very heavy burden to bear. Bearing this alone can be devastating, and both self-care and balance are required. Finding an inclusive community committed to self-reflection and transparency and trained in nonviolent communication is equally necessary. What drives me to fight for total animal liberation is that I was able to turn my embodiment of powerlessness into powerful action.

In doing research for this essay, I asked my mother if she remembered the name of our neighbor's cow. She responded, "Oh the one we ate?" I gasped, shocked by this information. She shared that our neighbor had sent us packages of "roast beef" after we had finished buying milk from her. At fifty years old I was as shocked as I probably would have been if she told me at age seven. If she had told me at the time, I wonder if I would have had the courage to stand up and say "I won't eat this." Would I have made the connection between nonhuman animals and food sooner?

©Jo-Anne McArthur

III
Overcoming Personal Challenge: Opening the Door to Activism

Through Empathic Eyes:
A Survivor's Story

Jasmine Afshar, army veteran

We regard crimes against the vulnerable as the most abhorrent in our society. Those who target children are intentionally seeking out the most vulnerable victims to exert power over for their own gain. When individuals are abused and exploited in their youth, it affects their physical and mental well-being for the rest of their lives.

At age five, my mother gave me the option to begin visiting my father's house on weekends. Before long, he moved in a woman and her young daughter. Soon after, she started behaving in strange ways, such as pouring water on me in the middle of the night while I slept and depriving me of meals when my father wasn't home. When I tried to tell him, she convinced him that it was my "childish imagination" and all was dismissed. One weekend when I returned to my father's house, I found most of my clothing and toys had been sold, but his girlfriend claimed she thought they were her daughter's items from when she was younger. She escalated the interactions to sexual assault when she began touching me with her hands and my bath toys during my bath time. It was excruciatingly painful, but when I tried pushing her away, she shamed me for misbehaving.

Finally, one evening at dinner, I threw my fork down and ran to the phone to call my mom. All I could divulge was, "Help me! She touched me in places she's not supposed to, and she keeps calling me fat," before the phone was ripped out of my hand. Very soon the door swung open and I was hoisted up by my stepdad and put in the car, as a tussle not meant for children's eyes took place in the building that had become the center of darkness in my life. Many memories from this time in my life have been suppressed. The psychological trauma is still being undone over twenty years later.

I remember smelling the feces from nearly a mile away the first time I stepped onto a farm. The dairy industry demands the repeated sexual assault of the females trapped behind bars with the intent of growing as many cows as fast as possible into dairy laborers. Workers tie the females to a rack and stick their arms into the cow's vagina to find the cervix. Then they insert a rod with defrosted semen collected from a male bull—stimulated through anal electrocution—into the cervix of the restrained female. Bulls often endure this process biweekly. When anal electrocution is not used, physical stimulation or arousal through manual manipulation of an AI doll is the common alternative.

As I stepped onto the farm, I began to see a wave of individuals rolling and flicking their tongues in the air; a desperate and ravenous version of dogs with peanut butter stuck to their mouths. I made my way toward a building on the side of the property, and upon entry, saw long rows of pens not much larger than the beings confined by them. The newly born calves had the largest, most soulful eyes with eyelashes that seemed to extend beyond the bars that bound them. As we walked by, they slammed their frail bodies toward the back of their pens to distance themselves from those who looked like their kidnappers. While examining the conditions of the facility, I passed by an individual whose curiosity exceeded her desire to retreat. I knelt next to her pen and extended my hand. This startled her; however, after a minute, she began to slowly inch forward before wrapping her tongue around my hand. I attempted to give her a tender pat on the head. Her anxiety was fleeting, as she began shuffling with pleasure from being scratched. Bouncing back and forth, I taught her a game, and like a puppy, she started to bounce around, hitting the sides of her pen with every movement. She was never given a name or identity to match her unique and exuberant personality, so I offered her the name MILA. It grew to stand for My Inspiration to Liberate Animals. Seeing such a vulnerable, inquisitive individual caged for profit compelled me to make a promise to devote every piece of myself to animal liberation.

Later, I realized I had given MILA a false impression that the interaction she experienced that day was one she could expect from humans. What awaited her was forced impregnation like that experienced by the mother who birthed her and the theft of every being that left her womb. The memory of that day haunted me so much that I went back to see what had become of her on my birthday nine months later. I had an employee search for which lot she might be on, and I looked for her number to no avail. As a last-ditch effort, I called out the name she had only heard that one day, and, to my surprise, she came bounding forward. Her eyes were hazy and her fur was patchy. Like other cows, she had succumbed to the overwhelming environmental stress and had begun tongue rolling. I fell to my knees sobbing. The lively, curious being I once knew now stood before me damaged and broken. This was supposed to be the ideal farm. a humane, family-owned "grow lot." Yet, because of humanity's inclination toward domination, we treat animals like objects, and even the best treated objects fall short of the needs of an individual. Today, I would not be able to find MILA. She was sent to another farm, where the remainder of her life will be spent as a tool, and the milk meant for her children fed to the humans of the world instead. She will be killed around four years of age even though she could live to twenty if given the chance.

I existed in the world without aspirations until I turned twenty-two. Every time I felt a seed of hope, it seemed to be ripped away from me, and I wanted to do everything in my power to prevent others from feeling such despair. After my childhood abuse, my stepdad who had saved me developed cancer and died. In school, I was harassed and bullied because I looked and thought unlike others. After high school, my mother gave me the options of full-time college, the military, or homelessness. I knew I would waste money in college because I did not care about structured learning at the time, so I joined the army, naively thinking I would be able to help the world that way. The first day of boot camp, a drill sergeant approached me and whispered in my ear, "I will make sure you don't make it to graduation. Barbies and hajis don't belong in my army." I took it as a harmless scare tactic that is commonly displayed in movies, but reality would prove me wrong. Before every physical fitness test, he discreetly pulled me aside and made me work out until the walls dripped from the humidity and my body lay entirely lifeless. The night before the final physical fitness test, he came into the women's sleeping area and informed us that he wanted us to move all the lockers and bunks into a separate room before the sun rose. This meant we would be fatigued the following day for our mandatory test. No man was required to do the same. He added extra weight to my sack the day of our eleven-mile march, causing me to develop a pelvic hip fracture. I left basic training with degenerative disc disease, arthritis in my back, slipped discs, a pelvic stress fracture, carpal tunnel syndrome, migraines, and fibromyalgia. When I went to my next duty station, I was asked to "power through it" unless it became intolerable.

I woke up one night a couple months later screaming and profusely bleeding. The sergeant on staff rushed to get two soldiers to carry me to the on-base medical clinic. Poking, prodding, and testing commenced to find out what was causing such immeasurable pain. After searching for about four months to no avail, the doctors began to question whether I was imagining the pain. My mom took it upon herself to begin researching potential causes, and she linked me to a site for endometriosis. I exhibited all the symptoms, including the inability to find physical anomalies on scans and other tests. I brought the potential diagnosis to my gynecologist, and she accused me of being a hypochondriac, which was reinforced by my on-base physician when I requested a second opinion.

I could not understand why my pleas for help were being ignored. After another month of attempted therapy, the army realized it would cost more to fix me than it would cost to provide me benefits after removing me from service. Since I was a broken tool, the military no longer had any need for me. A month after being discharged, I went to see a civilian gynecologist, who agreed to check for endometriosis, which had spread throughout nearly my entire pelvis. The surgeon told me I would likely experience chronic, lifelong symptoms. Had it been caught sooner, it could have potentially been effectively suppressed. I have had seven surgeries for my endometriosis. With each year that passes, my illness becomes more of a hindrance and also becomes more normalized, blinding those around me to my daily battles. I was told at one point that my best option was to learn to sit with the pain. Then, after seven years of fighting, I met a vegan local gym owner who saw through the facade I had created to mask the pain. He had me lay down and pressed gently into different stress points on my body, each movement and exertion of pressure creating a deeper sense of ease and contentment.

I thought I knew the depths of pain, until I had to stare someone in the face who was trapped in constant pain. It was dark; the wind whipped and slashed across our faces. We walked for what seemed like miles. It wasn't until we began to smell the putrid scent of death, feces, and ammonia that we knew we were approaching the city-like entity confining innocent beings to unimaginable conditions. We arrived at a large bush that concealed us on all angles from the building less than half a mile north of us. I sprinted around the two-hundred-foot-long barns. You could hear the mother pigs smashing their foreheads against metal, driven mad from confinement. My sense of urgency grew as babies and mothers began to vehemently wail, and I found an opening.

The team and I stopped for a moment to observe the moonlight caressing the cesspool of pig waste poisoning the earth, our bodies, and the animals trapped just feet away. We entered to see babies who should never have been born trampling one another to get to the nipples of their mothers. The mother pigs did not have enough nipples to accommodate all of them, but the babes were so hungry they chewed on whatever flesh they could find. I expected to see some fight from the mothers, but there was nothing. They lay there, submitting to their babies' hunger, instinctually feeling a responsibility to feed them at all costs. I walked toward one mother, who stood in defense as I slowly approached. I reached out my hand, knowing she had the power to damage it should she choose. Instead, she gently pressed her doughy, fuzzy nose against my open palm. I reached further to extend a touch of comfort, yet she flinched so hard you would have suspected I struck her. As she warmed to the idea of a soft caress, I glided the palm of my hand down the length of her spine in the hopes of alleviating pressure that had built up from stagnation. Tears streamed down my face as I watched an exaggerated version of the sensation of pain relief I had experienced just a week earlier at the gym. When I left the industrial-sized farm, I knew that my touch would be the only kind touch from a human that this mother pig would ever experience.

Hardship does not discriminate based on species. Pain is pain, regardless of the victim. If we can alleviate the pain unjustly inflicted on another being, we should never hesitate to do so. Especially when we, as a society, could abolish it entirely. I understand what it is like to have someone control your every movement, sense of reality, and basic needs while manipulating everyone around you to believe they are acts of benevolence. Yet when it is done to nonhuman animals, it is intentionally and legally obfuscated with lies about humane treatment.

I know what it is like to be sexually violated, to have someone pin you down and touch you without consent because they perceive you as an object to be controlled. When an animal's consent is violated, it is frequently done with an entire human arm forcibly penetrating their sexual organs to birth replacements for those whose bodies have begun to fail them, even though those beings with declining health are only children themselves at just a quarter of their natural life span.

I have felt a fraction of the physical torment that relentlessly stalks nonhuman beings. Even though I experience chronic pain daily, I cannot fathom being in their place for a day. I know the helplessness of having my pain ignored and my medical needs neglected. However, the animals see no relief. Their injuries, illnesses, and suffering go ignored until they are driven mad and eventually killed.

When I was rescued, my parents were celebrated for their impassioned display of breaking down the door and threatening my dad and his girlfriend for a victimized child. When the truth was brought to light, all who found out wept. When rescuers expose the lies of "humane washing" within industries that exploit animals and try to provide rehabilitation to the damaged victims they rescue, they are tried in the court of law with felony charges of theft and massively fined. Not only is animal suffering far worse than what many humans can ever imagine, but the powers that be have a vested interest in ensuring there is no way to save the victims.

None of this came full circle for me until I personally experienced persistent and immense discomfort daily, paired with being shown the suffering of another person—a pig. The video I saw in early 2016 began with a lone pig being coerced into a room by a human. When the animal breached the room and saw the red-stained floors and smelled what I only imagine they acknowledged as the stench of death, their eyes widened with utter fear. Their eyes were the same color as mine, and their desperation to seek safety reminded me of some traumatic moments in my own past. The human gripped the terrified being by the feet and hoisted them upward, causing their thrashing and struggling front half to come crashing down. I felt the same shock wave of fear when my body was violated as a child. Nausea overwhelmed me as a shiny knife struck the pig and blood spilled outward. I felt faint and full of sadness for the disregard of this individual who was desperate for life. Only then did I understand the urgency of destroying the perception that animals are commodities to be used. When I think about why I am compelled to take direct action and speak unapologetically on behalf of the animals, I realize that no deep philosophy is needed. The answer is simple—they are me, and I am them. Once you have experienced hell and crawled your way out, it becomes impossible to turn your back on those left behind, especially when they are closer to the flames than you could have ever imagined possible.

If I were a female cow in the dairy industry, a hen in the egg-laying industry, a sow in the pork industry, a queen bee in the honey industry, or any other female animal that humanity exploits, I'd be dead, because my reproductive organs don't function adequately. I can smile each day because I know whenever a knife is taken to my body it will be with anesthesia and medication, and, most importantly, I will—most likely—wake up. I can smile because I know my value within this society is not strictly dependent on my bodily systems. I can smile because I have the luxury of human privilege. The fate for the beings who suffer in exploitative industries is much bleaker. Society views them as a vessel to grow organs, tissue, and by-products, entirely neglecting the sentient individual enduring unimaginable suffering to accommodate human desire. I have no more inherent value than them. Our bodies and autonomy should not be perceived differently because of a superiority complex inherent in the human species.

I'm tired of it all. Tired of the smell of urine that burns my throat and lungs, making me feel suffocated whenever we document the suffering of nonhuman animals. Tired of hearing the piercing cries that remind me we aren't coming through in the ways they need from us. Tired of the gory slaughterhouse footage that exists because we don't have the will to stop unnecessary violence when it is within our ability. Tired of the blood staining everything it touches, including our hands, in a way that cannot be washed away. Tired of the manipulation, the corruption, the lies, and deceit; the hiding and the billions of dollars spent to sell the public misinformation. I'm tired of human privilege, privilege that is causing an irreversible mass extinction. I'm tired of the talking, pleading, and convincing, when we as rational beings know this is wrong and unnecessary. I'm tired of seeing fear-stricken faces, exhaustion, and mutilations scarring the bodies of the most innocent of those who grace this planet. I'm tired of the notion that it is only those who are evil who are culpable for our horrifying history of destruction. No longer do we have the option to point the finger anywhere else but at our own mirrors.

For the past few generations we have declared a one-sided war on the world and its inhabitants. A new framework of advocacy is needed, one using every tactic and approach, on every level, to ensure injustice no longer persists. We will need to support the aboveground and underground movements equally, as both serve as propellers catapulting the animal liberation movement forward. We need all voices and strategies so long as they are striving to remove the notion of human supremacy that leads to the exploitation of nonhumans. It is not just the blatant abuse we oppose; it is the very notion that we have a right to dictate the movements, relationships, and lives of nonhuman animals when there is no significant distinction between humans and nonhumans other than the way we look and speak. The supremacy that is believed to exist was built upon a foundation of deception. We cannot rightfully own or use sentient beings capable of self-rule, and we must use all necessary means to free animals when they are unjustly imprisoned, as we would for any innocent captive. We must remove the lenses that have blinded us and begin to see the world through empathic eyes. Until they are free, we as a society can never be.

From Addiction to Healing to Activism: An Olympic Medalist's Journey

Dotsie Bausch, Olympic medalist and founder of Switch4Good

I grew up in Kentucky, where I was raised on the regional cuisine of meaty casseroles, BBQ, macaroni and cheese, and of course, fried chicken. I was the typical all-American kid, and I ate the typical all-American diet. When I went off to college at Villanova University, I saw no reason to leave my meat-and-potatoes diet behind. From the outside, my first year of college looked pretty good. I was a successful journalism and philosophy major, became a member of the crew team, and joined a sorority. Like many, my freshman year was the first time I was really away from home, and I loved my newfound independence.

Unfortunately, this thrill wore off, and by my sophomore year things began to go downhill. The joy I once felt had somehow regressed into feelings of self-doubt, fear, inadequacy, and loneliness. On top of that, I had developed a toxic relationship with food and my once-comforting all-American diet and was diagnosed with severe anorexia and bulimia. By this point, I was already malnourished, and within weeks, my hair began to fall out, my teeth began turning black, and my skin took on a grayish hue. My eating disorder was a way to cope, but it wasn't enough, and so it joined forces with another addiction: cocaine.

The combination of restricting, bingeing, and using made me reckless and wild. I was trying to suppress my feelings with these behaviors, but I was only able to escape for short periods of time. The feelings of loneliness and self-doubt always came back, along with the new issues I was creating with my relentless addictions. I thought a change was what I needed, so I left college for New York City to pursue modeling. When I wasn't hungover or self-medicating, I landed some jobs, but neither the city nor success changed how I felt inside.

In addition to drugs, I was also addicted to exercising. I would spend up to eight hours a day at the gym hammering away at my body, trying to shrink it to nothing. I wanted to get so small that I would disappear. Self-hatred was running amok inside me. My parents barely recognized me, and they attempted multiple interventions, but my eating disorder was too strong, and I refused to listen to their pleas. After years of struggling and seeing no way out, I attempted to commit suicide by running into the middle of a freeway. I thought it would be a quick way to go, but I survived, and instead of trying again, I slowly began to seek help. It wasn't easy, but I worked with a therapist four times a week for two years, and she provided me with the tools to heal.

Near the end of this journey, my therapist asked me to rediscover ways to move my body in a healthy way again. It was important that I learned to move for movement's sake, rather than to burn calories or to punish myself. I picked cycling, really quite randomly, because it felt like something novel to me. I never cycled during my eating disorder, because I thought it didn't burn enough calories, but once I was no longer inhibited by my addiction to exercise, cycling just seemed right. From the beginning, cycling became my way of switching gears and changing myself. At first, I simply loved how it made me feel. It was absolutely freeing, and I felt like a kid again. Very unexpectedly, I began to get good at it.

I started entering amateur races, and I found that not only was I good, I thoroughly enjoyed it. In 2001, I won fourth place at the U.S. Nationals, and the United States National Cycling team took notice. This launched my career as a professional cyclist, and I spent the latter part of my twenties and all of my thirties traveling the world for races. Along that path, I won eight National titles and two Pan American gold medals and even set a world record. I ended my professional cycling career just months before my fortieth birthday, taking home silver at the 2012 London Olympic Games. It was a powerful moment to end on, for I had defied others' expectations and my own in more ways than one.

I've experienced several rebirths in my life. The first was my full recovery from my eating disorder, the second was my transformation into a professional cyclist, and the third was going vegan. From someone who has changed so drastically in life, let me tell you this—never limit yourself. I never thought I could recover from my eating disorder. But I did. I never thought I would stand on the podium of the Olympics. But I did. And I never thought I would be vegan. But I am.

Unlike my two previous transformations, my discovery of veganism was abrupt and certain. Although I didn't seek it out, once I knew, there was no doubt. Throughout the first half of my racing career, I ate meat and dairy. Like most, I never really thought about where my food came from or what it went through to make it to my plate. One night I was up late, mindlessly flipping channels, when I stumbled upon an exposé that showed the horror of slaughterhouses. Workers were kicking, shoving, electrocuting, and dragging live animals to their deaths. To say I was shocked and horrified is an understatement. Still shaken by what I had seen, the next morning I immediately cleaned out all animal flesh from my kitchen. I just could not see myself being a party to suffering and torture. However, I still held some hope that what I saw was an anomaly or an exception to the rule. I believed that there were laws against this kind of treatment. After all, this was America. The government protects and serves its people, so that must include innocent animals. I began to research, trying to make sense of the atrocity I had witnessed. What I found is that this disdainful treatment is not an anomaly. It is real, and it happens to millions of animals every single day.

During that time, I was laser-focused on the 2012 Olympic Games. This, of all times, was when I decided to completely upend my diet and go vegan. The truth is, I didn't know if I could make the Olympic team eating that way. Neither did Olympic coaches and officials. Would I have enough strength? Would I have enough stamina? And good grief, would I ever get enough protein? I was met with criticism immediately. Small-minded coaches and skeptical sports scientists asked what I was doing and why was I doing it. The pushback was relentless. "It's a really big risk," they said. "You may lose your dream of going to the Olympics. You are much older than the others, and you will need adequate protein to recover."

I was thirty-six at the time, which is great-grandmother old for an intense Olympic sport such as team pursuit cycling. I had only three and a half years before the Games, which would put me on the Olympic Team just six months shy of my fortieth birthday. Coaches grilled me about this "plant-based BS," as they called it. They were basically saying that vegans can't be Olympians. I don't know what I found more offensive—the "you must eat meat" message or the condescending attitude.

I knew deep in my heart that *this* was *my* moment. The Olympics might bring temporary fame and glory, but my decision to be vegan had the power to shape what I stood for and who I was for the rest of my life. I told my coaches, "I don't care if I fade away on this diet. I don't care if I shrivel into a raisin, because this is more important than anything I have ever done or ever will do, and it's much more important than any Games. These are lives we are talking about. Living, breathing, creatures who feel love and pain and sadness, and I will not idly stand by and eat the flesh of animals because I think it will make me strong for a sporting event. It's just not right, and for once in my life I am going to stand up for what's right."

After this bravado, I raced home to research what in the world I was going to eat. Thank goodness for Google! I discovered a whole new world of food, which was not only accessible but also tasted far more glorious than any meat I had ever consumed. What happened next still stuns me. I began recovering between workouts in literally half the time of teammates who were ten years my junior. I became stronger, faster, and more resilient. I was turning into a plant-eating, muscle-producing, endurance-building machine! And it was all because I stopped eating animals and their by-products. I trained hard, put in the work, ate in line with my ethics, made the 2012 USA team, and gave it my all at the Games. Winning my Olympic medal may be one of the proudest moments of my life, but not because of the obvious. It is because I earned it later in life and still hold the record for the oldest competitor ever—male or female—in my discipline, and I earned it on a plant-based diet!

I returned home, full of pride and unleashed energy—yes, even as a forty-year-old—and decided to dive deep into veganism and activism. During my research, I became particularly disturbed by the dairy industry. It just didn't make sense to me that we were drinking the mothers' milk of another species, and the cruelty involved seemed much worse than the meat industry. There are approximately 264 million dairy cows worldwide, who every single year endure a vicious cycle. Dairy cows are forcibly impregnated, carry their beautiful babies for nine months, give birth, and are only allowed to experience the joy of motherhood for the first twenty-four hours of their newborns' lives. When this time is up, the calf is taken away from its mother, either to be sent to slaughter (if male), or deposited into the same hopeless system as the mother (if female). This cycle of terror happens over and over again, until the mother cow is considered "spent" and can no longer produce enough milk for profit. She is then slaughtered, no different than a cow raised for meat. Dairy is indeed the very bottom of the dirty barrel on the cruelty food chain.

There are few things we cannot change, and I truly believe that we can change our food system. Together, we can stand up and say no more. We can make different choices. We can stop supporting the industry with our hard-earned dollars. Every time you buy a cow's-milk latte or eat cow's-milk yogurt, you are encouraging this abominable treatment of mothers and their children. I believe we can do so much better, so, earlier this year, I decided to do something about the dairy industry.

It was actually the Olympics that compelled me to take action. In early 2018, I was watching the Olympic Trials when a milk commercial came on. The ad claimed, "9 out of 10 Olympians grew up drinking milk. It has natural proteins and balanced nutrition." First off, I bet 100 percent of Olympians grew up drinking water, too, and as someone so eloquently posted on Twitter, "I bet 9 out of 10 serial killers grew up drinking milk, too." As for nutrition, cow's milk can encourage hormonal-based cancer tumor growth in humans, which is far from health-promoting. I was struck instantly by the need to tell the truth, so I got six other vegan Olympians together to tell their stories. I enlisted the incredible Asher Brown at Pollution Studios to produce a network-quality anti-dairy commercial that aired on NBC during the Olympic Winter Games closing ceremonies and on ABC before and after the Academy Awards broadcast. This was the beginning of Switch4Good, the dairy disrupter team here to reveal the truth.

When we stand up for what's right, we gain not only confidence but also momentum, and momentum can carry a movement into the stratosphere and start a revolution. A revolution is my dream for Switch4Good, which launched officially as an anti-dairy non-profit organization in late August 2018. We are two hundred athletes strong and growing. We welcome a wide range of active individuals into our family. For too long, the dairy industry has been funding multimillion-dollar marketing campaigns that mislead consumers. The truth is that dairy is not a health food, and we are exposing the industry's vast lies while unleashing a strategic fight that advocates for social, health, and environmental justice.

Looking back on my journey, I see there are so many different roads I could have taken, and so many different lives I could have touched. I could have continued to model and influence young girls. I could have been hit on that freeway and devastated my loved ones and the innocent driver. I could have ridden that Olympic glory and been content with post-career sponsors and campaigns I didn't believe in. But I chose to follow my passion and to stand up for what I think is right. Among everything I am—daughter, wife, mentor, Olympian—I am an activist, and that is what I am most proud of.

Giving My Struggle Purpose:
Overcoming Depression through Animal Advocacy

Matthew Braun, former investigator
of farms and slaughterhouses

When I was sixteen years old, I started seeing a therapist for depression. It had been building slowly, and, by the time I realized what was happening, it turned from a constant sadness to thoughts of suicide. I remember not doing any of my trigonometry homework in tenth grade because I was certain that I wouldn't be alive at the end of the school year. When the last week of the school year arrived, I crammed in enough of my missing homework assignments to just barely pass the class. High school is a battleground of passive aggression, where every aspect of life, from the clothes you wear to the classes you choose, is subject to scrutiny. As I struggled to figure out who I was during adolescence, I strived to stand out from the crowd, yet at the same time I craved acceptance. For a while I wore exclusively black clothing, but then changed to wearing the brightest orange and green pants and sneakers I could find. I pierced both of my ears at a time when people who identified as male generally only pierced one. Those four years of high school felt like a lifetime, but I survived, and shortly after graduating I found exactly what I had been searching for. I found veganism.

My best friend was vegetarian and struggling to cut out dairy and eggs to transition to a vegan lifestyle. While hanging out at a diner, he would agonize over whether or not to order eggs. After a few nights of witnessing him struggle with this decision, I started saying that if being vegan was something he really wanted to do, then he should stop complaining about it. Defensively, he bet me twenty dollars that I couldn't be vegan for one month. I accepted the challenge and won the bet, but to my surprise, I noticed a significant change in both my physical and my mental health. This motivated me to stick with it, and I became a full-fledged vegan on April 6, 2006. This decision marked me as part of a group of people that made up less than 1 percent of the population. I relished this fact, because it felt like an unparalleled way of differentiating myself. I wish I could say that I made the change to save animals, to reduce my carbon footprint, or even to improve my personal health, but the exclusivity of the lifestyle was the primary reason I made this change. At the time, the average person couldn't tell you what veganism was, and, for somebody like myself who shunned anything mainstream, it had an intriguing allure. In 2006, plant-based proteins and dairy-free ice cream weren't easily accessible like they are today, so it took dedication and self-discipline to convert to a vegan lifestyle in a small city in upstate New York. This amount of devotion immediately established a mutual bond when meeting other local vegans, which was a welcomed social hack for an introverted nineteen-year-old who was constantly trying to fit in and struggling with depression. I told everyone I met that I was vegan. I liked being able to teach people a new word, but this was also my way of flying a vegan flag before T-shirts with animal rights messages were readily available. This is how I met other vegans at punk shows, restaurants, and college. The instant camaraderie with other vegans made me feel accepted.

In addition to being the perfect combination of community and counterculture, being vegan gave my life a sense of purpose. Because I went vegan for trivial reasons, it took a few years before I learned about the intensive breeding, confinement, and slaughter of nonhuman animals. It was then that my lifestyle became about more than myself. Learning about the disgusting common practices within animal agriculture made my personal problems and social anxiety seem insignificant. It seemed wrong to feel bad for myself when I knew cows were being repeatedly forcibly impregnated and then separated from their offspring so the calves couldn't drink their mothers' milk. At that point I was no longer living vegan because of pride, or to win a bet, or even because of how energetic and healthy it made me feel. It became all about the animals.

Vegan living helped with my depression for several years, because I was eating healthier, connecting with other vegans, and living a life that aligned with my ethics. But eventually my depression returned with a vengeance. I realized that being vegan didn't really require me to do anything; it merely required me to abstain from purchasing or patronizing anything that perpetuated the notion that animals are food or property. I started to feel worthless again. I wanted to do something that I could be proud of.

After my friend with whom I had initially made the vegan bet landed a traveling internship with an animal rights organization, I hit rock bottom. I was twenty-seven and working at a hat store in a mall, which sold many products made of wool. I was making a living by selling products that I knew were unnecessary and unethical while my best friend was visiting college campuses across the United States to talk to students about animal rights. I knew that something had to change but I was unsure of what to do. I checked myself into the hospital with suicidal thoughts in October of 2013, and the doctors kept me there as an inpatient for eight days. In order to feel like I was worth the resources necessary to keep me alive, I felt I had to be making a positive impact on society. With help from a counselor in the hospital, I realized that there are plenty of careers and entry-level jobs that are not inherently cruel. They reassured me that it was not too late for me to switch career paths or to gain experience in a field that was important to me. I began volunteering at a community garden and later I helped prepare food for people in low-income communities. These small acts were the first ways in which I actively contributed to a good cause. It was fulfilling to work at something that had meaning and was helping people in my community, rather than working for a corporation, but the depression still lingered.

I ended up moving to Philadelphia with some friends, and it was there that I was finally able to get involved in animal rights activism. I started out by leafleting on busy street corners and at events with large numbers of people like concerts and free outdoor movie screenings. It felt wonderful to give back to the animals from whom I had taken so much. Advocating for nonhuman animals gave my life meaning, because I could finally define myself by what I was doing instead of by what I wasn't doing. Between the physical move and the activism, I felt the grasp of depression loosen, and my feelings of worthlessness and hopelessness started to fade.

Activism was my passion and so I continued to leaflet and do clerical work for an animal protection organization while looking for a new job. I was trying to find an ethical source of income to avoid ending up back in the hospital from frustrations similar to those that I had while working for the hat store, but I was getting desperate. I interviewed with a number of nonprofit organizations, but as finances became tighter, I also submitted several applications for corporate jobs. On the day that I was supposed to go to an in-person interview for a corporate position, I got the news that a nonprofit animal protection organization was interested in contracting me as an eyewitness investigator. I skipped the corporate interview, landed the investigator position, and never looked back.

An eyewitness investigator is someone who gains employment within animal-exploiting industries and films their everyday practices. Investigators often witness extreme cruelty and substandard living conditions for animals. The intention is for animal rights organizations to release the footage to the public to educate people about the rampant abuse found in puppy mills, circuses, vivisection labs, farms, and slaughterhouses. Whenever possible, organizations will try to seek criminal charges against the animal abusers caught in the act. As awful as the job sounds, it was a dream come true for me, because I was able to make a living by doing something to help animals. The work I ended up doing was physically, mentally, emotionally, and spiritually draining. Each night after working a full shift at a slaughterhouse I would write a report, upload my footage, and review it to look for key parts that would be beneficial to the organization. It was similar to working a second job. I always tried to do the report and cataloging before going to sleep, when the events of the shift were still vivid, but some nights I fell asleep during this process.

I have tremendous respect for each investigator in the animal rights movement and gratitude for the activists who share their footage. These videos are some of the animal rights community's most effective resources, and they wouldn't exist without the brave humans who go into enemy territory to erect glass walls at slaughterhouses and commercial animal farms in the attempt to prevent future animals from being bred into a similar fate. There are several safety risks that eyewitness investigators have to accept in doing this work. These factories and facilities are dangerous for employees due to sharp objects, machinery, chemicals, and handling live animals. I was told during orientation that doing this work would take time off my life. Even if everything goes according to plan, breathing in the chemicals and dander at slaughterhouses and commercial farms takes a toll on one's lungs over time. Thankfully I never came close to being discovered, but that's another factor that everyone who is an investigator has to think about. The people who own and operate these facilities exploit animals as their livelihood, and they likely wouldn't react kindly if they discovered that they were being investigated.

To mentally justify performing the duties of these jobs, I had to constantly remind myself that if I was not there doing this awful work the right way and documenting the conditions, then somebody else would be doing it, and nothing would change. The animals would still be suffering and dying without anyone there to bring their suffering into the light. The chickens that came through the slaughterhouse where I spent the largest amount of my time were very young. Chickens used for meat have been genetically manipulated to grow to the size of a full-grown chicken in just five or six weeks when normally it should take five or six months for them to reach this size. Many of the chickens were still chirping when they were hung on the shackles that took them to their death. Despite having a breast deemed big enough for human consumption, they hadn't developed the clucking sound normally made by full-grown chickens. Contrary to what some people believe, chickens raised to be eaten are not kept in cages at the farms. Unlike the completely separate breeds of chickens used for egg production who are often crammed into cages with other chickens, "broiler" or "meat chickens" are commonly raised in a filthy crowded shed. Several broiler chickens die every day from inability to reach food or water, being pecked or trampled by other chickens, or from diseases caused by intense confinement. The absence of a cage does not equate to a better life for these birds. They are packed so tightly into these sheds that they often cannot spread their wings. Once they are large enough, they are literally thrown into cages to be transported to the slaughterhouse. It is inevitable that more chickens will die during transport, so slaughterhouses are ready with a dumpster for what they call "dead on arrivals" or DOAs. Every chicken who makes it to a slaughterhouse has already endured a life of hell before they arrive.

I worked overnights in the live hang room of a slaughterhouse in Tennessee. It was my job to pick up chickens by their legs and force them into shackles where they would hang upside down, hence the term "live hang." Once they were in shackles, they disappeared into another room to be dragged through electrified water that is supposed to stun them prior to having their throats slit. The intent was that they would bleed to death before being submerged in scalding hot water to remove their feathers. My coworkers and I were expected to shackle between twenty-five and thirty chickens every minute. By the end of each night, we had killed approximately 120,000 chickens.

One night my coworkers and I had finished hanging a truckload of chickens and were rewarded with a brief respite before the next truck. This was not usually the case, and in reality, it had more to do with the forklift operator encountering difficulties loading the next cage of chickens onto the conveyor belt. Nevertheless, several of the shacklers abandoned their posts during this two-minute delay. What happened next would have a lasting effect on me. Many of my coworkers were missing when the first birds from the next truck started to arrive. I watched as the first chicken to reach the conveyor stood up, spread her wings, and ran. She made it farther than she normally would have because the conveyor was not full of chickens and because there were so few live hangers at their stations. It was probably the first time in her short life that she had been able to run, and it may even have been the first time she could spread her wings. She did not look scared like you might expect. In fact, she looked happy as she ran toward me. Maybe she thought that she was finally going to be free. Her happiness was short-lived, because I had to reach out, grab her by the leg, and hang her upside down in a shackle. I think about her often, and sometimes it brings me to tears. When people eat animals around me, I am reminded that somebody ate her, too. It's hard to think about any of the tens of thousands of chickens that I hung in my five weeks at this plant, but this particular individual had a lasting effect on me. I will never forget the look in her eyes.

Not long after working in this facility, I stopped working as an eyewitness investigator. The atrocities I was witnessing and the loneliness of being on the road by myself eventually got the best of me. I was exhausted, and it had become clear that this was not going to be a sustainable career. Perhaps it's because I was preoccupied with the work, but as stressful and horrific as the farm and slaughterhouse jobs were, I never felt hopeless. It was hard to imagine seeing the end of animal exploitation, but I was trying to be a catalyst for that change, and it was enough to keep my head above water.

Shortly after I stopped working as an investigator, I used that experience to acquire a touring internship with a different animal protection organization. I toured the country talking to people at rock concerts, schools, and YMCAs about animal rights. This gave me the opportunity to be part of a team and to share my experiences as an eyewitness investigator to educate the public about how chickens are raised and slaughtered for people to eat. At first it was hard to start these conversations, but after a while I noticed that the majority of people either are not aware of it or are not comfortable with the treatment of animals used for food, clothing, entertainment, and animal testing. My mission became clear. I had to do as much outreach as possible. I had to talk about animal rights to anyone who would listen. It was not enough just to tell people that I was vegan; I needed to ask them why they were not vegan. I toured for two years and only stopped after I had secured a full-time position within that same animal protection organization.

Now I am a resource for activists and aspiring activists and help them organize effective outreach events and win campaigns for animal rights.

A playful bet at nineteen and a hospital stay at twenty-seven were the two events that caused me to make monumental changes in both my actions and my ideologies. It is tough for me to think about how close I came to taking my own life and how much I have done with it since then. I followed my dream and, with a lot of hard work and luck, I was able to turn my passion into a career. Depression is not something that just goes away, but I have taken the necessary steps to keep it in check in my daily life. I can still enter a state of hopelessness or despair when things go wrong or when I worry about certain things, like my finances, but I do not feel hopeless when I think about animal liberation. It is easy to see that there is hope, because year after year more progress is being made for nonhuman animals. Circuses are closing, countries are banning clothing products made from animal skins, alternatives to animal testing are being developed and supported, and vegan restaurants are opening everywhere.

When I start to feel depressed about the plight of animals, I think of these victories, and I remind myself that the leaflets I have handed out, the protests I have attended, the footage I have captured, and the conversations I have had are partially responsible for the changes that are happening. I am part of a global change that is affecting billions of lives, and it is my participation in activism that enables me to finally feel like I am doing more good than harm.

Activism as a Fast Track to Growth: My Spiritual Awakening

Zafir Molina, truth seeker and movement artist

For the past few years, I have been deeply affected by the suffering that humans inflict on animals. Long before I was vegan, my mother influenced me to consider the feelings of animals, such as speaking about the cruelty in animal entertainment. When I wanted to take my little sister to the circus, she wouldn't let me because of the abuse that elephants and other animals experience. I told her she was exaggerating and dismissed it, thinking that it was a thing of the past. It seemed so cruel that it was hard to believe anyone in this day and age would support it.

Later, I became vegetarian, but after listening to a TED Talk called "Toward Rational, Authentic Food Choices" by psychologist Melanie Joy, I made the connection and decided to go vegan. She proposed a question that I couldn't answer: "Why do you eat certain animals and could never imagine eating others?" I knew why I wouldn't eat some, but couldn't justify why I had eaten others. She then showed slaughterhouse footage, and it was at that moment I realized that I was part of the violence. We were senselessly murdering animals, and it hurt me to watch. This was a contradiction to what I felt was right and wrong, and this contradiction would lead me to question everything. As I walked around in shock with an unknown feeling that my life had just changed, I would hold myself accountable for my actions and make sure that I was no longer the reason anyone was suffering based on who they were and what they looked like. I couldn't say that I didn't know anymore, and the more I learned, the worse I felt. The truth was so dark that it brought intense feelings of anger, disbelief, and loneliness.

Because my perspective had shifted, seeing "nonprofitable" newborn piglets killed by being slammed onto a cement floor was traumatic. I saw sheep forcefully inseminated by being placed on machinery that held their legs open, then moved around like objects with no regard to what they were feeling. I experienced states of shock, and reality didn't make sense. Being empathetic to the suffering of nonhuman animals hurt. Other times I felt numb, as I tried to fathom that it was happening to trillions of animals all over the world. Most days I feel extreme frustration. We are funding animal cruelty, killing the planet, and killing ourselves—for taste, for pleasure, and for money. We have been indoctrinated to believe that we own animals, that they are here for us—that they are property.

I had eaten animals for twenty-nine years of my life. Although I was never a big "meat eater" (probably my intuition speaking), I never once thought about the process. I knew I was eating an animal, but when I saw animals in person, I never thought of eating them. I was completely disconnected from what was actually happening. I was taught that animal flesh, eggs, and dairy were healthy until I came to realize that it's all a business, a system of greed justifying violence. It's all done for money, not survival, not need, not health, and not for the people. I was showed glamorized violence instead of being told that cows are put in rape racks, artificially inseminated, their babies taken away from them.

When I was seventeen, I went to my home country of Bolivia to visit my dad. He lived in a rural area where they killed animals for food. I never witnessed a killing, but my dad, being the sarcastic man he was, decided to tell me I was eating the baby goat I had interacted with the day before. I remember being appalled; the thought of it was extremely disturbing. Yet I continued to eat the flesh. Now I realize that instinctually I knew it was wrong, and I was so disturbed by it because I had shared a moment with that goat, with *someone*. But the normalization of eating these "foods" made me think that this was just the way things were, this convenient "circle of life" or "top of the food chain" idea.

When I became an activist, I began to show the cruelty behind animal agriculture and tried to provide solutions, but it seemed like so many weren't motivated to make the change. I understood it was disconnection—similar to what I had experienced with the goat—yet it was still so difficult to accept. We are people who value our rights, but some of our choices have victims; what about *their* rights? Injustice exists when one group bends the rules to benefit their side. The perspective that animals are lesser than because they aren't human is speciesism. Everywhere I look now, I see hypocrisy. People demanding justice, while at the same time causing someone else to suffer. We desire peace and love, yet our actions fund the opposite.

My intuition, even as a child, was too strong not to speak up about injustices, including the exploitation of life. As early as I can remember, I was always sensitive to unfairness, but was told life was not fair. I was rebellious when it came to the rules of society: how to be a "real" man and "real" woman, how to love, who to love, and how to look. I remember in middle school I hadn't shaved my legs "good enough," so a boy teased me. I told him to shut up, and, from then on, I decided I was going to be the girl who didn't shave her legs. Though I may have gone home and cried, I was unknowingly building inner strength to not allow others to define me. It was painful, because I did have the desire to belong, but it made me strong enough to accept truths that are not favorable and gave me the courage to stand alone when I needed a hug the most. I believe this is what has allowed me to embrace veganism the way I have, and eventually activism.

The realization of the systematic exploitation of animals by the human race led me to a more acute awareness of the human bent for oppression. Once my eyes were opened, the reality I found myself living in led me to mental isolation, while simultaneously opening the door to my biggest spiritual awakening. It became hard for me to relate to the circles I was part of, the fact that the people I loved and cared about were supporting violence. My voice shook when I told others about veganism and they denied it, turned a blind eye, or justified eating animals. I became angry at the inability of the people in my life to take responsibility for what they were part of. I felt the loneliest when I was around people—physically we were at the same place, but mentally we were in two different worlds. That anger turned into sadness as I realized that this system we live in thrives on separation and exploitation, and then I realized I was now part of yet another separation: vegan and non-vegan. This challenge forced me to look at all parts of myself, and I realized that I had to let go of all of my resentment in order to move forward. It was difficult to do, because it was emotionally, spiritually, and mentally exhausting to witness so much violence and injustice, but it was then that I realized how important it is to speak the truth without holding on to resentment. Though I felt unable to relate to some of the closest people in my life, it gave me the opportunity to get to know myself differently. I was experiencing authenticity because I was practicing self-honesty. By listening to my intuition, I created a reality that aligned with my values. The expectations of society used to hold me back, but when I accepted that not fitting into a culture that didn't align with my values was the best way of being different, I freed myself from expectations, experiencing mental liberation. This is when I felt my spiritual awakening truly take off. I had a desire to live honestly and was open to evolving. I was not my appearance, my career, my finances, or my house—those things didn't matter like I was taught to believe. What matters is humanity, earth, and animals—life.

Contrary to what some might think, becoming an animal rights activist deepened my empathy toward humans. I realized that we have all been misled and that some of us don't even have the basic necessities for survival. I also realized the importance of fixing all injustices from the core. After all, a racist is taught to hate, a sexist is taught to believe their gender is superior, and a person from China is taught that it's okay to eat dogs, just as Americans are taught that it's okay to eat chickens. All forms of discrimination that lead to injustice have been learned. If people don't know there's another way, how can they do better? If people are not told the truth about their "food," we can't necessarily expect them to make better choices. I felt empowered when I learned the truth, that everything we need to be happy and healthy is provided by Mother Earth and if we unite, we can inspire the understanding that all beings have the right to safety and health. That Earth is home to all of us, human and nonhuman animals. Activism was never part of my "plan," but I also hadn't known that I was part of the world's largest holocaust of all time. I have no other option than to take action, as everywhere I look I see violence, injustice, and an absence of humanity.

I can't believe the things I do as an activist. For example, protesting inside a grocery store. This may seem "crazy" to some, but these businesses sell the bodies and secretions of murdered animals, and they are disguised to look normal, healthy, and humane with no respect for the beings that were violated. Activism has helped keep me sane in this world of such violence; doing something about it is the difference. Activism has put me in situations I wouldn't otherwise experience. I am an organizer for one of the Los Angeles chapters of Anonymous for the Voiceless, a worldwide grassroots activism network for animal rights. In cities all over the world activists bring the truth to the streets (a truth otherwise unknown to the masses) by gathering in locations with heavy foot traffic and holding screens with footage of standard practices in the animal agriculture industry. We wear Guy Fawkes masks and form a human "Cube of Truth" with the footage and signs that spell out TRUTH. Other activists reach out to bystanders and engage in conversations regarding how animals are treated and killed for human consumption. The mission is to abolish animal exploitation by helping others make the connection to something they already believe is wrong. For example, the American culture believes that eating dogs is morally wrong, because we understand that they are sentient beings just like us and we value them as individuals. Animal rights activists have made this connection to all animals. Because so many people either stay away from looking at what happens to animals or have not been shown what they are paying for, it's hard for them to make this connection. The power of the Cube of Truth and its accompanying outreach arises from its ability to expose the public to animal exploitation and cause people to consider their thoughts and beliefs about the reality of the system. We change our actions when we change the way we think. Outreach often presents a simple question: If we have the choice to side with justice for animals, why wouldn't we? Whatever the outcome of the conversation is, individuals have now been exposed to the truth about animals. Because animal rights activists are often considered to be extreme and outspoken, many don't consider the personal challenges that come with speaking this unpopular truth. Through activism, specifically outreach at Cube of Truth demos, I realized that even though I was respectful, I still felt resentment and anger toward those who were causing harm to animals. The suffering of these animals is constantly on my mind, but I also realize the importance of speaking to others as allies. I don't look to prove anyone wrong, but rather to speak the truth about the injustice toward animals and find common ground in the reality that we all want a better world. I came to understand that the truth is enough, and how I deliver this fragile message to the masses is what really matters. My compassion for people deepened, because I discovered that we have all been provided limited and false information, and I also see this as an injustice.

Activism was a fast track to my growth on all levels. It has challenged me to face fears straight on, showing me the power of speaking the unapologetic truth, because it is the only thing that will shift our level of consciousness for the greater good. I learned to think for myself and trust the voice within, and through that I found my true purpose—to be kind to the world around me and to be courageous in speaking the truth.

How Veganism Transformed My Relationship with Food

Alexandra Paul, actress and cohost of *Switch4Good*

I was a kid who didn't think much about what I was eating, except I definitely had an eye for sweets. In sixth grade, I coveted Andrew Dakin's butterscotch pudding in his bag lunch. Andrew would happily trade it for my mother's homemade cookies, which invariably had oatmeal diluting the sweetness of the chocolate chips. I admired from afar any sandwich made with delectable store-bought bread, too, since my mom insisted on baking her own, full of cracked wheat and bran. I am thankful now, but Mom was what we called in the 1970s a "health-food nut." She was actually just British, and in England it wasn't a thing to buy processed food. TV dinners, which my siblings and I thought were the most exciting thing one could eat, were an abomination to her. She felt we needed to eat fresh foods like meat and dairy alongside lots of fruit and fresh vegetables. We had cow's milk on our cereal and glasses of it at meals, had deli slices on our sandwiches, and ate meat at every dinner. We followed a pretty typical diet, except we had less soda, fewer desserts, and no sugary cereals in the house.

My mom also believed in the power of one person to make a difference. For a long while she wouldn't buy iceberg lettuce, to support Cesar Chavez and the farmworkers' demands for better working conditions; we boycotted tuna because dolphins were being caught as bycatch; she refused to buy anything from Nestlé because the company was selling unnecessary baby formula to poor mothers in third world countries; she didn't eat foie gras because of the torture to ducks. When I read Frances Moore Lappé's *Diet for a Small Planet* at age thirteen, I started drawing my own moral lines about what to eat. The book argued that it was bad for the environment to eat meat, so I became a vegetarian then and there. My parents worried a bit (where are you going to get your protein, your iron?) but a couple months later I started high school at a boarding school three hours away, so they couldn't do much about it. That first year away, I wrote a book report about Peter Singer's animal rights treatise *Animal Liberation* and widened my reasons for being vegetarian to include animal suffering. I stopped using Revlon and L'Oréal shampoos because I learned they were tested on bunnies. I felt good about my choices.

What I didn't feel good about was my body. I had always been slender—skinny, even—but as puberty hit, I gained a few pounds. I might not have cared, but the two beautiful senior girls in the freshman dorm put a scale in the bathroom and complained about how fat they were. If they were fat, that must mean I was obese! I didn't know how to go on a diet, and wasn't sure I was willing to, but my sophomore year I got very sick and lost ten pounds. I didn't like being ill, but I liked the weight loss. Swearing to myself I would never be sick like that again and that I wouldn't gain the ten pounds back, I started removing foods I thought were unhealthy from my diet. For the next few months, I became more preoccupied with my weight and what I ate, and lost another fifteen pounds. When my parents put me in therapy, I was relieved to be forced to eat again. The problem was, my appetite felt uncontrollable—I couldn't stop eating. To solve that problem, I started throwing up with regularity. Being bulimic allowed me to binge without gaining weight, at least not at first (like any addiction, in the beginning the behavior solves problems, but after a while it stops working and just causes them).

I binged and threw up from age sixteen to twenty-eight. I felt an emptiness in my chest that only food seemed to fill, and I often threw up daily. During that time, I graduated from high school, modeled in New York and Milan, and started an acting career. I ate normally in public, knowing that once alone I could eat ice cream and chocolates until my stomach was distended. Through it all, I stayed a committed vegetarian and also gave up wearing animals or products tested on them.

During my twenties, my career as an actress was busy, I started my own nonprofit, and I had great friends who shared with me a fiery idealism about making the world a better place. The one dark cloud was my bulimia, for which I was seeing a therapist weekly. Even though on the outside my life was going very well, I continued to throw up daily. I couldn't imagine not having the powerful urge to binge. I kept my kitchen completely empty so I wouldn't be tempted to overeat.

When I was twenty-eight, I went to Overeaters Anonymous, a twelve-step program for the myriad of disordered eating that humans experience: overeating, undereating, purging, spitting, obsessing, anorexia, and orthorexia. Within a month, I had stopped throwing up, and that hole I'd kept trying to fill disappeared. In meetings, I heard stories of overcoming bulimia from people who sounded a lot like me, and calling my sponsor every day meant I had someone to whom I was accountable daily. This compulsion that I had experienced for twelve years was gone. My weight even stabilized a bit lower than it had been, which was a relief, because I had been afraid that without the insurance policy of purging calories, I would gain weight. But because I no longer binged, my appetite normalized. I was far from perfect—I was supremely aware of what I put into my body, and I made sure I exercised vigorously every day to keep my spirits up and my weight down—but I was so grateful to be out of the cycle of craving/bingeing/purging/loathing.

Twenty-seven years later, I am acutely aware that even though being bulimic feels a million miles away, I could still be there again in a second. This feeling of vulnerability is why it took me so long to go from vegetarian to vegan. John Robbins's *Diet for a New America*, a book with a similar sounding name to the one that inspired me to become vegetarian, educated me about the terrible lives that dairy cows and egg chickens endure. Later, when the Internet bloomed with undercover videos, I saw horrific footage that confirmed it. But I was terrified to take anything out of my diet, for fear that the equilibrium I had found with food would be lost. Memories of eliminating foods when I was anorexic flooded back, and I feared that denying myself would set off a binge. At least this was what I kept telling myself, for decades. I am embarrassed about this, but it took me thirty-three years to go from a teenage vegetarian to a full-fledged vegan. That it took so long is my biggest regret in life.

In October 2010 I finally made the change. By this time, I hadn't thrown up in nineteen years. I also had not eaten meat or fish for over three decades, hadn't worn makeup tested on animals for twenty-five years, and hadn't worn leather, wool, or silk for twenty-one years. It was basically the dairy in desserts that remained. That evening, I got off the plane from visiting my vegan brother Jonathan, and called my husband Ian as I was driving home to share with him that I was finally ready to become vegan. I had one last frozen yogurt—it wasn't even that good—and from then on, I have never looked back.

The transformation happened pretty quickly, and it surprised me. I thought that being an ethical vegan would be a sacrifice, but instead it added to my life in a myriad of ways. My biggest fear of feeling deprived and reverting back to my disordered eating never happened. I believe that is because for the first time my diet was aligned with my values, and eating plant-based was more authentic to me. My inability to be authentic was a major contributor to the hole I used to feel within me, so it makes sense that veganism improved my relationship with food and eating.

What I noticed first was balance. I felt more at peace in general, and especially with food. I attribute this to the fact that I was no longer consuming violence, and it felt good to not contribute to animal suffering. I also felt my heart crack open. I have always been emotional and empathetic—I am an actress, after all—but when I became vegan, I started looking at individuals more deeply, honoring their uniqueness. I became a better person because I softened. I have never been hard, but my heart extended outward more. I saw more clearly the injustices done daily to humans, animals, and the earth. I rethought what it means to be a loving parent to a cat or dog and realized I could never ride another horse again. I marveled at my own predictable speciesism: I put kittens above hamsters; hamsters above frogs; frogs above spiders. I watched myself as I interacted with people who are considered by the status quo to be lower on the societal rung, and saw that I still held biases and stereotypes.

Becoming vegan has given me moral courage. It is not popular to believe that animals have a right to the same autonomy as humans, and that we must not exploit them in any manner, and so I have developed a thicker skin. I fear disapproval far less than I used to. I don't mind being the one with the "radical" views because one can never go wrong by choosing the side of peace and kindness. I don't judge as much anymore, maybe because I have been humbled that it took me so long to make this change, or maybe because as a vegan I am somewhat of an outsider, so I don't look at the world through the lens of the mainstream. I am also more authentic, because veganism allows me to express my values daily through what I eat, what I choose to wear or not wear, and what products I buy or boycott. Ingrid Newkirk, the founder of PETA, has been quoted as saying, "Be kind, be kind, be kind." I have taken that on as my mantra, and living a vegan lifestyle has made that vow easier to fulfill.

My kind of vegan activism is not confrontational. I don't talk about the cruelty of our food system or the health benefits of a plant-based diet unless someone else brings it up. I prefer to be a role model and inspire others to give up animal products because they observe through me how it can help them live happier, healthier lives. I maintain my weight and take care of my appearance, because I hope to be a positive physical reflection of what being vegan can do. I've swam fourteen-mile ocean races, proving that you don't need animal protein to be strong and fit at any age. I eat next to friends ordering steaks and don't say anything. They usually apologize to me for their food choice anyway, even though I haven't said a word. It is always more effective if people change because they themselves decide to, but if sitting next to me helps jolt them out of the denial of what eating meat means, then I am okay with that.

This acceptance of others' choices extends to my personal life: I am in a mixed marriage—Ian is an omnivore. At first, I continued to buy milk and eggs for him when he asked, but one day I realized I couldn't do it anymore, and he understood. A few years ago, he decided to stop bringing meat into the house without me asking him. Now, the only animal food in the kitchen is his egg whites, which he buys himself. I have not insisted on any of these changes, although I harbor a secret wish that he will one day eschew all animal products for ethical reasons. Because it took me thirty-three years to go from vegetarian to vegan, I recognize that everyone has their own journey, and I cannot judge anyone else for taking what time they need to make the change.

For me, simply being an ethical vegan is not enough. As much as I believe in serving as a role model as a catalyst for change, I need to actively help our society understand how animals suffer under humans. The animal rights community has so many loving, passionate, smart people in it, and I am honored to be part of it. I attend a weekly pig vigil here in Los Angeles, where around one hundred activists give water to the truckloads of pigs entering the Farmer John slaughterhouse and document the reality behind the pork and sausage sold so merrily everywhere. I hold signs on street corners to protest whaling, animal testing, circuses, and fur. I have been arrested four times in the last three years for doing sit-ins at a slaughterhouse and an Amazon office, for trespassing on a chicken farm, and for participating in an open rescue at a massive duck farm. I have rescued a pig from a factory farm and a calf from a dairy facility and have had the pleasure of seeing them grow into healthy, vibrant beings at animal sanctuaries. The scared piglet I could easily cradle in my arms as we left the concrete pen of the factory farm (why do we even say the word farm? It is a factory, plain and simple) is now a happy adult five times my weight. The calf we rescued was so sick from living in a filthy, isolated box that she barely survived, but three weeks after freeing her from the hutch I saw her run into a paddock and kick up her hind legs in joy. She was *frolicking,* something her calf sisters left behind would never do. It fills my heart to know I made a difference in these beautiful individuals' lives. My life is so much richer now that I no longer participate in the cruelty and unfairness of animal exploitation. I went vegan to save animals, but veganism also saved me.

©Jo-Anne McArthur

IV
Campaigns & Outreach:
Anchors of Change

How to Speak about Animal Rights: What I Learned from Working in Corporate Sales

Alex Bez, founder and director of Amazing Vegan Outreach

I am the founder of Amazing Vegan Outreach (AVO), a nonprofit organization that began offering professional learning and development services to animal rights activists in early 2018. The events that led me to this point in my life began back in 2012. At the time, I was working as a corporate sales manager when one day I found out that a colleague of mine was vegan. Curiosity got the best of me and so I walked into her office to find out why. She recommended I watch the documentary *Forks Over Knives*. After watching it, I began to understand the health benefits of eating plant-based foods, and more importantly, the repercussions of eating animal-based products. This sparked even more curiosity within me, and I spent the next few months doing a lot of research. Eventually, I came across the documentary *Earthlings*.

Watching *Earthlings* was a pivotal moment in my life. Learning how we treat the most vulnerable beings on the planet broke my heart. I wept when I witnessed what we, as humans, are capable of doing to other living and feeling beings. As the credits rolled at the end of the documentary, I made the easiest decision of my life. I would no longer participate in the exploitation, torture, and death of other animals. To be honest, I wouldn't have considered myself a huge animal lover at that time. However, the concepts of justice, equality, and freedom had been instilled in me from a very young age. It had never dawned on me that we were discriminating against other living beings just because they happen to look different than us. I felt extremely guilty that I had participated in the unimaginable suffering of others for over thirty years.

Although I would never have imagined it before being vegan, finding delicious food to eat was actually one of the easiest aspects of veganism. The hardest part was coming to grips with the reality that I lived in a society responsible for, and seemingly apathetic to, the suffering of nonhuman animals. The amount of judgment and mockery I received for caring deeply about this issue was much more difficult to stomach than a burrito packed with beans instead of meat.

Reflecting on my pre-vegan life, I recognize that I didn't always have the strongest drive to help others. In fact, for the majority of my adult life, my strongest motivation was to further my career and make as much money as possible. Working in sales, I was accustomed to generous paychecks, and at the age of thirty-five, I was earning triple what I would have considered a respectable salary. I had enough money to buy almost anything I wanted: a new BMW, a large downtown apartment, expensive clothes, lengthy vacations—basically everything I had envisioned up until that point. I was on pace for an early and comfortable retirement. By most standards, I had a great job, a great life, and nothing to complain about.

During that time, I never imagined leaving my dream job. That is, until a book reading by Dr. Will Tuttle in Toronto, where I ran into an old friend with whom I had worked at Apple years earlier. Michael told me about a group he knew called Toronto Cow Save and suggested I join one of their slaughterhouse vigils. Although the idea at first seemed a bit strange, I thought I might as well check it out. After all, I didn't know any other vegans besides my coworker who first introduced me to it and my girlfriend at the time. After that vigil, my perception of life began to change.

I vividly remember standing outside of a slaughterhouse for the first time, waiting to meet the individuals arriving to be killed. It was a cold, fall morning in Toronto. The first truck arrived, packed tightly with cows of different colors and sizes. Of course, logically, I knew that cows were killed for foods that I had enjoyed for the majority of my life. However, I had never come face-to-face with an individual cow, let alone one who was about to die. Thinking back to that moment, I was afraid to be there. Not because I was concerned for my own safety, but because I was afraid to face the victims I had been exploiting my entire life. After all, an expensive, medium-rare steak with a side of buttery, mashed potatoes had been my favorite meal for over a decade.

As the truck rolled to a stop, I tentatively approached the side. Peering through the small holes in the metal walls, I saw gentle, furry giants staring back at me. Each one of their breaths pushed small clouds of vapor out of their nostrils into the cold air. Their heads swayed back and forth, trying to see what was happening outside. They were understandably restless and nervous after having been trapped in this metal cage on wheels for countless hours. Looking down, I saw that all of the cows' legs were covered in their own excrement. When I looked back up, I was face-to-face with a black dairy cow. Her eyes were opened wide and I could instantly sense how terrified she was. At that moment, I decided I had to do something to help the individuals trapped in this mercilessly cruel system.

Eventually, the need to help them consumed my life, so in 2017, I decided to dedicate myself full-time to the liberation of nonhuman animals. I regularly attended slaughterhouse vigils, protests, and marches, and also spoke with people on the streets. I even traveled to South America, Central America, and Europe to help start animal rights groups and inspire other vegans to speak up for the victims of speciesism. Establishing my organization, Amazing Vegan Outreach, seemed like a natural overlap between my previous life as a sales leader and my new life as an activist. Given that my professional background included a full decade of teaching others to communicate effectively, it only made sense to share these same skills with the activist community. The vision of having highly skilled animal rights activists spreading the vegan message all over the world was too tempting to resist. Although it came at the expense of giving up the comfortable standard of living to which I was accustomed, I was highly motivated by the opportunity to help end the suffering of so many individuals. I was also sure that activists would appreciate the opportunity to learn communication skills, which would significantly increase their success rates. Outreach is not much different than sales. In fact, it's almost identical. Here are a few things I've learned from working in sales for twenty years and from speaking with over one thousand people on the streets about animal rights.

How to Speak about Animal Rights

Most of us are familiar with the sayings "Knowledge is power," and "With great power comes great responsibility." Being aware of the atrocities happening to animals, we hold the power to create a non-speciesist world. Speciesism, like racism or sexism, is the basis for dis-crimination and oppression based on physical characteristics that labels groups of individuals as "lesser than." With the power to help these victims comes the responsibility to represent their interests to the best of our abilities. This raises the question: What is the most effective way of delivering an anti-speciesist message so that it results in the greatest amount of positive change?

There was a time when I would recite the ethical, environmental, and health benefits of veganism as often as possible to whomever would lis-ten. I also studied and learned rebuttals to all of the common objections to veganism. Sometimes I would take a more passive, lead-by-example approach. At other times, a direct and unapologetic attitude when dis-cussing speciesism seemed appropriate. There is certainly no consensus among the animal rights community as to the most effective approach to inspiring individual behavioral change during animal rights conver-sations. This is likely due to a general lack of data and empirical analysis of different styles of outreach and their effectiveness.

As initiators of the animal rights conversation, we choose (either consciously or unconsciously) between different strategies and struc-tures for these interactions. We can debate others, argue with them, lecture them, teach them, question them, coach them, or combina-tions of the above. We can support them in their gradual journey to veganism or we can pressure them into making changes immediately.

We can ask people to simply reduce their consumption of animal products, or we can adamantly state that no amount of animal exploitation is acceptable. When deciding between these different approaches, it is important that we make a conscious choice based on the intended outcome while considering the benefits and drawbacks of each.

Identify the Intended Outcome

The first question when considering and analyzing different approaches should be: "What is the intended outcome?" Would we like people to walk away with more information? Are we simply hoping to create a more positive impression of veganism? Would we like to generate curiosity around speciesism and veganism? Would we like people to take steps toward being vegan after speaking with us?

Defining the desired outcome is the first step in gauging the effectiveness of our actions. Only then are we able to measure our effectiveness against a specific target. Developing a sound strategy is key to achieving success in any endeavor, including animal rights outreach conversations. The more important the outcome, the more important examining the pathway to the intended goal becomes.

Identify the Best Process to Achieve the Goal

Assuming the ultimate goal is for people to go vegan or to take the first steps toward ridding themselves of a lifetime of speciesist conditioning, the next logical question would be: "Which communication structure best supports the intended outcome?" Before tackling this question, activists working to inspire change in the world should not forget how difficult change can be. Humans are creatures of habit, the reason for which can be explained through evolutionary theory. As we learn new skills and adapt to our environment, we begin to perform certain tasks in a state of unconscious competence—meaning, we do not have to consciously focus on executing these repetitive tasks in order to perform them well. Some examples of this are walking, balancing while riding a bicycle, shifting gears while driving a car with manual transmission, and even deciding which products to purchase at the grocery store. After having accomplished these tasks successfully many times, our minds relegate the mundane tasks to autopilot in order to preserve bandwidth for other, more complex, and unfamiliar tasks.

Given that food choices are often a result of habits developed over decades, inspiring individuals to change these habits must include a compelling reason for change. There is no reason more compelling than one discovered by oneself. And herein lies both the science and the art behind amazing vegan outreach. It is vital that we inspire the desire for someone to change, while not telling them what they should do or how they should live their lives. If we intend to inspire behavioral change, they themselves must recognize the problem, consider the solution, and voluntarily implement the next steps. How, then, do we as activists generate that motivation within others to take the first step?

The Coach Approach

Proven to inspire behavioral change, coaching is perhaps the most effective outreach approach if the end goal is for others to go vegan. Coaching involves engaging someone in a strategic thinking process where the aim is to help that person identify their own values, goals, obstacles, and solutions, resulting in a specific action plan. The benefit of coaching over debating, discussing, demanding, arguing, teaching, or preaching is that the person being coached is much more likely to follow through on a self-determined action plan. When encouraged to come to their own conclusions, people are more likely to take the necessary steps to align their future actions with their current values.

It's important to recognize that most people do not need to be convinced that exploitation, abuse, and killing are wrong. It is rare to find people who do not hold anti-speciesist values—justice, peace, compassion, and respect. Rather than convincing them of these values, our aim should be to help them *explore* the values they already possess. Once someone is encouraged to verbalize how they *feel* about violence toward others, they are more likely to explore a solution that involves no longer participating in the actions they *themselves* have identified as being unacceptable.

Coaching Tools

When speaking with others, applying a coaching strategy can make the difference between an average experience for the other person and an exceptional one. The first, and most important, strategy is rapport building. A coach has many tools at their disposal to build rapport and ensure someone feels comfortable enough to explore their emotions and values related to speciesism. One of the most underutilized tools within society is nonverbal communication.

Paralinguistics refers to the aspects of communication that do not involve words. These include body language, facial expressions, eye contact, gestures, body position, pitch, and tone of voice. It is important that as coaches, we recognize how much information is communicated without speaking. In order to have the largest impact on the thousands of people with whom we will speak over our lifetime, it is wise for activists to study communication. By learning and consciously employing advanced communication skills, coaches can ensure they are inspiring others and making progress toward the intended goal.

Investigating values is another key skill for a coach. When we ask the right questions, we help others better understand their own values related to animal abuse and exploitation. By bringing these preexisting values to the surface, coaches help others explore speciesism from their own perspective. This significantly reduces the chances that the ego will feel threatened and reduces the temptation of debating someone over the specific attributes of veganism.

The reason why debating as a means to inspire behavioral change has proven to be ineffective is that decisions like these are not often made from a rational, logical place. Emotion and ego often lead others to make intellectually dishonest arguments in order to "save face" during a debate. Very few people are comfortable being proven wrong on such an important topic by a stranger on the street, let alone a friend or family member. When challenged about deeply engrained cultural norms, people will say just about anything to defend what they were taught since childhood—that eating animals is natural, necessary, and normal. A skilled coach avoids creating situations where others feel like they must defend their beliefs and actions. Often, people leave debates more convinced of their own position because they have had to work so hard to defend it.

It is worth highlighting that ego is arguably the largest hindrance to receiving and accepting information that contradicts deeply engrained belief systems. A skilled coach avoids triggering the ego in others by removing their own ego from the conversation and remaining relatively neutral. Approaching this topic from a place of humility, vulnerability, and understanding will only help to disarm the other person's natural defenses.

Once an individual explores their perception of animal exploitation, and they themselves recognize that their actions are not aligned with their values, the coach can enter the "solution phase." This involves inviting the individual to suggest potential solutions to the problem. When the individual has had a chance to explore potential solutions, a coach can then reinforce those and suggest other potential solutions based on their expertise. This then becomes a collaborative problem-solving exercise, as opposed to a confrontational debate.

Van Gogh said, "Great things are done by a series of small things brought together." Those who regularly experience high levels of success in outreach conversations are often employing many coaching techniques successfully. Everyone has the opportunity to motivate people with whom they speak to align their actions with their values. Doing so requires two things: an understanding of coaching methodology and a lot of practice.

The Challenge with Coaching

Despite coaching being the most effective method for inspiring behavioral change in others, it is rarely used in outreach conversations. Professional training and mindful practice are the best ways to develop the necessary patience, curiosity, active listening, and rapport to motivate others to change. Once we accept that people believe what they say, not what they hear, our conversations should hopefully take a more supportive and curious tone. Less talking, more listening. Next time someone asks, "Why are you vegan?" we should resist the temptation to upload all of our vegan knowledge into their brain. Instead, we could ask them, "What do you think is motivating so many people to go vegan nowadays?"

I'm quite a different person today than when I approached that truck outside of the St. Helen's slaughterhouse in November 2014. I suppose that my core values haven't changed all that much; however, my actions are much better aligned with those values today. Money and material goods are not as alluring as they used to be. More important to me now is living life purposefully. Helping others is perhaps the most rewarding feeling in the world. The largest commission check I ever received could never top the feeling of rescuing two piglets from a factory farm in Canada, or three geese from a Christmas market in Hungary, or a baby chicken from a slaughterhouse in Costa Rica. Teaching a roomful of salespeople how to make more money will never compare to teaching a roomful of selfless activists how to inspire positive change in the world.

The awareness that comes with being an animal rights activist is both distressing and empowering. Despite exposing ourselves to humanity's darkest side, we also find ourselves in the company of the most kindhearted people. I am often contacted by these kindhearted people, who are struggling to cope with the immense amount of suffering that exists in this world. Their stress is compounded by an inability to rescue animals trapped in the system and by society's widespread apathy. Of course, for those who accept that pigs, cows, dogs, and humans suffer as equals, there can be no justification for speciesism.

Thinking back to the times that I have personally felt demoralized and hopeless—and there have been many—you might be surprised to learn who usually makes me feel better. It's not other vegans, or even my closest activist friends. It's non-vegans. It's that conversation on the street after someone sees video footage of a cow being stabbed in the throat and throws out the beef burrito they had just purchased, swearing to never eat meat again. It's the police officer, called to deal with protestors at the slaughterhouse, who decides to go vegan after seeing two hundred pigs packed inside a truck. It's the slaughterhouse worker who tells you that he hates his job and wishes slaughterhouses didn't exist. It's the message you receive from someone you haven't spoken to in years saying that they have been following your posts on Facebook and want to go vegan.

People are waking up. I have no doubt that we will see significant and positive changes in the way nonhuman animals are viewed and treated within our lifetime. For that to happen, we must continue leading by example, developing as activists, and inspiring others to live in alignment with the vegan values they already hold in their hearts.

Lost Souls:
Fighting the Harms of Animal Experimentation and beyond

Cory Mac a'Ghobhainn, organizer
with Progress for Science

The scene is brilliantly lit with deep harsh shadows: it is some sort of surgery room. There's an operating table with straps, a circular bank of lights suspended overhead, and gleaming instruments. People in lab coats are gathered around the prone figure before them. The object of their interest is not sedated. In fact, he is thrashing about, pulling at his restraints, clearly in pain and panic. It's hard to see exactly what the lab coats are doing but it seems highly invasive, an assault on dignity and self-autonomy. Why is the victim—and it's clear that this is a more apt term than "patient"—conscious? He doesn't know why these humans are causing him such trauma.

This is a scene from a documentary. I'm not sure exactly when I saw it, where I saw it, or who I was with, and I have not been able to find it again in Internet searches. All I know is it was sometime in the early seventies when I was a student, and it shocked me. This was my first exposure to something called vivisection—animal experimentation—because the struggling figure was not a human, but rather he was one of our cousins, a large ape. My mind struggled to reassure itself that this wasn't something happening in the present, and that it was limited to movies like *The Island of Lost Souls*, that Hollywood slice of dread and despair about a mad scientist's quest to surgically create human/animal hybrids. This film embodies for me that most gruesome of terms— "vivisection"—from Latin *vivus* or "alive" plus the ending of "dissection" from Latin *dissecare* or "cut in pieces."

The movie's images stayed with me, but I refused to give them any sort of real-world credence and, like all things we don't want to confront head-on, my mind slipped around the subject as though I could live in a different sliver of reality. Of course I now know that incredible cruelty happens to animals in the name of science, sometimes almost Dr. Moreauvian-style science—that cats, dogs, rats, fish, even elephants, are cut open, drilled into, drugged, and poisoned by the scientific and medical communities. But back then I didn't want to admit it all *really* existed. I don't know how I squared this denial of the real world with the frog in biology class. What contortion artists our minds become in order to sleep at night.

My memory may have shrugged animal experimentation off to the side, but reality certainly hasn't. A compilation of data on the number of animals used in US research, experimentation, teaching, and testing shows around 2 million in the 1970s (at about the time I saw the horror film) and the 1980s. Recently published USDA reports (for 2016) show about half that number, but this figure should come with a big caveat: according to Speaking of Research, a pro-vivisection advocacy group:

> Precise figures for the number of mice, rats, fish and birds used in research do not exist and thus it is not possible to accurately estimate the total number of vertebrates used in research. Across the EU, 93% of research is conducted on animals which are not counted under the U.S Animal Welfare Act. If the same was true in the U.S then the total number of animals used in research would be approximately 12 million, however this is only an estimate and we have previously suggested the total figure could be as high as 27 million.

In the United States, rats, mice, and birds are not counted in research and testing. Although the Animal Welfare Act (AWA) of 1966—the only federal law in the United States that regulates how animals in research are cared for and treated—was amended in 1970 to include all warm-blooded animals who are commonly experimented upon, the term "warm-blooded animals" was defined so as to exclude rats, mice, and birds. These animals are actually believed to constitute an estimated 95 percent of animals used in research in the United States.

Though the AWA covers how animals in research are housed and cared for and to some extent regulates the pain they suffer, it does not cover what is done to them. Animals are used for chemical, drug, product, food, and cosmetics testing. They are used in education—in high school biology lessons and university medical training—and in curiosity-driven "let's see what happens when we do this" type of experimentation. The animal research industry is very opaque. Who these animals are and what happens to them is usually closely guarded information—the animals kept almost entirely anonymous, each just a faceless number.

Very occasionally, a research animal will become named and their story revealed. Double Trouble was a red tabby at the University of Wisconsin–Madison where sound localization experiments were performed on cats who were then killed. Among other procedures, steel coils were implanted into her eyes and a stainless-steel post was screwed into her skull to immobilize her head so that electrodes could be inserted in her brain. Due to public outcry after these studies came to light, the UWM cat lab was shuttered in 2015. Britches was a baby macaque monkey born in 1985 in a laboratory at the University of California, Riverside, and torn away from his mother shortly thereafter. To determine the effect of blindness on human children, a study was devised wherein his eyes were sewn shut and a sound device emitting piercing metallic sounds was strapped to his head twenty-four hours a day. Fortunately, Britches was rescued by the Animal Liberation Front on April 20, 1985 and lived out his days in a sanctuary.

I didn't know any of this back in my undergrad days, and I wouldn't for a long time. Though I'd gone in and out of activism through my adult life—marching against the Vietnam War and later against Bush II's Iraq war, joining various kinds of protests in Mexico City's Zócalo in the nineties, and later hanging out at Occupy encampments in San Francisco—I had never been involved in the animal liberation movement. I floated in and out of spates of "ethical" vegetarianism, driven by vague notions of how animals were abused. Finally, I came across a video produced by a farmed animal sanctuary, and upon learning about the heartbreak of a mother dairy cow separated from her baby, I went vegan.

After I moved to Los Angeles, a protest at a McDonald's near my house made me into an activist. I wasn't sure that standing on a curb next to someone in a cow outfit and waving at cars driving by was really going to do much, but I joined them anyway. From there I kept looking for and taking part in other actions and demos. I met people, I learned about campaigns and strategies, and I read books. Instead of hopelessly thinking every night before I went to sleep about all the animals who at that very moment were packed into long-distance semis, were trying desperately to back out of cattle chutes, were getting electrocuted, having bolts rammed into their head, being dipped alive into scalding tanks, and having their throats slit, I could think about how I could be part of a worldwide effort to stop it all. This quickly became the driving force of my days, and some time later I was asked to join a local grassroots group dedicated to ending animal experimentation at the University of California called Progress for Science. And so began my entanglement with the fight against vivisection.

At that time, Progress for Science was conducting campaigns focused on two UCLA researchers who were involved in drug-related experiments on monkeys. Our group's activism sought to shine a spotlight on the waste of diverting money and resources from both human-based clinical studies and on the inefficacy of using other species, as well as to expose the cruelty the animals were subjected to. We sought to hold these professors personally accountable by staging protests at their homes. Various groups and individuals had worked on UCLA vivisector campaigns over previous years, with some of the actions being pretty rowdy. I've heard first-person accounts of black-bloc activists wearing ski masks and chanting in front of a researcher's house with police squad cars blocking streets and LAPD helicopters overhead. Famously in 2007, a garden hose was inserted through one of the researchers' windows and turned on, flooding the house and causing significant damage. Later a firebomb was left at a front door: it didn't go off. As one result of these actions, one professor decided to "throw in the towel," announcing he was giving up working on animals altogether.

There are many strategies to end vivisection, such as public-awareness campaigns, petitions, boycotts, legislative campaigns, and corporate and university pressure campaigns using the secondary and tertiary targeting of lab suppliers and airlines transporting lab victims. Progress for Science, while engaging in raising public awareness around the cruelty and ineffectuality of experimenting on animals, also believes that researchers should be held accountable.

To that end, we continued with some home demos: we held candles; we played music and sang songs of liberation; we partnered with a deaf animal rights activist group and staged a rally where we signed "free the monkeys right now!" in ASL; we recited poems and read letters to the researchers' monkey victims; we woke up at dawn to leaflet one professor's neighborhood. One such morning resulted in the researcher losing a restraining order, a Strategic Lawsuit Against Public Participation—or SLAPP—against us, paying Progress for Science $10,000 in legal fees. We managed to shame UCLA by filming the entirety of their expletive-filled (some of it in Russian, bizarrely) counterprotest to one of our vigils. One of our activists got falsely arrested, then immediately cleared based on bogus claims by the same experimenter. We were constantly engaged—we irritated, we beseeched, we demanded.

These two campaigns are now finished. One of the researchers took our chanting advice and left town, transferring to an out-of-state university and continuing the same work there. The other appears to have stopped using animals, her published research papers indicating that she started concentrating fully on clinical studies with humans. So, did we win? Were we the reason for the change? Without her making a statement to that effect, we will never really know. We just know the monkeys won.

Those supporting animal-based research claim that activists are dead wrong. They argue that it saves lives and that many of the miracle drugs we now have on the market were developed using all the millions of nonhuman animals who are tested on every year. It would be foolish and counterproductive for us to claim that there have been zero benefits—centuries of studying the bodies of other animals have taught us much about our own physical beings, about our broadly shared circulatory systems, our organs, and our nervous systems. But is animal research always predictive of human outcomes? Do other creatures with their similar but still different physiologies and genomes really serve as good enough analogues for human beings? The Food and Drug Administration (FDA) seems to cast doubt on that claim, estimating in 2004 that:

> 92 percent of drugs that pass preclinical tests, including "pivotal" animal tests, fail to proceed to the market. More recent analysis suggests that, despite efforts to improve the predictability of animal testing, the failure rate has actually increased and is now closer to 96 percent.

After having undergone mandatory animal testing, "more than half of the few drugs approved are later withdrawn or relabeled due to serious or lethal adverse effects in humans." The results of these miserable figures can be devastating. Two cases in point: In the late fifties an estimated ten thousand babies were born around the world with severe limb deformations with only 50 percent surviving. What they all had in common was their mothers had taken the drug thalidomide, a sedative that had been tested on animals and "proven" safe. Once these birth defects were linked to the drug, researchers started conducting tests on pregnant animals of innumerable other species that also failed to produce similar malformations. Animal tests also indicated the arthritis drug Vioxx was safe, but, when marketed, it caused over sixty thousand deaths in the United States alone.

Though more and more evidence piles up showing that animal experimentation is not necessarily predictive of human outcomes and can result in demonstrable harms and sometimes even death for humans, these are not the main reasons we oppose it. Central to ethical veganism is the idea that all lives have meaning; that every animal is unique and inherently valuable. Animals are not objects to be used for our entertainment or profit, nor are they items to be listed in lab catalogs. But vivisection is a lucrative business, not only for the research universities that receive huge taxpayer-funded grants, but also for the supporting industries: the outfits that breed and sell the animal victims, the airlines that transport the animals, and the companies that supply the lab equipment—the little guillotines that slice off the heads of mice, the cages, the food, the feeding systems, etc. It is another instance of profit trumping life.

It is worth considering that animal abuse—despite laws we put in place banning animals in circuses, animal-based cosmetics testing, and selling from puppy mills—will always find a way to rear its ugly head as long as it is profitable. Not only are the animals suffering, but the elevation of profit is causing our planet's ecosystem to buckle under the abuse we throw at it, and human populations—starting with the poorest and most vulnerable—are increasingly under threat. Big money is a powerful all-encompassing overlord.

The end of two of our UCLA campaigns marked a turning point for my group Progress for Science, and also for me personally. While continuing to advocate for animals in labs and to call out the work of UCLA vivisector Michele Basso, we began to focus on other issues, if not as organizers then as allies. We have led AR contingents several years running in both the Women's March and International Women's Day March. We have held political prisoner letter-writing sessions for folks the state has unjustly silenced behind bars—in particular in support of the members of the MOVE 9, a family of black and animal liberationists imprisoned en masse for the shooting of a cop during an armed police raid against the men, women, and children in their communal home in Philadelphia in 1978. Along with a local homeless advocacy group, She Does, we created an altar at the annual Hollywood Cemetery's Dia de los Muertos event in memory of several individuals who have died in the streets of LA. I also give art classes to formerly homeless people living in transitional and permanent housing facility near LA's notorious Skid Row as part of my work with Art for Animals' Sake. Every Monday as we work, I have listened to individuals recount the events of their lives, which are so very far from my own sheltered existence.

As for many, the 2016 presidential election was jarring in a way that seemed to leave me mentally breathless. Though I as a white person was not going to ever feel the full effects of this plunge into chaos and intolerance, it reinforced for me that holding demos at vivisectors' homes or standing on street corners and chanting "It's not science, it's violence" was not enough when on those same streets are more and more tents of the unhoused, when on those streets people whose first language is not English are being harassed, when on those streets unarmed black people are being shot by police with few consequences. When people are feeling trampled under, it's hard for them to care about unknown animals in hidden labs or in slaughterhouses.

Maybe there is an additional way to fight these harms wrought by our destructive economic system. Maybe we as activists need to make some adjustments by following animal oppression to its roots—realizing that the view of life as hierarchical, with some lives having more value, greatly affects otherized humans such as immigrants, refugees, people of color, people of fluid or nonbinary gender, children, women, the unhoused, and the poor—the list goes on. Learning about the commodification of life is crucial where social justice is concerned: not only are animals used for profit but so are workers, more so those in the most exploitative jobs—prison, slaughterhouse, agricultural, and sweatshop workers.

The word intersectional is often used in the animal rights community. Coined in 1989 by Kimberlé Crenshaw in a paper for the University of Chicago Legal Forum, "Demarginalizing the Intersection of Race and Sex: A Black Feminist Critique of Antidiscrimination Doctrine, Feminist Theory and Antiracist Politics," intersectional initially referred to how being a black women in the United States must be viewed in terms of being black and being a woman and how these two states interact and reinforce each other. Intersectionality holds that each form of oppression is unique and that these forms of oppression intersect because people's different identities intersect. Animals reside in this concept of intersectionality differently. A rat in a lab is not there because she has two or more identities; she is in that cage because rats are victims of systems of oppression that at their roots exploit both nonhuman animals and humans.

While we can recognize how forms of oppression are linked, what is not intersectional is to compare or equate oppressions: human slavery and its to-this-day legacy in the United States is not "like" the exploitation of animals, as some animal rights advocates maintain. The animal rights movement is not the new civil rights movement, which a look at the news media on any given day will forcefully demonstrate to be still *not over*. Should we show up at an MLK Day march holding posters equating the two? Is the profit-motivated forced insemination of a cow, though also a violent assault on her life and self-determination, really like the domination-driven rape of a human? We celebrate new vegan options at fast-food chains, forgetting not only the animal bodies that went into the rest of the menu, but also the exploited workers who serve it all. We repeat Dr. King's words "Injustice anywhere is a threat to justice everywhere" without looking at all the other "everywheres."

Maybe only by learning how oppression works, learning who the few exploiting the many are and how they do it, and by radically reenvisioning how we humans share the planet with all others will we bring about animal rights in any sustained way. All else seems like a Band-Aid on a gushing wound. There will always be animal rights activists who have the privilege to feel the most strongly about the tragedy of the place animals occupy in this exploitation, and to work exclusively on various campaigns to end it, but in fighting injustice it's important to know what it consists of and to not, by ignoring the plight of disadvantaged and abused humans, inadvertently reinforce it.

There is another, more practical reason for looking at animal oppression as just one piece in the larger picture of systemic oppression. When animal rights activists join with and/or support other liberation movements, we give lie to the commonly held belief that "You PETA people only care about animals," a belief that delegitimizes our struggle on behalf of animals. At rallies and marches for human-focused causes, I am seeing that groups and organizers from other movements are joining in. A dramatic example of this is activists in Palestine lending not only moral but also practical and logistical support to the people in Black Lives Matter, beginning with the Ferguson protests a few years ago. Animal rights groups, though, are rarely represented in coalitions. We haven't really learned the skill of being and making allies. Good allies support one another first, form relationships, and only then share what drives their own causes to then-receptive, appreciative ears.

With this in mind, myself and a few other women formed a group called Animal/Human Rights Allies. Our purpose is to expand our knowledge of and commitment to other struggles and, as vegans, show other movements that we animal activists do care about humans, and our modus operandi is to actually show up. We have started marching, protesting, and physically supporting the actions of our fellows fighting for immigration rights, Black Lives Matter, labor strikes, women's marches, and for anyone else who needs help un-fucking the world. We don't let it stop us that we are often surrounded by people who do not include speciesism in their list of isms to be fought—we are there because their causes, which are often our causes, too, are important and just.

We are also there because by being in the same space, in the same room, or on the same sidewalk, maybe one day the animals we advocate for will no longer be on the table, but will get a seat at the table itself. One day. So, let's be good allies. The animals, including the lost souls in the vivisectors' labs, really do depend on it.

The Least We Can Do: Communicating the Animal Rights Message

Natasha & Luca, "That Vegan Couple,"
social media influencers

If you've ever watched toddlers learning how to walk, you'll notice how unsure they are of where their feet will land. Despite looking unbalanced, they eagerly put one foot in front of the other. A toddler's enthusiasm for learning to walk is admirable, and in time, their clumsiness is replaced with confidence and balance. With practice, experience, and many failed attempts, walking becomes fluid and natural. This is akin to most people's introduction to animal rights activism. Once their blinders are removed and they've recognized the agonizing reality of suffering and violence to which they have unknowingly contributed by eating and using animals, a deep heart connection is often made with the animal victims, and a strong sense of urgency to rectify injustice takes over. This sense of urgency often begins with awkwardness as the new vegan learns to navigate uncharted territory. Over time, confidence, skill, and greater awareness are developed.

That's certainly how we felt when we decided to go vegan at age thirty-one. We found it difficult to reconcile that we hadn't known the truth sooner. How could we have been so ignorant about what we ate? Alongside feelings of shame and guilt was the need to do something: to immediately take action and let everyone else know about the truth we had just woken up to. This moment of awakening is a powerful and serious event, yet most of us aren't quite sure where to start on our new-found path. Just like the toddler learning to walk, new vegans tend to take their first steps awkwardly. Sometimes overenthusiastically, other times painfully, they put one foot in front of the other and try to master the art of communicating the truth to people who don't often want to hear it.

We went vegan together after watching an incredible speech on YouTube by an activist named Gary Yourofsky. "Best Speech You Will Ever Hear" changed our lives. After watching it, we sent an impassioned email to all the people in our contact list telling them about the speech, the fact that we had become vegan, and that it was our moral obligation to share this life-changing and lifesaving information with them. The responses we got from that email back in 2011 were an exact representation of what we would experience in the coming years as we continued to advocate for animals. A few people replied congratulating us, telling us that it was an admirable decision, but not something they could do. One person—a former vegetarian—wrote back and dismissed everything we had said because this was in no way the "best speech" they had ever heard. Another person wrote back in absolute tears; after watching the speech, which contained animal exploitation footage, she was shocked to her core, and thanked us profusely for waking her up and helping her choose vegan. And that was it. The vast majority—99 percent of people we personally wrote to—ignored the email. They simply didn't respond or acknowledge it in any way. Their silence was far more frustrating than the former vegetarian's comment about it not being the "best speech" ever. We noticed how quickly our annoyance turned into anger. How could *those* people be so ignorant and selfish to ignore the very thing that just changed our lives forever? We tried reminding ourselves that we had been *those* people only a few days earlier, but still, their silence cut deep. The challenge was on—how could we communicate the vegan message in a powerful enough way that nobody would ever ignore us again?

The truth is, we couldn't. We've learned over the years that people will still ignore you no matter how perfectly, politely, or politically correctly you try to speak about veganism. The vast majority don't want to hear it and will try their hardest to block out the truth. Once when we were performing outreach in Boston, an elderly lady yelled at us: "Shut up, I don't want to hear anything!" A month before that incident, a young man cried with gratitude after a powerful conversation that no doubt changed his life. The lesson is, no matter how people react, say it anyway. Outreach is a powerful way to effect change. Even when people react angrily, the message they hear may be something they pause to reflect on and consider later on.

We find that many new vegans are shut down by their loved ones about their decision to go vegan, and as a result, they are disheartened and stop talking about veganism to anyone. But it's important to remember that our job is not to make sure every single person we speak to goes vegan. Our job is to simply plant seeds and trust that seeds eventually sprout. Irrespective of how the conversation goes, a seed is planted, and that person can't un-know the truth. The challenge is to walk away from each conversation with the ability to detach from the outcome. If we mentally and emotionally invest in the outcome of every conversation, we may be at risk for a breakdown. In order to make vegan advocacy sustainable for our mental health in the long term, we must simply focus on the seed that was planted, not if or when it will sprout. The question many people ask is, why bother planting seeds? Why bother having those uncomfortable, difficult conversations with people who don't want to hear about veganism? Why put ourselves in a position where so many non-vegans will disapprove of our actions and see us as preachy, angry, pushy vegans? The reason is that going vegan is not the most we can do, it's the least we can do. This has been our tagline for years now, and we say it because it perfectly sums up what we want to convey to the world. Not paying other people to needlessly slit the throats of innocent animals so we can eat their bodies and secretions is merely the least we can do. Not paying other people to rip the skin off defenseless animals is the least we can do. Not paying people to torture and mutilate terrified animals to test products we purchase is the least we can do. Not participating in the largest slaughter of sentient beings every single day is the very baseline. If we can't see that ripping a baby away from his mother at birth just so we can have a slice of cheese is morally unjustifiable and totally unnecessary, then we have a major problem on this planet. If we do wake up from the somewhat hypnotic trance of carnism and go vegan, we must realize that it's not the most we can do. It's just the beginning.

From the victim's perspective, it's not enough for us to simply not participate in the violence. The victim would want us to actively intervene. We must take the next step by advocating for animals and working toward their liberation. We need to fight for them the same way we would want someone to fight for our lives, the way we would fight for the lives of our beloved cats and dogs, and the way we would fight for our children, parents, and partners if they were the ones being trucked to execution. That is the power of being an animal rights activist, and not just a vegan. The more we believed that going vegan was not the most we could do, but the least we could do, the stronger our activism became and the more determined we were to plant the seeds of truth and awareness. There are countless ways to plant these seeds, as we have learned from our many forms of activism over the years. From our perspective, it's a numbers game. We saw that emailing all the people we knew about veganism only gave us one immediate positive reply for a change of heart. If we want to have thousands of positive replies of change, we need to reach many, many more people than those in our contacts list. The power and magic of social media gives anybody with an Internet connection the ability to share the truth about animal agriculture and exploitation, and help people transition to a vegan life. Just like our carnist blinders were removed by a video on YouTube, social media is largely how we help other people remove their blinders. It is the easiest, fastest, and most effective way we know to reach the largest number of people around the world with the vegan message. In five years, we've had more than 23 million views on our YouTube channel alone and millions more on our Facebook and Instagram posts. Using social media is the key to spreading the animal rights message as fast as possible.

Not everyone wants to be in front of a camera, or is cut out for making videos. Even if you are comfortable in front of the camera, it's still a skillful juggling act to balance entertaining your audience while speaking about the serious topic of mass slaughter. Luckily, using social media as a tool for animal rights activism doesn't rely solely on making videos. The simple act of sharing other people's videos and writing your own captions is incredibly powerful and effective. Social media works with algorithms—basically, the more interaction (likes, comments, shares) a post gets, the more the algorithm favors that post and continues to promote it. Therefore, sharing great videos from other activists with your followers not only ensures your audience will see the video, but also adds to the exponential growth and popularity of that video, thus maximizing how many non-vegans will see it.

An interesting transition we have made over the years is taking our online activism to the streets and then back online again. In short, the focus of our online activism has always been to educate people about all things vegan related. But this conversation was very much a one-way dialogue. We would make a video and post it online, but we weren't conversing with anybody in real time. Once we started getting more involved in street activism and outreach in public about what happens to animals for food, clothing, entertainment, testing, and the pet industry, it became a two-way dialogue. But speaking to just one person at a time was not an efficient use of time, so we started to film our outreach conversations and upload those videos to social media. All of a sudden, a conversation with one person could reach the hearts and minds of thousands of people with a click of a button. The impact of this has been phenomenal. No matter how the seed was planted and received, everybody watching the outreach video is learning. Non-vegans watching the video are hearing how nonsensical carnist objections to veganism sound, and they're also learning new information about why veganism is so important. Vegans watching the outreach videos are learning how to answer carnist objections, and, perhaps most importantly, they are seeing other vegans doing more than just being vegan. They are seeing other vegans get active and advocate for animals. This fosters courage and confidence in not-yet-active vegans to speak out, and it helps boost the participation of those who are performing outreach and attending animal rights events.

During a Q&A session after an activism workshop we led in Detroit, Michigan, one of the audience members asked us what we thought the worst thing a vegan could say during vegan outreach. Our answer was "saying nothing at all." To stay silent is to consent. There is no right or wrong way to say that we have a responsibility to stop killing innocent beings. There may be more effective ways to communicate our message and to ensure that seeds sprout later on, but even then, the most strategic, compassionate, respectful approach can still be met with resistance and anger. So, when we help vegans become activists and equip them with outreach tools in our activism workshops, we encourage them not to overthink their outreach. Waiting to become the "perfect" activist with all the right answers before having a conversation might mean you'll never have the conversation. There is no such thing as a perfect conversation, and the animals can't wait for vegans to master all the answers to all of the questions they will face.

We encourage people to speak with conviction and passion, strength and compassion, but most importantly, to just speak. We can have more of an impact on people if they feel our words are coming from our authentic, heartfelt selves, rather than a finely polished script using all of the "right" words. Speak for the animals the same way you would want someone to speak for your life. The extraordinary ripple effect of being a animal rights activist can't be underestimated. First and foremost, it helps to educate the public and create the change we need to liberate our animal cousins. Second, it's incredibly empowering for vegans. Many of us often feel helpless and hopeless, but getting active helps us feel like we are doing more than simply not participating in the violence. We're actively helping to stop it, and this is incredibly empowering.

Animal agriculture is a mammoth, trillion-dollar industry. To the individual vegan, taking on this industry can seem like a David versus Goliath task. But the power is in realizing that we don't have to go into battle with Goliath directly to stop the unnecessary violence in the animal agriculture industry. This is a clear-cut example of power to the people. Consumers decide what industry produces because industry responds to consumer demands. As educators and activists, we focus our attention and energy on reaching and changing consumers, who will in turn change what industry produces. Over the years, part of our role has been not only to educate non-vegans about the fact that, as consumers, they are directly paying for violence toward animals, but to also empower vegans in how we can use the supply-and-demand economic theory to our advantage when reaching out to non-vegans.

We personally have found—and have heard from countless other activists—that the sense of helplessness is significantly reduced when becoming an active vegan. When we surround ourselves with like-minded people, united by the goal of saving lives and creating lasting change, it generates a powerful connection that helps us rise together and push the animal rights movement forward.

Saving Joe and Legal Wins
for Captive Animals

Brittany Peet, Director of Captive Animal Law
Enforcement for PETA

When I was a kid, I used to visit a bear named Smokey who lived at a park in Mount Pleasant near my hometown in Michigan. My family and I would watch him pace around on a concrete slab in a little round cage. I guess I was too young to recognize that Smokey was deprived of everything, even though there was nothing in his cage to keep him occupied except a tire swing and a bowling ball. I vaguely recall some other visitors commenting on how small his cage was, but most, like me, were oblivious to his misery. It was a different time back then, a time when the public simply viewed captive animals without much thought about what it meant. Visitors didn't demand change. There were no protests. Smokey died in that cage without ever setting foot outside of it for who knows how many years.

I was just a kid, but *what if* people had spoken up and taken a stand? Would I have joined in? Would my eyes have been opened? It's hard to say, since I spent many hours of my childhood sitting and playing on the skin of a bear my father had shot and killed. As the years passed, I came to deeply regret the part I played in keeping Smokey behind bars and for believing that a bearskin rug was acceptable. I eventually realized that animals deserve better than to be caged for human amusement. My dog Wesley is to thank for my change of heart.

I never had a dog before Wesley and, frankly, I really didn't know anything about "life with a dog." That quickly changed. Wesley had a *huge* personality. I learned every single one of his idiosyncrasies and habits—and he learned mine. He comforted me when I was struggling through my law classes and met me with sheer joy every time I walked in the door. He could be hilarious and he could sulk. I came to realize that Wesley wasn't "just" a dog; he was a complete individual. I stopped eating animals shortly thereafter: I realized I couldn't claim to care about them while continuing to eat them.

My growing interest in animal issues prompted me to take some animal law classes. When I finished law school, I knew I couldn't devote years of my life working eighty-hour weeks for corporations, and so I applied for a fellowship with the PETA Foundation. Being accepted for the fellowship was thrilling, as I would be able to work on issues that really mattered to me, including rescuing bears and other animals from roadside zoos and other awful places.

My desk is piled high with pressing cases, but in 2013 alarm bells starting ringing when an employee of an Alabama roadside zoo, called the Mobile Zoo, contacted PETA about a chimpanzee named Joe and other animals who were in serious trouble. We learned that some animals were living in their own waste because there was a lack of staff to perform basic cleaning tasks, and animals weren't provided with adequate veterinary care. Even when they had diarrhea and were vomiting, they were denied treatment. Care was so lax that an ostrich fell into a tub and died of hypothermia.

The pictures and eyewitness descriptions haunted me. During the day when I enjoyed my lunch, I knew that Joe and other animals were being fed moldy fruit and rancid meat. At night while I lay in my clean, warm bed, I knew that Joe and others rarely knew a moment's comfort. I'd wake up with an overwhelming urgency to make things happen. By 2013, Joe had lived at the Mobile Zoo for fourteen years after being dumped there by a notorious breeder and exhibitor named

Steve Martin (*not* the actor) who exploits animals for the film and television industry. Chimpanzees are highly social, but Joe had no one to play with or turn to for comfort, and he was confined to a cage that was about the size of a small dog pen. The ceiling was so low that he couldn't climb—which is something as fundamental as breathing to a chimpanzee. Visitors pelted him with peanuts. Driven to despair by the lack of companionship and everything else that's natural and important to a chimpanzee, Joe had resorted to pulling out his own hair.

The heartache I felt helped drive PETA's intense two-year barrage of complaints to state and federal agencies and local law enforcement as well as an extensive online and grassroots advocacy campaign. These efforts were a resounding success by any measure. The U.S. Department of Agriculture (USDA) cited the Mobile Zoo for seventeen violations of the federal Animal Welfare Act (AWA) following PETA's first complaint to the agency, and the Occupational Safety and Health Administration slapped the facility with a $2,000 fine for allowing a worker to come into direct contact with Joe. We filed more complaints, and Alabama wildlife officials seized eleven endangered gopher tortoises the facility had illegally obtained and released them back into the wild. But two years into the campaign, Joe and the other animals remaining at the roadside zoo were still stuck there.

It's impossible not to be moved by the plight of captive chimpanzees, with whom we share nearly 99 percent of our DNA. Seeing Joe's fingers grip the bars of his cage as he looked out in what can only be described as desperation broke my heart. Even though I was emotionally spent, my determination to secure a much better life for Joe never wavered.

Finally, there was a breakthrough. The antiquated "split-listing" of captive chimpanzees—which meant that only *wild* chimpanzees were protected by the federal Endangered Species Act (ESA)—was eliminated, opening up the opportunity for PETA to sue the Mobile Zoo and its owner, John Hightower. Our rightful claim was that the roadside zoo was in violation of the ESA by keeping Joe in solitary confinement without adequate space and enrichment.

When Hightower was ready to talk settlement, I felt sheer joy. Initially things were moving along nicely, and we found an appropriate and accredited sanctuary that was willing to take Joe. Then, the roadside zoo threw a wrench into the discussions. Among other unfounded claims, its sole caretaker asserted that Joe would either kill or be killed by the males in the chimpanzee group at the sanctuary that PETA had suggested and wanted him placed elsewhere. Of course, I should have seen this coming. This is a common refrain from "caretakers" of abused and neglected animals. They insist that the animals can't be introduced to others, claiming that previous attempts have failed. In my experience, such claims have been wrong 100 percent of the time. When animals are shoved into cramped pens with unfamiliar cage mates and there are established social hierarchies and scarce resources, aggression and antagonism are almost inevitable. Reputable sanctuaries take great care in easing traumatized animals into their new situations. Animals aren't just placed into a new environment with high hopes and fingers crossed—introductions are done with tremendous planning, patience, and expertise.

To keep things moving, we agreed on another sanctuary, and a transfer date was set. Then, four days before Joe was due to hit the road, we learned that the Mobile Zoo had done an about-face. It was now leaning toward sending him to a Michigan roadside zoo that was *notorious* for keeping a young chimpanzee in solitary confinement and allowing tourists to take photos with him. The Mobile Zoo claimed that it was opposed to Joe getting a vasectomy at the agreed-upon sanctuary—it wanted him to breed. Preventing even more animals from being born into a world that has no place for them is a fundamental tenet of any legitimate sanctuary. The demand that Joe be able to breed was bizarre, given that he had been held in solitary confinement and that the Michigan facility housed only two male chimpanzees. It seemed clear that the roadside zoo was doing whatever it could to block his rescue. To say this was maddening is an understatement. It was time to turn up the heat. We let the Mobile Zoo's attorney know why the sanctuary was a better home for Joe and that the transfer to the facility in Michigan wouldn't make the case go away and would likely result in additional violations of the ESA that PETA would pursue. We began preparing to seek a temporary restraining order as a last resort to prevent Joe's transfer to Michigan. We pushed our rescue date back by one day, but we continued our last-minute planning as if it were still going forward. If we were able to salvage the settlement, I didn't want Joe to wait one more day to get out of that hellhole. Days went by and we heard nothing. The roadside zoo made us wait until just about the very last minute, but the call finally came: the rescue was on! Everyone involved headed to Alabama.

Despite the joy of the occasion, Joe was a pathetic sight. He had very little muscle mass and was missing all the hair on his forearms and calves. What mattered most, though, was that he was healthy enough to travel. The sanctuary team would be driving him to its Florida facility, and I—along with our fabulous videographer, Neel—would fly to meet them there. We didn't think that we could take any more surprises, but soon enough, we were hit with a welcome one. By happenstance, the most renowned primatologist in the world, Dr. Jane Goodall, was going to be in Tampa, Florida, a city on the transport route. The sanctuary's director contacted Dr. Goodall's assistant to see if she wanted to meet Joe. The opportunity to capture an interaction between Joe and the distinguished primatologist on film was invaluable. Neel and I immediately resigned ourselves to exchanging our two-hour plane ride for a ten-hour road trip.

But we should have known that we weren't out of the woods yet. When we got to the Mobile Zoo on the morning of the transfer—all of us balls of nerves and anticipation—we were crushed to be informed that "the vet's not coming." The news was devastating, because "no vet" meant "no go." In order to transport most animals between states, a health certificate—an attestation that a licensed veterinarian has visually inspected the animal and that the animal is fit to travel—is required. But the certificate can *only* be signed by a veterinarian who is licensed in the state the animal is leaving. And we didn't have one. Our settlement agreement *required* the Mobile Zoo to have an appropriately licensed veterinarian on-site at the agreed-upon time to complete the health certificate and oversee the transfer. The roadside zoo's attorney shrugged and blithely said that there was nothing that they could do. There was a lot that *we* could do, though, including going to court to enforce the agreement if we had to. We started calling every veterinarian in the area in order to find someone who could sign Joe's exit papers, but they already had packed days with existing clients or didn't feel comfortable signing a health certificate for a chimpanzee.

As hope was dwindling, a car pulled into the Mobile Zoo's long driveway and a man got out. The roadside zoo's veterinarian—who had apparently never been asked to come in the first place—had finally been called. The facility's attempt to thwart the rescue seemingly fell apart after they learned that we could enforce the settlement in court.

Joe was examined and given a sedative. I could only wonder what was going through his mind. Excitement that something was happening to break up his interminable days of boredom and monotony? Or perhaps curiosity, an emotion that chimpanzees feel so keenly. Fear? Even if he couldn't understand what was happening, he soon would. Finally, he was wrapped in a comfortable fleece blanket and tucked into his transport crate with a white teddy bear. The awful, filthy cage was now behind him forever.

As Neel and I followed the transport van, the sanctuary's vet texted a precious photo of Joe curled up with a red plaid blanket, clutching his teddy bear, and let us know that he was starting to stir. Unfortunately, the Mobile Zoo's last "gift" to Joe was more abuse. It had ignored the veterinarian's instruction not to feed him the night before his transfer, and he had vomited several times as a result. Thankfully, he was awake when he vomited, so he didn't choke or inhale the vomit—a real risk that could have killed him. After looking him over, the veterinarian was confident that he was going to be okay.

Hours later, Joe met someone who spoke his language. He and Dr. Goodall became friends immediately. They vocalized to each other and bobbed their heads in greeting, and Joe truly seemed to enjoy their meeting. It was a thrilling moment, one that Neel was able to capture so that it could be preserved and shared. Only two hundred more miles stood between our little convoy and the paradise awaiting Joe.

When we finally pulled into the long driveway of the sanctuary, the van's rear doors were flung open, and for the first time in years, Joe was able to hear and smell others who were just like him. This was the most exciting thing to have happened to him in nearly two decades. The sanctuary's Special Needs Facility is designed for new arrivals like Joe and for those who require a little extra TLC. As we carefully maneuvered his transport crate inside, the residents began to wake up and hoot greetings. After all this time, Joe could communicate with other chimpanzees. Instead of a low-ceilinged, cramped dog kennel, Joe now had two rooms stocked with toys, blankets, and nesting materials. Wasting no time, he began to climb as high as he could. We left to let him get settled in. Joe was home.

It had been an exhilarating, infuriating, and exhausting day. Neel and I were dead-tired and famished. We went through the local Taco Bell drive-through on the way back to the hotel and customized our own vegan feasts, then devoured every zesty bite. That night, in my comfortable hotel bed, tears leaked from my eyes knowing that Joe was in one, too, for the first time. The next morning was surreal—after all these years, after so much struggle and so many obstacles, was this really happening? Neel and I couldn't wait to get back to the sanctuary—Joe was going outside!

The opening to his outdoor space was several feet off the ground, with mesh surrounding it so that he could climb up or down to get in and out. But he had no time for such trifles. The instant the door opened, he leaped out. Everyone gasped, but he was completely unfazed. He ran through the grass, tore through an upturned tire, and began to climb. He climbed to the top of the enclosure and started to swing—the technical term is "brachiate"—across the mesh roof. This is a quintessential chimpanzee behavior, but it was probably the first time that Joe had brachiated in his life. Within just a few days, he was introduced to a chimpanzee named Geraldine, who was known to be gracious to new residents. When the door between their enclosures opened, there was no hesitation. They immediately embraced and groomed each other—a gesture of trust and friendship between chimpanzees. They then ventured outside, where they played and chased each other in the Florida sun.

Joe's happy ending was the beginning of the end for the Mobile Zoo. Within just a few months, the USDA revoked its AWA exhibitor's license following years of violations, and soon after, it was raided by local animal control officers. Hightower was charged with twenty-eight counts of cruelty to animals. He pleaded guilty to fourteen of them and was sentenced to pay $3,500 in restitution and be on probation for two years, and he was ordered never to own animals professionally again. The rest of the animals at the roadside zoo were confiscated, and PETA worked with our friends at a Colorado sanctuary to rescue the facility's three remaining North American black bears, Elsie, Bella, and Dusty.

Today, Joe looks like a different chimpanzee. His wasted body has grown muscular and strong. His days of plucking himself bald are behind him, and his hair is thick and healthy. He has many friends and spends his days climbing, roaming, and getting into mischief with his pals. When I first returned to the sanctuary for a visit a few weeks after he arrived, he was still in the area for those with special needs. He took a moment to greet me, but he was more interested in chasing his new rambunctious friend Timmy through their enclosure. In a testament to just how far animals can come when they're transferred to a sanctuary, on subsequent visits Joe was too busy being a chimpanzee to bother with the likes of me. He lives on a lush island now, with trees, hammocks, and tall forts to investigate and navigate. At the risk of cheapening animals' emotional lives by ascribing human emotions to them, I look at Joe and see a happy person. There is always injustice inherent in confining wild animals, but until all cages are empty, these animals can have some semblance of a normal life when the focus is on their well-being rather than on human entertainment.

One of the first hard lessons I learned when I started advocating for animals is that I won't win every battle. Doors are slammed. Calls go unanswered. Pleas are sometimes ignored. But the losses are precisely what keep me going. There's a need to both honor those we couldn't help in time and continue fighting for those we can save. Sometimes victories come quickly—other times, progress is excruciatingly slow. Knowing that animals are languishing while we fight for their rescue is difficult. The frustration involved in working cases is exacerbated by seeing reports from government inspectors that document a lack of veterinary care, social isolation, and squalid living conditions. It *should* be easier to free animals from these situations, but we're fighting for those who are unfortunate enough to have been born during a time when they had few legal protections.

Not so long ago, animal rights lawyers didn't exist. Today, elite schools offer fellowships in the discipline, and constitutional law scholars are weighing in on issues affecting animals. Legal wins for animals are occurring, and they aren't anomalies. I'm fighting for other chimpanzees like Joe now, and I'll never give up. My dog Wesley was the catalyst for where I am now, and perhaps Joe's story can motivate others to take action. If you don't think you're "big" enough or important enough, this I've learned: One person *can* make a difference. While rescues like Joe's mean so much to the individual's life who has forever changed for the better, we can band together in the broader fight for systemic change. And we can find more effective ways of attacking the problems. Persistence is one of our strongest advantages in these battles, and if we keep fighting, *we will win.*

In some ways, it doesn't seem that long ago when I watched Smokey the bear in that cramped cage, but in other ways, it feels like a lifetime ago. Back then I was simply too young and conditioned to believe that keeping animals behind bars for human amusement was unacceptable. Today, my life's work is getting them out.

©Jo-Anne McArthur

V

Bearing Witness, Civil Disobedience & Open Rescue:

A Movement Rising

The Power of Protest: Learning from Nonviolent Social Justice Movements

Chase Avior, actor and filmmaker

I have learned that the most fulfilling purpose in life is to help those in need, but it was a long and rough path that led me to this realization. Growing up, I was socially awkward and was bullied by other kids because of my strange behavior. Sometimes I would overwhelm people with my intense energy, and other times I was harsh and avoidant because I didn't understand how to regulate my emotions, which got me into a lot of trouble. Much of the bullying was done by authoritarian adults who would physically hurt me and cast me off to sit in isolation because I wasn't compliant with some of their oppressive rules and dogmatic beliefs. I was completely dominated my entire childhood, which made me feel powerless, and because my power had been stripped away, I lashed out at the world. The wounds that resulted from being bullied caused severe depression and anger, which led me to become a bully myself. I used violence to make myself feel superior, much in the same way that speciesism works—humans oppressing nonhuman animals from an ego-driven mentality—until I developed my ability to empathize. Having been subjected to bullying, I know the feeling of being scared and defenseless, and I see that same terror in the eyes of every animal headed to the slaughterhouse.

I stopped eating animals in 2009, and off and (mostly) on for the past several years, I've been sleeping in my car so that I can live without worrying about money very much and dedicate most of my time to volunteering for animal rights. I left behind my growing career as an actor, which some might call me foolish for because I could have made a lot of money, but my priorities changed. I enjoyed the excitement of Hollywood, but justice was always on my mind, encouraging me to take immediate action for the animals I used to exploit, and I fell in love with this calling. Now I use my skills as an actor and filmmaker to create motivating videos about animal rights. I'm building a strong following on Facebook and YouTube and I currently have over forty supporters donating to me monthly on Patreon to help keep my work going. My activism is bold and uncompromising, which results in some folks dismissing me as a "crazy vegan." This all raises two questions: 1) How did I get to the point where animal rights is so important that I am sacrificing money, comfort, and social acceptance? and 2) Why do I think controversial tactics are the most effective?

In 2009, my life was forever changed when I saw the science fiction film *District 9,* which tells the story of a group of aliens who come to earth and are discriminated against simply because they aren't human. The humans segregate the aliens from society and perform violent experiments on them. The next day I was eating a steak as usual, and for the first time I seriously thought about the individual who was killed for that piece of flesh. I suddenly understood that I had been discriminating against animals simply for being different. Like the aliens in the film, animals are sensitive beings with friends and families who want to live as much as humans do.

I ate animals for twenty-six years, until the day I finally looked at it from the victims' perspective and realized that we don't have the right to kill them. I couldn't find any real difference between humans and animals that justifies us committing unnecessary violence against them. I had been telling myself that animals aren't as intelligent as humans, but realized that this isn't a justification for taking an individual's life. I came to recognize that nobody gets to choose how they're born and that it was prejudice for me to say that only humans (and certain animals like dogs and cats) deserve the right to safety, but that cows, pigs, and chickens deserve to have their throats slit.

I watched slaughterhouse videos of these innocent creatures scream-ing and struggling to stay alive—baby animals who were killed at ages representing a fraction of their natural life span. I realized that animals need us to speak up for them in the same way we would speak up for ourselves if we were in their position, so I became an activist in search of the most effective methods of change.

There are many important forms of activism such as conversational outreach, social media outreach, bearing witness at slaughterhouses, animal rescue, sanctuary operation, legislative change, and creating vegan alternatives, but my focus is primarily on the power of disruptive protests. We learn from the women's rights movement, the gay rights movement, and the civil rights movement that disrupting oppression is essential to dismantling it. As history clearly shows, protesting draws attention to the issue, communicates the severity of the problem, and empowers people to take collective action. For example, the lunch-counter sit-ins of the civil rights movement in 1960 were successful in getting media coverage and public support precisely because these pro-tests were disruptive and controversial. These nonviolent acts of civil disobedience shined a light on the battle against racial segregation in the southern United States. The whole country was watching news reports of peaceful protestors being assaulted by white, racist custom-ers and then arrested by police. This polarized the issue and caused an uproar of public discussion about racism and the struggle for equal-ity. White people who were neutral about segregation saw that acts of violence were being perpetrated by the oppressors, not the oppressed, and these brave acts of nonviolent resistance motivated the public to seriously discuss the issue with their families and social circles.

The initial four-person sit-in at Woolworth's lunch counter in North Carolina inspired over one thousand college students to join the disruptions in constant waves and led to copycat actions in fifty-five cit-ies with about seventy thousand protesters and three thousand arrests. People who were already against racial segregation found themselves empowered to push their activism to the next level as these daily protests paralyzed business and sent a clear message to society. After only six months of protests and mass boycotts, Woolworth's desegregated its lunch counters. Demonstrations like the sit-ins helped ignite the movement, and in 1964 the Civil Rights Act was passed, making it illegal to discriminate on the basis of race.

Martin Luther King Jr. explained the efficacy of this approach when he said, "Nonviolent direct action seeks to create such a crisis and foster such a tension that a community which has constantly refused to negotiate is forced to confront the issue. It seeks to dramatize the issue so it can no longer be ignored." MLK was arrested twenty-nine times for protesting against segregation, and many racists thought Rosa Parks was rude for disrupting prejudice when she sat in the whites-only section of a bus, but their activism threw a wrench in the running wheel of discrimination and inspired millions to take to the streets.

I believe our main goal as animal rights activists should be to make speciesism socially unacceptable like civil rights activists did with racism. This will be achieved by educating and inspiring the public and collectively speaking out boldly and frequently. As activist Lauren Gazzola said, "We can only challenge what is normalized by normalizing the challenge to it." Change is not always popular, so resistance to it is understandable, but that should not scare activists into silence. According to the website ElectionStudies.org, when Americans in 1964 were asked what they thought of the civil rights movement, 63 percent said that activists push too fast and 58 percent said activists hurt their own cause, yet today we look back and revere their actions.

A few decades ago, members of the LGBTQ community could not be open about their sexuality without fear of losing friends, family, and their jobs, and even being assaulted or killed. Yet today society has shifted immensely, and same-sex marriage has been deemed a constitutional right. This astounding victory was largely set in motion by loud and energetic protest groups such as ACT UP that empowered gays during the AIDS crisis of the 1980s and 1990s to come out of the closet and demand equal rights to medical treatment. While there is still a struggle to eradicate racism, sexism, and homophobia, these lessons from history teach us that massive social change happens when a group of people publicly refuses to tolerate discrimination and takes serious action.

It's important to consider what causes individuals and communities to hold prejudiced beliefs in the first place and what causes them to shift toward justice. Sociological research by Yale professor Nicholas Christakis shows that the strongest predictor of human behavior is adherence to the social norms that dominate our culture. In short, "People eat animals because other people eat animals." Humans are social creatures who tend to follow the crowd to avoid awkward interactions. What we see now when we walk into a grocery store or restaurant is a social norm where violence against animals is considered acceptable and speaking out in defense of the victims is taboo. One of the goals of disruptive tactics is to challenge the normalized violence against animals and our silent compliance that allows it to continue. The purpose of disruption is to create a new social norm, one that publicly takes a stand against animal cruelty and empowers others to do the same.

As this form of activism continues to spread, disrupting speciesism will become the new norm until speciesism itself becomes socially unacceptable. For this to be accomplished, the animals need every vegan to become an activist and to speak the truth at every opportunity so people realize how much they're suffering. The power in numbers is crucial, as is nonviolence. Nonviolent protesting means being love-based while standing in the way of tyranny. In accordance with the principles of nonviolence set forth by both Gandhi and Dr. King, the premise is to demonstrate anger at oppressive systems and ideologies, while striving to remain compassionate toward individuals who are part of these systems. We must remember that we were all programmed by the ideology of speciesism, and it can be very challenging for some people to escape the conditioning and the pressure to conform. However, none of this is an excuse for animal abuse, so we must intervene and defend the victims. We speak loudly during protests to be heard by everyone and to convey a sense of urgency, but, instead of condemning people, the goal is to highlight the animals' perspective, emphasize the injustice of human supremacy, and empower everyone to make better choices. Choosing nonviolence helps our movement be seen in a more positive light and creates the space for a serious conversation among the public.

It's understandable that some people inside grocery stores and restaurants get upset when we disrupt speciesism, because our message is challenging their habits and beliefs, but we have an obligation to the victims to speak the truth despite discomfort or denial, and protesting outside is simply not as powerful as disrupting business inside. A person who reacts negatively at first might simply be grappling with the cruel reality of speciesism and their own suppressed feelings of guilt, but when they go home and pet their dog or cat, they may come to accept our message of ethical consistency. For those who express anger at us for speaking out, we must consider what type of person gets mad at someone for standing up against animal cruelty. These individuals are not our target audience. We're not trying to win over the people who say "Mmm . . . bacon." Our primary target audience is the people who actually do care about truth and justice—many of whom are not even in the store, but are the thousands of people watching the protest video on the Internet or hearing about it in the news. Our actions empower these people to take a stronger stance in the same way that protests during past social justice movements empowered folks to publicly pick a side and get active. There are millions of people who are ready for this message and it is those people who we are reaching.

I've been to more than two hundred protests in the past several years, and I often see people applauding us and even joining our demonstrations. Educating the public on how to go vegan is important, but we also need to inspire them to talk about animal rights with their friends and families and to join collective demonstrations. We need to expose companies that are hurting animals, create a strong community of animal rights activists, and invite society to join our movement.

In training for nonviolent direct action, we learn of the "Spectrum of Allies," which is a half pie chart that includes these sections from left to right: Active Allies, Passive Allies, Neutral, Passive Opposition, and Active Opposition. From the perspective of animal rights activists, our Active Allies are our fellow activists, and we need to grow that section by empowering our Passive Allies, who are A) vegans and vegetarians who are not yet activists, B) genuine animal lovers who happen to still be eating animals because they haven't made the connection yet, or C) human rights activists who are already fighting for justice but who have not yet truly considered animal rights. These Passive Allies are people who are trying to do the right thing, and once we mobilize them into Active Allies we will have a bigger, stronger community with immense leverage over our Active Opposition on the far right, which are companies, individuals, and government agencies that have an in-depth knowledge of the cruelty and continue to cause it or support it anyway. The Active Opposition will likely never change unless we force them to by making animal slaughter unprofitable or illegal. Our Passive Opposition might be the people who heckle us during a protest, but who probably wouldn't hurt an animal themselves. Their public scorn for our message can make us shy away from speaking out, but it's best to continue speaking for the more receptive members of the audience. I used to be one of those hecklers until I stopped my selfish perspective and became more neutral. When I went vegan, I became a Passive Ally and when I started doing activism and really challenging speciesism in society, I became an Active Ally. As activists, it's best to aim for the low-hanging fruit rather than the hard-to-reach branches, so our time is better spent mobilizing our Passive Allies into Active Allies.

In her TED Talk called "The Success of Nonviolent Civil Resistance" political scientist Dr. Erica Chenoweth explains her research on hundreds of social movements over the past 106 years, which shows that 100 percent of the time it takes a maximum of just 3.5 percent of the population engaging in consistent, nonviolent direct action to create massive social change such as gaining rights or overthrowing a corrupt government. On average, nonviolent campaigns were twice as successful and four times larger than violent campaigns, because peaceful demonstrations are naturally more inclusive for a wider range of people such as the elderly, children, folks with disabilities, and so on. Mass participation is key. It's all about people power. For example, 3.5 percent would be eleven million people in the United States and just four thousand people in the city of Berkeley, California. This mobilization has the power to create a domino effect that starts in one city, then spreads to a whole state, and then the nation, but Erica Chenoweth's numbers only apply to tactics of direct action such as protesting. They do not apply to consumer veganism, which is technically just an economic boycott (albeit an important one, especially when tens of millions of people are participating).

It is our duty to shut down animal-abusing industries and make animal exploitation impossible by physically getting in the way and making it illegal. Direct action prompts people to take to the streets and disrupt "business as usual." Politicians and companies feel extreme pressure from a mass, nonviolent uprising, as do individual members of society, because many people don't want to be on the wrong side of history when the times are changing. The social science is telling us that nonviolent direct action is likely the quickest way for a movement to reach the tipping point by challenging and changing unjust norms and laws.

Any reservations we might still have about disruption can be answered with one simple question: If we say it's right to protest for humans, but wrong to protest for animals, isn't that speciesism? The victims need us to take this seriously. Remember the worst pain you've ever felt. For me it was a kidney stone that caused me to fall to the ground screaming in agony. I felt helpless and desperate for someone to take away the pain. This is what animals experience every day, but their cries are hidden behind the walls of slaughterhouses. The discomfort that activists or the public might feel during a protest is nothing compared to the absolute horror animals are going through. These are gentle, innocent creatures—babies and their mothers—yet we stab them in the neck and call it humane. They need us to speak out against speciesism at every turn so that society will recognize the truth and find the power to fight for freedom.

What I've learned from activism is that there is nothing extreme about speaking out against oppression or sacrificing our own comfort for the sake of helping those who are suffering far worse. What is extreme is to stay silent. Nothing will change if we don't stand up, speak out, and demand animal liberation now! Soon, our 3.5 percent will shut down every slaughterhouse in the nation, because that's what the animals deserve, and the majority of people will side with us. We must be brave and remember that most growth takes place outside the comfort zone. As William Faulkner said, "Never be afraid to raise your voice for honesty, truth, and compassion against injustice, lying, and greed. If people all over the world would do this, it would change the earth."

Throughout my life, I have struggled with major depression and have been suicidal many times because of how brutal this world can be. Though the darkness still creeps in at times, I'm much more able to cope now that I am part of a community of dedicated activists. I'm grateful I survived so that I can stand up for beings who are vulnerable like I was when I was bullied as a child. Although poverty has been hard on me, and not having easy access to a stove, refrigerator, or bathroom is a challenge, living in my car is worth it, because it gives me more time to help animals. And I'm still privileged compared to the individuals being tortured in factory farms and slaughterhouses. Eating meat for twenty-six years means that I'm responsible for the needless murder of over two thousand animals, and I owe them for that. We all do. There's no greater purpose than to make this world a better place, and activism has brought me enlightenment through dedicating my energy to the animal rights movement.

Bearing Witness to Babies before and after Motherhood

Amy Jean Davis, founder of Los Angeles
Animal Save

Before I read *The Answer*, the law of attraction seemed like pseudo-science, but I learned in this book how our reticular activating system (RAS) judges each of the 400 billion pieces of sensory data per second as relevant or irrelevant to our reality, and then prompts us to notice more of what is relevant. So, I began envisioning the future I wanted as if it were already real, and my life changed dramatically. I see how what I think about all the time attracts more of the same.

A couple of years after I read *The Answer*, I learned that humans don't need animal products for nutrition whatsoever, and that everything we do need is available from plants. I had already been vegan for a few years, but I was what is known as a Personal Choice Vegan—a vegan who considers what they eat to be a personal choice and doesn't bring up the subject of veganism unless asked. Once I learned that there was zero necessity to eat animals, and that the consumption of animal products was linked to various illnesses, I couldn't understand why anyone would eat them. This is when I became a social media activist, using Facebook and Twitter to spread vegan information. An activist group called Toronto Pig Save reached out to me about coming to a vigil for pigs and thought that if I attended, a media outlet or two might come out to the vigil because of my *American Idol* credential (I was a top-24 finalist in season 7). I thought to myself, *I should do this to help the animals.* Even though I didn't really know what bearing witness meant or what the experience would be like, I agreed and headed to Toronto.

I still remember the moment I first looked inside a transport truck full of baby pigs. Their skin was colored so softly and delicately, and they were looking at me with wide, terrified blue eyes. They looked like big pink dogs, crammed on top of one another, scared and confused. It felt like lightning hitting the center of my chest, as if my heart might burst from the sadness and helplessness I felt all at once. At the same time, it was very surreal. To meet these victims face-to-face; to smell them; to hear their raspy breathing; to see the red marks on their skin; to have my eyes burned from ammonia; and to be standing there on the median in the road, free to walk back to my vehicle and drive home to a soft, cool bed without someone dragging me to a gas chamber. It's a moment I will never forget.

About a year later I founded Los Angeles Animal Save. The Toronto activists had asked if I wanted to start a group in LA before, but the notion of being an activist was still a new layer of who I was becoming, and the thought of being an *organizer* was intimidating. Once I started the group in December of 2016, I immediately knew I should have started right when I came home from first bearing witness in Toronto. Some say that bearing witness is an obligation, and I completely agree. Additionally, I feel that organizing is an obligation for me.

At the Farmer John slaughterhouse, next to downtown Los Angeles, around seven thousand pigs are killed a day. The exterior of the massive building is covered in murals of happy pigs laying in mud and under trees; one pig is even wearing an LA Dodgers hat. On the back of one of the structures there are painted pigs flying into the sky with little wings they've sprouted. These are the pigs who have been electrocuted, their throats slit, and the life drained from their bodies. To say these murals are disturbing is an understatement.

Working with the local police department, activists stand in front of the slaughterhouse gate to bear witness as trucks arrive. Because we have pedestrian right-of-way on the sidewalk, the truck drivers are legally required to stop. An officer informs the drivers that a demonstration is in process, which allows us to approach each truck to give the pigs water and love for a few minutes. The pigs inside the trucks are anywhere from four to six months old, the same age as my daughter at the time of writing this. Yet these innocent babies spend a mere three weeks with their mother as she lay on the hard-slatted ground in a farrowing crate until the farmers move them to a "nursery." Farrowing crates (where mother pigs are kept) and gestation crates (where pregnant pigs are kept) are so narrow that these animals cannot turn around. Father pigs live in boar crates, on concrete or slats, and are taken out a couple times a week to have their semen harvested. The agony these animals endure cannot be described. One undercover investigation witnessed a boar who fell sick and wasn't able to stand up. Due to a leak in a pipe over his crate, the skin on the underside of his body began to rot.

As a new mother, my world has become full of perhaps the strongest kind of love—a mother's love for her child—and it has also become more terrifying. Animal rights activists are deeply aware of the egregious cruelty committed against animals, but to know firsthand how a mother feels for her baby while knowing that billions of mothers are forced to stand helplessly by while their children are taken from them is a crippling thought. The thought of someone taking my baby away, for any reason, causes a knot in my stomach and immediate tears in my eyes. Then, considering a baby's experience—just wanting her mother, but getting the rough hands of workers taking her to her death instead—how can this be the world I live in? How is it that I live among human beings who pay for this kind of violence? Human beings who are familiar with love, yet deny it to 70 billion sentient, scared beings each year, reserving it for whichever animals their culture has taught them are acceptable to love? These human beings are members of my own family, whom I watch dote on their dogs and cats, then turn around and sink their teeth into the mutilated bodies of animals who are every bit as sentient.

Every Sunday night I watch truckloads of innocent baby pigs crammed together in their own feces, urine, blood, and vomit be driven through the slaughterhouse gate. I see their eyes as they look around timidly. They must be wondering, what's next? Where are we going? Unfortunately for them their fate is a violent one, carried out by humans who are also victims of the system. Cruelty against animals is intimately linked to cruelty against humans, yet in this country and in most countries in the world, societies stand on a foundation of institutionalized violence and oppression against the most vulnerable—human and animal alike. We employ the poor and undocumented to work in factory farms and slaughterhouses and pay them meager wages to commit atrocities to animals who did nothing but be born of a particular species. Had they been born a dog or a cat, their chances of ending up in the loving home of a family are higher. Instead they are born in windowless sheds, have their testicles removed without anesthesia, and their heads slammed into the ground if they don't grow big enough, fast enough.

I will continue to utilize the law of attraction to envision a world where humans engage in compassionate behavior instead of vile actions and apathetic indifference. And I know so many others envisioning that same world. This vision is in the spaces between attending a vigil or protest or a legislative hearing hoping that elected representatives will vote on the side of the animals. It is in the spaces between where instead of getting lost in the deep sadness of recognizing our current level of consciousness, I choose to empower myself by recruiting my subconscious brain to keep me as powerful of a peace creator as possible. I was an activist before I was a mother, but now that I am a mother, I have a new kind of motivation that fuels my activism. All babies are innocent and deserve to be protected.

Turning Repression into Liberation

Wayne Hsiung, cofounder of
Direct Action Everywhere (DxE)

Rescuing a dying piglet from the worst place on Earth is "felony theft" and "rioting." Blowing the whistle on corporate misconduct results in a restitution ruling against activists in the hundreds of thousands of dollars. And it all adds up to a "pattern of unlawful activity." As of June 2019, over one hundred DxE activists have pending legal cases—misdemeanors, felonies, and civil claims—as a result of our investigatory and rescue work. I'm personally facing fifteen felonies, plus civil suits by two agribusiness corporations. Our legal docket seems to grow by the week; we even have a few more cases penciled in, which we expect to drop soon. But it wasn't always this way.

Humble Beginnings

When Patty Mark heard of the horrific cruelty at an Australian egg factory in 1992, she had no visions of pioneering a transformative tactic, "open rescue," to give power to liberation activists so often silenced or repressed. When an employee told her that "hens would somehow get out of their cages then fall down into [a massive manure] pit, where there was no food and water, and they would slowly starve to death," she knew that she had to get them out, and fast. "It didn't cross my mind for our action to be clandestine, only to somehow get ourselves in there safely so we could help as many hens as possible, to document conditions so people would become aware of what was happening, and to openly identify ourselves while doing what needed to be done." This bittersweet story of cruelty and liberation made national headlines, and open rescue was born. Subsequent years saw an awakening as the tactic of open rescue rose to prominence; even a member of the Australian Parliament joined activists in openly rescuing factory-farmed piglets. Activists worldwide were inspired at seeing everyday people proudly and publicly taking these actions, with groups like Compassion Over Killing and Mercy for Animals adopting the tactic.

Industry Pushes Back

The early 2000s saw the global rise of "ag gag" statutes, which criminalized certain acts of documentation inside animal agricultural facilities. Citing increasingly aggressive activist activity—releases of minks and other animals at farms, as well as property destruction—industry-friendly politicians passed the insidious Animal Enterprise Terrorism Act into federal law in 2006 via bipartisan unanimous consent, requiring no formal vote. The lone dissenting statement in the US House was made by Representative Dennis Kucinich, cautioning that the bill was "written in such a way as to have a chilling effect on the exercise of the constitutional rights of protest." A chilling effect was right. Open rescue all but disappeared in the United States for a decade beginning in the mid-2000s.

Waking a Sleeping Giant

Citing a unique Good Samaritan provision of California law, Penal Code Section 597e, to justify our entry into the farm, DxE's first open rescue was covered in the *New York Times* in January of 2015. Thousands of hens were revealed to be crammed in filthy sheds, many suffering from illness, even cannibalism, inside a "Certified Humane" Whole Foods egg farm. Dozens of investigations that followed, of some of the biggest sellers of animal products in the country, resulted in no legal consequences, despite numerous violations of animal cruelty law. It certainly wasn't for lack of evidence; social and mainstream media content publicly revealed not just our findings, but our investigators' identities. We wanted the opportunity to bring the issue to court, but ignoring scandal is corporate public relations 101. When an upstart grassroots group goes public with troubling findings, any response beyond a generic denial likely does a major corporation more harm than good. And so it went for over three years. Investigations of Smithfield, Costco, Whole Foods, even a dog meat farm in China came and went. We reached millions via the *New York Times*, *Nightline*, viral Facebook videos, and more. Our work expanded beyond a small team in the San Francisco Bay Area to independent teams throughout the United States, in Canada, and even Europe. Our mass gatherings— where inspired activists connect, learn, and take action for animals— have grown exponentially, from dozens to over one thousand. The minor annoyance that Big Ag had hoped would go away on its own has instead blossomed into a force which can no longer be ignored.

The Backlash Effect

"That's precisely why this industry is so obsessed with intimidating, threatening, and outlawing this form of activism: because it is so effective."

—Glenn Greenwald, Pulitzer Prize–winning journalist

The barrage of charges over the past year is not all bad, of course. It should actually be very good, provided we stay the course, supporting each other in whatever ways we can. It's also not unexpected. To the contrary, draconian repression efforts are an almost inevitable part of social progress, an indication that we're really doing *something*. And that something has provoked a calculated and coordinated effort between some of the most powerful government and corporate entities in the country. In August 2017, a six-car armada of FBI agents in bulletproof vests and armed with search warrants raided farm animal sanctuaries in Utah and Colorado. The subject of such an expansive use of taxpayer resources? Two dying piglets—of zero commercial value—that DxE rescued from a Smithfield farm in Utah. Then, in 2018, publicly available documents revealed that prior to charging these activists with felonies, the Sanpete County attorney in Utah who brought felony charges on a DxE turkey investigation was communicating and coordinating with the Utah Attorney General, who filed the felony charges in the Utah Smithfield case to bring the charges around the same time.

And these are just a few of the examples—ones we know about. More often these sordid arrangements are unspoken understandings, communicated in financial contributions rather than words. Agribusiness donates tens of millions of dollars to influence races at all levels each election cycle, but while industry has the power of money and politics, our passion and people power can level that playing field, and then some. More recently, we've seen our numbers at mass demonstrations escalate, even as the stakes have also risen.

In May 2018, forty activists of more than four hundred on-site were arrested on misdemeanor trespass, as activists rescued thirty-seven hens from a Petaluma, California, factory egg farm where whistleblowers had documented criminal animal cruelty (which was ignored by authorities). In September 2018, we returned to Petaluma. This time, fifty-eight were arrested on felony charges—including some simply there for photography/videography, never entering a barn—as activists attempted to provide lifesaving care to sick and injured animals. During the 2019 Animal Liberation Conference, seventy-nine were arrested on felony charges, with over six hundred in attendance, as thirty-two ducks were rescued from a Petaluma factory farm and slaughterhouse.

A movement sinks or swims with its response to repression. Prosecutions of civil disobedience must be met with even more civil disobedience, leveraging the passion of ordinary people into the power to transform society into a more just place for all. DxE saw an opportunity and went for it. We've continually refined our work, drawing on lessons from trailblazers like Patty Mark and Lauren Gazzola, an organizer who served prison time in connection with the Stop Huntingdon Animal Cruelty (SHAC) anti-vivisection campaign of the early 2000s. With inevitable legal battles certain to grab national headlines, the threats are rising, but not as fast as the opportunities. A handful of open rescue activists becomes dozens, then hundreds, until this massive force lays itself on the gears of the machine that is animal agriculture to bring it grinding to a halt.

But there is a greater ambition in our actions. Effective movements have not just addressed the symptoms, but the root causes, of oppression. And by taking these mass actions, DxE activists have highlighted one of the most fundamental tensions within not just our legal system, but our culture. This is the tension between animals as property and animals as living creatures who deserve moral and political consideration, i.e. legal "persons." By garnering public support and attention for these actions—and eventually winning in the court of law—we will be doing what has seemed impossible through normal legislative channels: enshrining the right to rescue animals from distress and, by doing so, forcing legal acknowledgment that animals are not things for corporations to use and abuse.

Some of the most impressive lawyers and scholars of our generation are now lining up to support us, from criminal law scholar Hadar Aviram—a chaired professor at UC Hastings and Fellow at Harvard Law School—to former federal prosecutor Bonnie Klapper, who busted drug gangs and now goes after criminal factory farms. As with iconic court cases from movements past, we hope our cases in California, Utah, and North Carolina will finally, after far too long, make animal rights into a real political question. We are, in short, taking a leap of faith. We believe that the people of this nation and planet are a compassionate people. That they want to preserve life, and not destroy it. And if we are correct, these cases won't just enshrine the Right to Rescue. They'll supercharge our movement and turn repression into liberation.

The Power and Duty
of Bearing Witness

Anita Krajnc, founder of the Save Movement

"When the suffering of another creature causes you to feel pain, do not succumb to the initial desire to flee from the suffering one, but on the contrary, come closer to him, as close as you can, and try to help him."
—Leo Tolstoy, *A Calendar of Wisdom:*
Daily Thoughts to Nourish the Soul

"One who knows the truth must bear witness of the truth to those who do not."
—Leo Tolstoy, *My Religion: What I Believe*

In 2006, I returned to Toronto after three years of teaching political studies at Queen's University in Kingston located at the point where Lake Ontario flows into the St. Lawrence River. I wanted to live by the lake, as that was my favorite part about the university campus, and so I found an apartment right on Lake Ontario in downtown Toronto. Soon I became aware of the existence of Quality Meat Packers, a pig slaughterhouse less than a mile away. The slaughterhouse's jarring presence entered my consciousness a few times a year when I passed the area on a streetcar and could see the ominous gray buildings with barbed-wire fencing and a tall, round chimney in the distance. I contacted an active animal rights group in the nearby city of Hamilton and asked if they could leaflet or something, but nothing came of it.

In the fall of 2010, I adopted Mr. Bean for my elderly mother when she came to live with me. Mr. Bean, a lanky beagle and whippet mix, was a rescue from Animal Alliance of Canada's Project Jessie. In the mornings, Mr. Bean and I would take long walks along Lake Shore Boulevard, and in the rush-hour traffic, we encountered a stream of transport trucks carrying pigs to the downtown slaughterhouse. One day, when the traffic was especially bad, we saw eight or nine transport trucks moving slowly. The pigs' snouts poked through the portholes and their sad, scared eyes looked out, pleading for their lives. By putting me in touch with my surrounding community, Mr. Bean sparked the epiphany that led to the formation of Toronto Pig Save. Our mission was simple: to expose slaughterhouses with firsthand community witnessing in the hopes of creating a wave of vegans and, equally important, more activists and organizers locally and abroad. In retrospect, it's surprising that when I moved near the slaughterhouse four years earlier, I never took the time to go see the pigs and stand up for them. I was already a vegan and an activist, but I rarely thought about the slaughterhouse, as life's distractions got in the way. My activism consisted of occasionally organizing or attending events like film screenings and demonstrations; I even considered going to vegan restaurants a form of activism. My self-perception before bearing witness was that I was a fairly strong animal rights activist, but that perception crumbled when I saw the extreme extent of the pigs' suffering and exploitation. These innocent, gentle beings had prompted a clarion call to action.

At the time, I was reading biographies by Romaine Rolland, a vegetarian pacifist and writer who won the Nobel Prize in Literature in 1915. He set up a vegetarian society and organized an anti-fascist league in the 1920s. He wrote biographies on Ramakrishna, Vivekananda, Tolstoy, Gandhi, and other exemplary individuals he considered societal role models. Each of these men had taken action in their local communities when there was an injustice, despite how busy they were in their lives and careers. I realized, as these individuals had, that there was no time to waver or pass the buck.

In Toronto Pig Save's first year, we focused on gathering footage and holding art shows that featured artwork and photographs of pigs by local and international artists to raise awareness and funding. A small group of us snuck along the railway lines late at night and early in the morning to gather slaughterhouse footage. On our late-Sunday-night surveillance missions, we saw thousands of pigs crammed in pens, held overnight to be killed the next morning. On weekdays at 6 a.m., we could hear the agonizing human-like screams a hundred meters from the building. It sounded like an asylum. They screamed as they were electrocuted with hard-wired cattle prods, which pushed them in single file along a corridor toward the door to the carbon dioxide gas chamber.

In June 2011, PETA organized a "human meat tray" demo in front of Quality Meat Packers and the organization's Canadian campaigner asked if Toronto Pig Save activists would join. PETA helped put the Toronto slaughterhouse on the map by garnering media awareness. To cover the event for Rabbletv—a progressive online Canadian media outlet where I volunteered—I stood at the intersection where the transport trucks turned almost a mile from the slaughterhouse. On my previous walks with Mr. Bean, I had only seen the pigs at a distance. Now, with the trucks stopping at the traffic light, I went up to the portholes. A sweet, innocent pig looked up at me with an expression of desperation and confusion. It's hard to describe the feelings I first had when witnessing these incredible creatures. There's an accountability that comes with bearing witness. You keenly recognize your responsibility to do everything in your power to stop this atrocity. Then and there, I made a promise to that pig that I would help organize a minimum of three vigils a week. Toronto Pig Save activists have kept this promise.

Most of our vigils were held on a traffic island we dubbed "Pig Island" about a kilometer from the slaughterhouse. The early morning vigils lasted three hours. We would alert thousands of drivers and passersby with our banners and placards, do vegan outreach, and point at the trucks, inviting them to join us and bear witness. We'd hope for a red light when the transport trucks came, giving us the chance to come right up to the portholes and see the pigs. It's the first time they had sunlight on their faces. At times, there would be trucks with pigs too despondent and frightened to approach us. More often, they'd come to us and nuzzle our fingers, greeting us with curious grunts. The most heart-wrenching instances were when they looked out with imploring eyes, as if to ask what was happening and wondering if we would be the ones to free them.

The regular vigils rejuvenated animal rights activism in Toronto and helped create many new activists and community organizers. Quality Meat Packers killed 6,000 pigs a day; 30,000 a week; 120,000 a month; and more than a million innocent pigs a year. Each day thirty transport trucks carrying two hundred pigs each traveled along the city's busy throughways, passing the Liberty Village condo development and then a dog park before entering the facility. It was hard to see the trucks and not be upset. But it took a grassroots group and regular vigils to make people pay attention and galvanize the animal rights community in the city. In April 2014, Quality Meat Packers went bankrupt. We had to wonder about the impact our vigils had on their business over the course of the few years we gathered there. After they closed, Toronto Pig Save moved its vigil location to Fearmans Pork Inc., a slaughterhouse in nearby Burlington. Earlier, we had also committed to holding weekly vigils to bear witness to the cows and chickens at Toronto's three slaughterhouses in the northwest part of the city.

The Save Movement defines the strategy of bearing witness as the moral duty and obligation of society to collectively bear witness and recognize the individuality of every animal, their desire and right to live a natural life, and our corresponding duty to help them. Toronto Pig Save developed an easily reproducible blueprint for communities to hold regular vigils at local slaughterhouses and put a face to the billions of individual farmed animals being killed in the animal-exploitation industry. Toronto Pig Save's commitment to organize three vigils each week was informed by historic community organizing approaches used by other social movements, which emphasized the importance of holding regular, intensive, on-the-ground actions using a love-based approach.

The strategy of bearing witness has been used to great effect by social movements for centuries, from the Quakers challenging slavery to Greenpeace setting sail for ground zero to protest nuclear tests in Alaska in the early 1970s and in the South Pacific during the 1980s. It's essential for the animal rights movement to be present in the face of the most egregious exploitation and injustice against farmed animals; bearing witness enables people to strongly empathize with their incredibly unjust and cruel plight. The Save Movement draws on the philosophies and practices of nonviolent approaches developed by Leo Tolstoy, Mahatma Gandhi, Martin Luther King Jr., community organizer Saul Alinsky, United Farm Workers cofounder Cesar Chavez, and environmental justice campaigner Lois Gibbs. The concept of bearing witness creates the opportunity to get closest to the animal standpoint, which generates the most empathy, compassion, and action. We absorb a small fraction of the animals' pain and learn a tiny bit of their story, which we share with others to help them wake up to this reality.

Leo Tolstoy said that only by having a firsthand presence can you approach knowing their truth. He bore witness as part of his research for an introductory essay to Howard Williams's *The Ethics of Diet*—a book about famous vegetarians in history. He wanted to see with his own eyes the reality of what happened to animals at slaughterhouses. Tolstoy's influential essay "The First Step" became the "bible" of the fledgling animal rights movement in Russia and elsewhere in the 1890s and early 1900s.

Bearing witness puts an end to the distancing effect in supermarkets, where slabs of meat do not have expressive eyes. When we see the fearful, pleading, curious, and affectionate faces at the vigils, it prompts us to want to help and share their stories. What would we want if we were in those trucks? In his book *On Life and Essays on Religion*, Tolstoy wrote, "A person knows the life of other beings only through observation and only so does she know of their existence. She knows of the life of other beings only when she wishes to think of it." Imagery is key to existence. When the imagery of observing animal suffering is imprinted on one's mind, it becomes a part of one's soul.

We need to change the cultural norm so that looking the other way is seen as an unacceptable response. Bearing witness acts as a living testimony to other creatures' suffering, which changes people in profound ways. Many non-vegan vigil-goers begin to transition to a nonviolent vegan diet once they see fearful, suffering animals trapped in trucks. Equally important, people who have never done activism before attending a vigil suddenly find it important to commit to being activists and organizers. Many begin to dedicate their life to organizing for social change.

A common dictum in a community organizing approach is "Everyone is a leader." I used to teach a university course in social movement strategies and tactics at Queen's University and was keen to apply the principles learned from other social movements and community organizing approaches to the Save Movement. Many people have asked how we keep people motivated to bear witness when it is so painful on a personal level to witness the brutalities faced by animals going to slaughterhouses. It's a paradox, which is aptly captured in a dictum by Ramakrishna, the nineteenth-century Indian prophet: "But my heart has grown much, much larger, and I have learnt to feel [the suffering of others]. Believe me I feel it very sadly!" The idea is that being present in the face of injustice makes you stronger, sacrifice is part of social change movements, and participation in creating change adds a meaningful element to one's life. Before the weekly vigils, I was depressed because I felt helpless. Now, I and so many other activists feel stronger and more determined than ever, as we see the movement growing exponentially and have a stronger sense of the enormous scale of the problem and what needs to be done.

Attending the animal vigils creates a strong sense of connection. People often speak of their Save community as vegan family and say that they found their tribe when they joined us. I felt this in my most important moments. When my beloved mother passed away on July 15, 2012, more than half of the people who attended her vegan funeral were members of Toronto Pig Save, people I had met in the previous year and a half.

Bearing witness is the most powerful experience I've ever had in the animal rights movement. It is the duty to be present at the darkest sites of injustice and to let others know of this injustice. In bearing witness, you follow your conscience, thus recognizing a higher "natural" law than any legalized violence against animals. We open ourselves up to understanding their experience, because if we were in that situation it would be the exact same for us. This stems from the understanding that we are all interconnected. When you are outside a slaughterhouse, it weighs you down and can make you feel sick. But it is also empowering to hold a slaughterhouse vigil as a community, as bearing witness together touches the collective spirit. You replace what was unseen and ignored—which is what enables animal exploitation and suffering—with light and active campaigns to organize for change. The more of us that shine a light on the darkness and try to help, the sooner we will achieve our aims of animal liberation.

On June 22, 2015, an incident occurred that changed the course of the Save Movement by putting the act of bearing witness into the media and public eye in a way that went beyond the social media videos and photos shared by activists attending vigils. I, along with three other activists, were participating in one of Toronto Pig Save's weekly vigils across the street from Fearmans Pork, Inc., in Burlington. When a truck stopped at the red light, we could see the pigs panting and foaming at the mouth. It was a scorching hot day. I went up to the side of the truck to give water to an eagerly thirsty pig, who immediately came up to me and reached her snout out of the truck's porthole to suck the water from my bottle.

Suddenly, the truck driver jumped out of his cab and shouted "Don't give them water!"

My response was, "Show some compassion." He demanded that I stop and so I quoted Matthew in chapter 25 of the Bible, "Jesus said if they are thirsty, give them water." I was following my conscience and believed the Golden Rule to be a universal and unbreakable tenet.

The driver shouted back, "They aren't human, you dumb frickin' broad!" He yelled again to stop giving the pigs water, but I put the bottle back against the porthole and the same desperate pig approached for more water. The thirst of this individual was what mattered to me, not the driver's callous request. Then, he yelled that he'd hit the bottle out of my hand if I didn't stop, but I said that this action would constitute assault. He said that he was going to call the police, but then he hopped into his truck and drove off.

Two months later, a constable showed up at my door, and I was notified of a criminal mischief charge—interference with property—for giving water to thirsty pigs, a charge that carried a potential sentence of ten years in prison and a $5,000 fine. This charge was shocking, as giving water to pigs at the vigils was a small act of mercy and something that we had been doing for two years and often in the presence of police, who expressed concern for our safety and on occasion empathized with our small acts of mercy.

The Save Movement gained worldwide attention through the Pig Trial with the help of my two vegan defense lawyers, James Silver and Gary Grill, and a group of animal rights organizations supporting Toronto Pig Save, including PETA, Animal Justice, and Direct Action Everywhere. My lawyers were able to put animal agriculture on trial by focusing on the ethics, animal suffering, and devastating environmental and health effects of animal agriculture. We also put forth ethical concepts, such as: pigs are not "stuff" or property, pigs deserve personhood, and giving water to thirsty animals is a universal law that transcends time and cultures.

The case resonated with the public, because people understood that my gesture in offering water to a suffering pig on a sweltering day was simply an extension of "Do unto others as you would have them do unto you" and it sparked the social media hashtag "Compassion is not a crime." When compassion is treated as a crime, it can create a historic moment in a social movement helping to further educate and mobilize people around issues of injustice. One historical example was the passage of the Fugitive Slave Act in 1850, which set a six-month prison term and a fine of $1,000 for anyone giving food to a runaway slave. Harriet Beecher Stowe was so incensed, she responded by writing her 1852 novel *Uncle Tom's Cabin*. As the second-bestselling book of the nineteenth century (following the Bible) it helped raise consciousness for the abolition of slavery. A second historic example of criminalizing compassion was the Russian government's attempt to stop Tolstoy and his family from engaging in famine relief in Russia in 1892 by trying to make it illegal to set up soup kitchens for the hungry. In the same way that the hungry should not be denied food, thirsty animals should not be denied water. The Golden Rule applies to all living beings, as stated by Tolstoy in *A Calendar of Wisdom*: "We should take pity on animals in the same way as we do on each other. And we all know this, if we do not deaden the voice of our conscience inside us." When animals are legal "things" in the law, their basic inalienable rights and fundamental interests—their pains, their lives, and their freedom—are invisible to civil law. Since animals suffer the same as we human animals, they deserve equal consideration of their interests and needs.

Almost two years later, on May 4, 2017, Judge David Harris dismissed my charge of criminal mischief—interference with property—because I didn't stop the truck or prevent those pigs from being slaughtered. While the judge recognized that compassion is not a crime, it was extremely disappointing that he missed an opportunity to move the law forward in regard to nonhuman animals as persons. He referred to the pigs as being property under the law. Is a sentient being, such as a pig, no different than a toaster? (To amplify the insanity and injustice, nonliving entities like corporations have legal personhood standing in the courts.)

The global media coverage of the Pig Trial put the plight of the pigs into the public eye and helped spark major worldwide growth for the Save Movement. When the confrontation with the truck driver took place in the summer of 2015, there were about thirty-five Save chapters in five countries. Riding the wave of international attention and financial support, the Save Movement was able to focus on a growth strategy by sending organizers to table at VegFests, hold slaughterhouse vigils in new areas, and organize new Save chapters. In 2018, nineteen Save Organizing Tours in North America, South America, and Europe took place. By September 2019, there were nearly seven hundred Animal Save chapters in seventy countries.

Given the power of bearing witness and its impact on changing hearts and minds, it is imperative to continue growing the Save Movement, making the moral duty to bear witness a new cultural norm. The sense of urgency also arises from the multiple issues resulting from animal agriculture, such as catastrophic climate change, world hunger, and threats to public health. Therefore, in 2018 the Save Movement was restructured and three sub-movements were created: the Animal Save Movement (which aims to hold a vigil at every slaughterhouse in the world), the Climate Save Movement (whose mission is to build a grassroots movement to solve the climate crisis by ending animal agriculture, reforesting the Earth, and phasing out fossil fuels), and the Health Save Movement (which promotes veganism to prevent and reverse diseases related to animals products and food justice programs). The Save Movement is now addressing a wide range of issues, developing intersectional campaigns, and forming broad-based coalitions and alliances.

After first starting to bear witness with Mr. Bean in 2010, being an organizer quickly became of upmost importance to me. I have been an animal rights activist since the early 1990s, but only since I joined with others to collectively bear witness at slaughterhouses has my level of commitment increased to the point of it being the number one priority for the rest of my life. I've learned the importance of being an organizer and the need to recruit millions of animal rights organizers worldwide. During the civil rights movement, Eric Mann estimates that there were tens of thousands of organizers and hundreds of thousands of activists working for equality. Gandhi said, "Social change will occur not in some "dim and distant future" but "within a measurable time, the measure being the measure of the effort we put forth."

I've also learned how important it is to constantly work on the love-based philosophy in community organizing. The challenges we face to save animals and the planet are so immense and urgent, it is easy to fall into the trap of getting angry and feel rage against not only the system, but the humans participating in this evil. It's important to reread works by Leo Tolstoy, Mahatma Gandhi, Martin Luther King Jr., and other practitioners of love-based organizing and communication. Tolstoy liked to quote the Bible's passage, "I came not to judge, but to save." He advocated returning love for hate and to kindly point out to the oppressor what is wrong and to organize the public in "noncooperation with evil" campaigns, such as boycotts and direct action, including nonviolent civil disobedience.

Every social justice movement in history has succeeded when enough people stand up. To witness suffering animals changes everything. By bearing witness to egregious animal injustice and helping to create a new cultural norm where people see it as their duty to not look away, we discover the unity of life. By combining bearing witness with love-based community organizing, we quicken the pace of achieving social, earth, and animal justice.

The Urgency of Animal Liberation: A Teenage Activist's Perspective

Zoe Rosenberg, founder of Happy
Hen Animal Sanctuary

As a young child, I would wake up early every morning to watch shows about animal rescue. At just six years old, I was viewing animal cruelty investigators take dogs and cats away from hoarding and neglect cases, fighting rings, and other atrocious situations. I dreamed of someday starting a dog and cat rescue. I even printed out photos of dogs at local shelters who needed homes and posted them around my school.

Dogs and cats weren't the only animals I cared about. On rainy days in early elementary school, I would run around the playground defending worms from the careless feet of other children. I would gently move them onto the grass and spend all of recess protecting them. When it wasn't raining, I was usually guarding caterpillars, spiders, and roly-poly bugs.

The idea of wanting to hurt animals was foreign to me from day one. My mother raised me a vegetarian, and I was never able to comprehend the idea of eating a dead animal. When I saw people I knew eating animals, I would approach them and ask why. I wondered why they were eating someone, when that someone didn't do anything to them. Usually, I would just get a shocked stare in response. As I got older, I stopped spending all of my time defending insects, and refrained from approaching adults eating meat. Society's influence made me a quiet girl who didn't dare speak her mind.

During third grade, I began to feel sick every day and so my mom took me to the doctor for blood work where I was diagnosed with an incurable autoimmune disease. From then on, my life would be filled with needles and finger pricking. After that, I became even more shy. It was the first time I had ever experienced real hardship, but life continued as I adapted to my disease. I didn't think that anything could ever shake my world as much as being diagnosed with an incurable illness, but when I was almost ten years old, everything changed again. This time it was because my family got seven baby chickens. According to my mother, we would definitely not be getting any more.

These seven chickens became my everything. The first thing I did when I got home from school was visit them, and I longed to be with them every second of the day. When one of the babies grew ill, I dug through the Internet in an attempt to find solutions, but after a few days she passed away. My heart was broken. However, while doing research I found a website that would allow me to aid hundreds of other chickens: NSW Hen Rescue in North South Wales, Australia. This organization on the other side of the world changed my life. The website showed videos of rescuers entering factory egg farms and taking hens away from death row. I watched in tears as innocent birds went from existing in misery to living joyful lives at sanctuaries. This was the first time I had heard about the cruelty behind the egg industry, and I immediately stopped eating eggs. Later, I learned about the atrocities of the dairy industry and became vegan. I quickly realized that veganism was not enough.

I sent an email to Catherine Kelaher, the founder and director of NSW Hen Rescue, and asked her how she has been able to bring light to animals suffering in the dark. In her response she explained what open rescue was. She said that she and other rescuers would simply walk onto farms in the middle of the night, with no masks on, and take animals out. She explained that I could take the route of negotiating the release of hens from egg farms, so that's what I set out to do. But first I had to start an organization. Sitting down at the computer, I busied myself with making a website. I called it "Happy Hen Chicken Rescue." Seeing all of my hard work, my mother agreed to help me negotiate the release of twelve hens from a local egg farm, but she assured me we would not be rescuing more than that.

I found Direct Action Everywhere (DxE) when I was twelve years old. DxE was doing everything I wished I could do. They were going into grocery stores and butcher shops and restaurants, speaking the truth about the world we live in—a world where animals are treated like garbage. After stalking DxE's Facebook page for several months, I received a message from one of their organizers, who asked if I would plan a protest in my hometown. My mom, feeling overwhelmed, insisted that I say no, but declining the request did not make me forget the message. Every day I thought about it, and the next month I messaged the organizer and agreed to plan a disruption at a grocery store.

In January 2015, DxE released their first investigation and open rescue. That was the moment I realized that open rescue really did mean going onto a farm, with no masks on, and taking animals out. DxE had gone into a Whole Foods factory farm and rescued a dying hen they named Mei Hua. It was her story that we were supposed to share at the Whole Foods disruptions, which were taking place in unison in various locations. And so, at age twelve, I led a group of eight other activists into the Whole Foods in San Luis Obispo. We spoke and chanted about the brutalities that animals face and the movement that is rising to change it. From that point on, I became convinced that direct action was the path to achieving animal liberation. I have been organizing for DxE ever since, and I am now in charge of managing the very Facebook page that brought me to where I am today.

On May 29, 2018, five years after I had emailed with Catherine Kelaher about open rescue, I had the opportunity to participate in a mass open rescue in Petaluma, California, during the Animal Liberation Conference. Open rescues usually involve small teams of activists and mostly occur in the middle of the night, but the Petaluma rescue was in broad daylight with around sixty trained activists and around four hundred others gathered in support. When I had gone to the egg farm with my mother to rescue twelve hens, the farm knew we were coming. This time, we were going unannounced. We were going to execute our legal right, according to California Penal Code Section 597e, to intervene at the site of suffering animals. Whether the farm would respect that right, we didn't know. I was leading Team Number One, the first team to enter the barns and the first team to leave with sick or injured birds. In addition, I was leading the animal care station. As soon as I was out of the farm with my team, I would be caring for sick, potentially dying hens in the animal care vans.

The pressure was on. After gathering my team and making sure we were set, we began our march to the facility. To throw off the farm, we had signs that said "Funeral Procession in Progress." Once we were almost to the barns, a farmer pulled his truck in front of us. My palms were sweating, but I found comfort in the hundreds of activists standing behind me. We had a plan to ask the workers at the facility to let us enter the barns and remove animals who were clearly ill. After less than a minute, it was abundantly clear that the hostile owner wasn't going to comply with our requests. But we had the legal right and, more importantly, a moral obligation to do right by the hens.

Stopping at the entrance to the largest barn at the facility, we put on our biosecurity gear, which provides protection to prevent the introduction and spread of infectious disease pathogens. As we were doing so, farm employees gathered around us, yelling in our faces to leave. We had the barn door open, but just before we could enter, they blocked our way and slammed the door on us. Walking quickly, we made it to the only other entrance, but the employees arrived seconds before us and locked the door with haste. Everything was moving so fast, and I wasn't sure of a backup plan.

In DxE we try to maintain strong security culture, which means if you don't need to know something, no one will tell you. This makes it harder for the animal agriculture industry to find weak links in our movement to manipulate information. As my mind raced, I heard a fellow activist scream that he had opened the door to another barn. I told my team to run, and we took off toward the opening. We were the first ones in, just as planned.

My eyes wandered upon thousands of eyes in every direction, begging me to help them and bring them to freedom. I knew we would have to leave most of these individuals behind. As we walked down the first row of the barn, I reminded everyone to look out for sick birds. Moving to open one of the cage doors, I realized that the locks weren't like the locks in facilities I had been inside of in the past. As I fidgeted with the latch, I began to panic. A few minutes passed and I started to think we weren't going to save anyone. My heart felt as though it had sunk fully into my stomach. Then, the lights in the barn went out. I moved to grab the flashlights and headlamps from our materials bag, only to discover that they had been lost during the shuffle with employees at the previous barn.

I glanced around and saw another team, who graciously loaned us one of their flashlights. I kept asking into my walkie-talkie if any of the other teams had figured out the cage latches, but I was met with silence. Just when it seemed that all hope was lost, an activist shouted that she had gotten one open. I launched into action and tried to pull a weak hen from the cage, but the hens ran to the back to get away from me. Each of my teammates stood on their tiptoes, trying to reach into the cage. We were so close, and yet it seemed that we wouldn't be able to achieve what we came to do.

No one could reach, and I figured we would have to wait for the hens to come to us. But then one of the activists in charge of filming the rescue insisted that he was small enough to get into the cage. After that, I began carefully climbing inside of cages to remove sick hens. I was terrified the wire would bend and a hen would get hurt, but the metal held up. With five hens in our arms, we started to leave the barn, but employees were at the exit to block us.

I asked one of my team members to find another exit, and a minute later, she reported that she had found another way. We followed her through a large sliding door, but to my dismay it led to even more chickens. My eyes widened. These hens were much sicker than the birds opposite to us had been. I wanted to show the law enforcement officers the dire conditions of the animals, so I decided to attempt one more rescue. I tried to open one last cage door, but it was jammed. Someone yelled that the employees were going to block our last chance of an exit; with a deep breath, I walked away, leaving the suffering hens behind.

We had no idea what would be waiting for us outside. The police could have been standing there, ready to drag us to jail and return the hens to their doom. Animal services could have been on-site, preparing to join us in our mission to save lives. The bright sunlight overwhelmed my vision for several seconds as I took the first step out. I looked up and saw hundreds of activists gathered by the other entrance. We needed some of them to walk with us and help keep the hens safe. Over fifty activists swarmed around us and I felt a sense of safety with the strength in numbers as we walked swiftly toward the entrance of the farm.

The march off the facility grounds feels like a blur in my mind. Looking back, I can appreciate the fact that this was the first moment that those beautiful girls ever saw the sky. While I was frantically managing people and trying to keep everyone safe, they were breathing their first breaths of fresh air. We cradled their fragile bodies in our arms, and when we reached the animal care vans, I jumped inside to ready the crates. One by one, I took the girls into my arms and gently laid them upon soft towels. I promised that soon we would be off to my sanctuary and they would never have to be afraid again.

A couple dozen police officers were now on-site, and we had no way of predicting what form of action they would take. We decided the safest move would be to keep the animal care van moving, in hopes that they wouldn't realize the hens were inside. Once all of the other teams had exited the barns, there were thirty-seven hens in the vans. Thirty-seven individuals who would no longer have to suffer at the hands of animal exploiters. We were taking them away from a place that had stolen everything from them.

It was a six-hour drive from the factory to Happy Hen Animal Sanctuary, where my mother would provide them with urgent veterinary care. Upon arrival, one of the hens, who I named Liberty, wasn't doing well. I could see in her eyes that she was beginning to give up. We rushed her to the animal care room and gave her fluids, medicine, and a warm place to rest. Checking on her the next morning was terrifying for me. I have awoken to so many animals who have passed overnight, and it is the worst feeling. I reached my hand into her crate and lifted her body. She was cold and hard. The egg industry had tortured her and neglected her so severely that she lost her life. I held Liberty's limp body in my arms, mourning her loss, and the losses of all hens who have died in this exploitative industry. She deserved so much better, but I am glad that at least she died free.

The remaining thirty-six hens continued their path of physical and mental recovery. Most of the girls had severe upper respiratory infections from breathing the toxic air inside the filthy barns. We quickly put them on antibiotics, and they all eventually recovered. One hen stood out to me from the beginning. She would come up to me, sit in my lap, and allow me to hold her. The other hens would run from me, afraid of human contact. But this girl was different. It was almost like she was asking me for help. I named her May, and after watching her for a few days I began to notice that she couldn't move around as well as the others. One night, I was putting everyone in the barn so that they could go to sleep, and I found her outside, unable to get up. She seemed to have lost all coordination. Lifting her weakened body, I carried her to the animal care room. After being observed by two veterinarians, it was decided that May had a neurological disorder. It was predicted that she hit her head on the wire of the cage, which damaged her brain stem. Since she was differently abled, she would need constant support for the remainder of her life. It pains me to think of the long death she would have suffered at the factory, a place where chickens are seen as things, a place where killing is preferred since it is cheaper than veterinary care.

In the end, all of the hens, except for Liberty, recovered. Forty-seven activists were arrested after attempting to return onto the farm property to save additional hens. Twelve girls live permanently at Happy Hen Animal Sanctuary, and the rest were transferred to other sanctuaries or adopted out to thoroughly vetted, vegan homes. This was the first mass open rescue in US history. Someday, there will be thousands of us, and we won't leave a single animal behind.

Over the years, my dedication to the animal rights movement has only increased. I was arrested for an act of civil disobedience at age fourteen, and again at age fifteen. The first time I was arrested was for running onto the Dodger baseball field in Los Angeles to expose the cruelty behind Dodger Dogs. DxE had conducted an investigation at Farmer John, which supplies pig bodies to Dodger Stadium. What they found continues to haunt the investigators in their sleep.

My second arrest was for chaining myself to the Cal Poly Slaughterhouse to prevent a cow from being slaughtered as part of a meat-processing class. I named her Justice, and demanded that Cal Poly release her to sanctuary. However, after two hours, the chain was cut and I was arrested and dragged out in cuffs while my fellow activists shouted "WHERE IS JUSTICE?" Hearing the impassioned shouts of my fellow activists, I realized that no matter what, Justice would not be forgotten. I hope that in her last moments of life she remembered the girl chained to the slaughterhouse chute. I hope she knew that the fight for justice would continue and grow louder in her name.

As I've been treated like a criminal for trying to help suffering animals, I continue to think of why we must make bold moves in order to shine light on animal exploitation—because in the darkness, behind shadows and walls, animals are killed. In secret, they are forced into giant prisons. Their wide eyes are ignored by turned backs. They scream into a barren nothingnesses, tuned out by the only humans who can hear them. And anyone who tries to disrupt this system gets punished.

As I write this, it's early 2019, and I am sixteen years old. I have seen countless rows of cages stacked high, filled with hens climbing over one another as they struggle to survive. I have seen hundreds of gallons of blood being poured into dumpster trucks outside of slaughterhouses. I have heard the terrified screams of chickens as their throats are slit, screams that will haunt me for the rest of my life. I have comforted baby cows as they desperately cry out for their mothers, and I have held the broken bodies of animal agriculture's victims in my arms.

As of today, my organization has rescued over eight hundred animals from factory farms, slaughterhouses, and other abusive situations.

Happy Hen Chicken Rescue is now called Happy Hen Animal Sanctuary, and we don't just rescue chickens—we have saved pigs, cows, turkeys, goats, sheep, quails, geese, and ducks from death, and we have shared their stories with the world.

When I first became an animal rights activist at age eleven, I started behind a computer screen building a website, creating Facebook pages, and writing stories. At the time, I didn't want to speak to anyone; I just wanted to rescue animals and let other people do the talking. I was deeply afraid of confrontation. Eventually I realized that the animal rights movement wasn't about me, and that in the bigger picture my comfort zone didn't matter.

In December of 2014, a hen that my mother and I had saved the previous summer passed away. Her abdominal cavity was filled with eggs due to a reproductive illness she had developed. Georgia had a huge personality and would always come to the door of my house to say hello. She quickly became one of my best friends. On the night Georgia died, I felt broken. I watched her collapse as the remaining life left her. I sat with her as she breathed her final breaths. I sang her a lullaby and told her she was safe. But, most importantly, I made a promise—a promise I will never forget. I promised her that I would dedicate my life to fight for animals like her, and that I would make sure that someday no more chickens would suffer, or I would die trying.

After Georgia's death, it took more strength to remain quiet than it did to speak out. When I was nervous, I thought of Georgia. I would repeat the phrase "I promise" over and over in my head. To this day, if my legs are shaking before a big disruption, or if I feel like giving up, I think of Georgia. I think of the vow I made to her as she died, and I know that no matter what happens, I have a moral obligation to speak truth to power. Georgia didn't deserve to die, and she is just one of trillions of animals who have died for human greed. If I have to leave my comfort zone in the dust in order to create a better world, then so be it. Regardless of any fear or anxiety, I began to speak my mind, to say what the animals would if they could.

Getting to personally know the victims of animal agriculture quickly changed my perspective on the world. I began to recognize the urgency of animal liberation. Every second of every day, animals are having their bodies dismembered so that humans can feast on their deceased bodies. I refuse to sit by while this genocide takes place. I have no doubt that in the days and years ahead, I will come face-to-face with more unimaginable cruelty, but I also have no doubt that someday sooner than we think, this cruelty and death will come to an end, and we will be living in a world where animals are treated with respect. I have no doubt that ordinary people will rise up to make that world real. Animal liberation is on the horizon, and that is a fact.

VI

The Sanctuary Life:
To Heaven from Hell

Farm Sanctuaries: Healing Animals, the Planet, and Ourselves

Gene Baur, founder of Farm Sanctuary

Farm Sanctuary was born out of investigations at stockyards, factory farms, and slaughterhouses as we found living animals who had been discarded like garbage. Our rescue work started in 1986 with Hilda, a sheep who was dumped on a pile of dead animals behind Lancaster Stockyards on a muggy August day. As we walked around the stockyard witnessing and documenting conditions, we came across a cement slab with the bloated and decaying corpses of cows, pigs, and sheep. The stench was overwhelming, and the maggots were so thick you could hear them moving. Then, we saw one of the sheep lift her head. We were stunned and immediately removed her from the dead pile. We brought her to a veterinarian, thinking she'd have to be euthanized, but she recovered and lived at Farm Sanctuary for more than ten years. Hilda died of old age and is now buried in the center of Farm Sanctuary's Watkins Glen shelter.

Thousands of animals have followed in Hilda's footsteps by coming to live at Farm Sanctuary. There are now hundreds of other farm sanctuaries around the world, caring for rescued farm animals and demonstrating how we can relate to them as friends instead of food. Billions of animals are exploited in the food industry every year, treated as inanimate commodities in an industrialized mass production system. They are conceived through intensive breeding practices and artificial insemination, overcrowded in warehouses, and then killed on the slaughterhouse assembly line, where their bodies are cut into pieces for complicit consumers. Farm animals are among the most abused creatures on the planet, yet their suffering, and their lives, have been largely ignored.

Farm sanctuaries create opportunities for people to know cows, pigs, chickens, turkeys and other animals as living, feeling individuals, not lifeless pieces of flesh on the plate. Sanctuary residents are refugees of an abusive system that most people unwittingly support through their eating habits, and these lucky ones serve as living ambassadors for the billions of others who sanctuaries aren't able to help. Meeting slaughterhouse survivors and hearing their stories can have profound, life-changing impacts.

While sanctuaries transform the lives of individual animals and influence how people view so-called food animals, ultimately, we need to transform our entire food system. Sanctuaries provide tangible relief for a small number of survivors, yet also struggle with the ongoing ethical impossibility of only being able to help a tiny fraction of those who deserve protection. The only feasible long-term solution is to replace animal agriculture with plant-based agriculture.

In addition to reshaping our connection to farm animals, there is also great potential for sanctuaries to play a role in reforming our relationship to food and the environment. Sanctuaries can grow food and promote wellness, connecting people to what we eat and how it's produced. We can model compassionate vegan living and create positive examples that stand in stark contrast to the violence of animal agriculture. The best way to prevent the violence and suffering born of factory farming is by inspiring and empowering consumers to eat plant-based foods and to transform our agricultural system.

In affluent societies, most of us grow up eating animals without thinking about the individuals whose bodies we consume and without considering the vast devastation wrought by animal agriculture. Thankfully, a growing number of citizens, including health professionals and other experts, are encouraging the vegan lifestyle instead of supporting our unhealthy animal-based food system. It's been estimated that we could save 70 percent on health-care costs in the United States by shifting to a whole-food plant-based diet. By eating plants instead of animals, we can feed more people with less land and fewer resources, while preserving rain forests and other increasingly scarce natural ecosystems.

Rather than destroying habitats and polluting the environment the way that factory farming does, sanctuaries can help restore and preserve diverse ecosystems by applying principles of nonexploitation and mutuality in place of the now-dominant agricultural paradigm of extraction. Just as sanctuaries heal rescued animals and create mutually beneficial relationships between people and farm animals, they can also create mutually beneficial relationships between humans, the earth, and wild species. Also, since farm sanctuaries commonly occupy land that had previously been used for animal farming, they can play an important role in transforming how agricultural land is used.

While farm sanctuaries have focused primarily on caring for rescued farm animals, we have sometimes failed to give adequate attention to environmental issues like effectively managing animal manure and protecting ecosystems. Sanctuaries can do more to become models of environmental stewardship and to integrate restorative practices, which I believe will also help attract and engage broader audiences.

The climate crises, species extinction, and the loss of biological diversity are linked to our system of exploiting animals for food, which destroys natural ecosystems for grazing and growing crops to feed farm animals. Animal agriculture occupies vast swaths of land around the globe, and in the United States ten times more land is used to raise animals for food than to grow food for human consumption. Researchers have found that 96 percent of the mammals on earth are either human or domesticated (mainly farm animals), while only 4 percent live in the wild. In the case of birds, just 30 percent live in the wild, while 70 percent are domesticated, mostly chickens. We are now experiencing the earth's sixth mass extinction. The last one occurred 65 million years ago when the dinosaurs vanished. Scientists say we are living in the Anthropocene era, a geological epoch dominated by human beings that will be marked in the fossil record by plastic and chicken bones.

Expanding programs to more fully demonstrate and enable vegan living will allow sanctuaries to reach people on many fronts, whether they are concerned about health, animal suffering, environmental destruction, or various forms of injustice, which are becoming better understood in the context of our food system. People who work at factory farms, as well as those who live near these toxic facilities, face elevated risks for injuries and other health threats, and they are disproportionately people of color who have been historically disenfranchised. At the same time, residents in lower-income areas have limited access to healthy fresh food, and they suffer disproportionately from diet-related illnesses.

While social scientists have referred to neighborhoods lacking in nutritious food as "food deserts," they are now beginning to apply the term "food apartheid," which more accurately describes systemic injustices around food and farming. Vegan activists can support and partner with a wide array of food justice activists and organizations in both rural and urban communities. Some of these, like Green Bronx Machine and Harlem Grown, empower New York City youth to grow fresh food in communities where it is sorely needed. Growing your own food and connecting with the earth can be profoundly restorative. In some instances, farm sanctuaries could even employ former slaughterhouse and factory farm workers as a concrete embodiment of healing and transforming our food system.

Farm sanctuaries can play an important role in inspiring and training farmers in humane, holistic, and regenerative plant-based practices, while also tapping the vast resources and infrastructure of government programs and institutions that have been created to support farming. Working with people at these agricultural establishments can encourage new ways of thinking that inspire them to evolve beyond the reductionist and extractive model that has dominated agriculture. There are passionate, purpose-driven farmers who want to reform the food system, and farm sanctuaries can work with them to advance our shared interests.

Engaging in food production allows us to speak more authentically as active and knowledgeable participants, not just critics, who are working to reform our agricultural system. As a vegan, I have avoided buying honey for years, because I don't want to contribute to the exploitation of bees, but the same bees who are used to produce honey are also trucked around the United States to pollinate many of the fruits and vegetables that vegans eat. Sanctuary grounds could provide pollinator habitats as part of creating a whole and vibrant food system, which includes mutually beneficial interfaces between domesticated and wild species, and between farmers and consumers.

By avoiding animal products and shifting to a whole-food plant-based diet, our nation could significantly reduce our risks for cardio-vascular disease and other debilitating illnesses. We could save billions of dollars on health-care costs every year, along with untold suffering and the premature deaths of millions of humans. This cruel system embodies abusive relationships, which impact us in disturbing ways, including undermining our empathy, which is a very important part of our humanity.

When humans wield power and control over others and exploit disempowered individuals, those with power commonly create narratives that denigrate their victims. This pattern occurs in abusive human relationships, and it also applies to unhealthy relationships with other animals, including farm animals who suffer egregiously and who are completely at our mercy. Rather than being self-reflective and con-sidering the consequences of our actions, we commonly validate and excuse our cruelty by minimizing the suffering and the lives of our victims.

Our society routinely harms and degrades farm animals in both word and deed, often in ways that are unconscious, but that reflect our iniquitous prejudice. Calling someone a "pig" or a "turkey," for exam-ple, unfairly demeans pigs and turkeys along with the person targeted with such name-calling. Farm animals are also debased with groundless stories that label and scapegoat them as somehow undeserving of our respect. Derisions like these reflect abuses of power that are normalized amid systemic cruelty and injustice.

University of California professor Dacher Keltner has researched and written about power. He describes its effects on people, including the troubling conclusion that "having power makes people more likely to act like sociopaths." He says that people with power are less inclined to understand others, and predisposed to stereotyping and to "judg[ing] others' attitudes, interests and needs less accurately." Although Professor Keltner is describing relationships between human beings, these same psychological patterns also apply in our relationships with other animals. It seems that the more we abuse other creatures, the more we need to justify our conduct by devaluing them.

Our relationships with other animals exist within contexts where humans have enormous power and influence, and this is particularly the case with farm animals. We control every aspect of their lives from conception up until slaughter, and we treat them like inanimate production units. Farm sanctuaries are a direct challenge to this commodification of sentient life. Being kind to other animals is good for both human and nonhuman animals, while killing them is harmful for everyone involved. Imagine what it would be like to work in a slaughterhouse where your job is cutting the throats of animals, one after another. Such violence injures the human psyche and is part of a system that represents one of our planet's most significant moral and ecological threats.

Farm sanctuaries have been established to confront the abuses of animal agriculture, to provide respite for some of its victims, and ultimately to bring about healing and wholeness. Today, with a growing convergence of issues connected to food and agriculture, sanctuaries have more opportunity than ever to work with aligned individuals and organizations on common goals. The good news is that most people share our basic values and interests and prefer kindness over cruelty, health over disease, and ecological sanity instead of environmental destruction and injustice.

In the Steps of Giants: Saving Elephants in Southeast Asia

Saengduean Lek Chailert, founder
of Save Elephant Foundation

I come from very humble beginnings in the remote mountains of northern Thailand. My grandfather was a shaman, or traditional healer, who helped the people of our community. Sometimes villagers would bring sick or injured animals to him for care, and he allowed me to participate in their treatment. In return for saving the life of a young man, he was given an elephant named Tong Kam, meaning Golden One.

My youth was spent in the shadow of this giant. A special friendship developed and it was then that my intrigue and love for elephants began. As a young woman, I became more aware of elephants' working conditions and of their suffering. I would hear their cries from the deep forest, and I vowed to change their lives for the better. With the knowledge that they were becoming endangered, I began raising public awareness of their situation and providing medical aid to elephants in remote villages who had injuries and wounds.

In the 1990s I began rescuing injured, neglected, and elderly elephants and in 2003 was able to establish a permanent homeland for them in the picturesque Mae Taeng valley near Chiang Mai. In an industry steeped in tradition, advocating for positive change in the ways that domestic and wild Asian elephants are treated has not been an easy battle.

The survival of both wild and captive elephants is dangerously compromised. There are 3,500 working elephants in Thailand. The beautiful giant deserves better than history affords. Lives stifled by merciless restraint, our efforts to rescue are a signpost for others to imitate. We work to create a space for elephants free from fear and harm, with access to natural requirements and a gently managed opportunity for friendship with their own kind.

At Elephant Nature Park, we have eighty-four elephants who have been rescued from logging and the tourism industry (riding camps, elephant shows, and street begging). Many of our elephants can be described as old, sick, lame, blind, or somehow compromised. Hence, we have a full-time veterinary team (nine vets on staff) to provide care and rehabilitation. Food and freedom play no small role in healing. A healthy diet is important for recovery. Tons of food are delivered daily to satisfy the requirements of our herd. As we deplore the chain, all elephants have a fetter-free night shelter with water access and enrichments. An ongoing necessity is the purchase of additional lands each year to expand both space to roam and the potential to rescue others from their life of hardship.

Save Elephant Foundation promotes responsible, ethical, and sustainable forms of ecotourism. We sponsor people from around Asia, including Myanmar, Sri Lanka, Laos, India, and Indonesia, to visit our project, in order to understand our compassionate approach to elephant husbandry. Our Saddle Off program was born of a desire to provide more opportunities for tourists to encounter elephants responsibly. We mentor elephant camps to transition to an ethical model, which allows their elephants to enjoy natural behaviors such as walking, swimming, playing with each other, and reveling in mud. Our support to these projects includes microfinancing and building chain-free shelters. There are currently over forty trekking camps that have transitioned by taking the saddles off their elephants and offering visitors the opportunity to observe elephants behaving naturally and in many cases volunteer with them. Our work in Thailand is quite broad. We also have developing rescue operations in Cambodia, Laos, and Myanmar.

Our rescue work is not limited to elephants. Wherever there is need, we try to help. Many animals pass through our gates injured or abandoned, neglected or abused, and others bound for the slaughterhouse. Akin to Noah's ark, we have dogs, cats, horses, water buffalo, cows, goats, pigs, monkeys, bears, sheep, chickens, ducks, geese, rabbits, birds, and other animals. Our dog shelter fluctuates at five hundred residents, as does our cat community, and our adoption program has created a global pack that shares happy pictures with us from their new forever homes. Our fully equipped mobile clinic is always ready to provide free treatment to any animal regionally in need, and our small-animal clinic offers free treatment, sterilization, and vaccination services, helping to control overpopulation.

We offer two weekly volunteer programs at Elephant Nature Park, one with elephants and the other with our dogs. Elephant volunteers gain insight into the conservation work of Save Elephant Foundation, while getting their hands dirty in cleanup, food preparation and delivery, shelter enrichment, and other community activities. Volunteers play an important role as ambassadors for elephants by educating travelers about the harm and exploitation behind traditional elephant tourism and encouraging people to visit them at a reputable sanctuary, instead of riding them on a jungle trek. Dog volunteers learn about our shelter history and the dogs under our care, while being responsible for walking, feeding, cleaning, and socializing with dogs.

Supporting the local community is of great importance to Save Elephant Foundation. We focus on empowering Thai women from the nearby villages, providing them with work and an opportunity to become economically independent. Various jobs include animal caretakers, housemaids, gardeners, cooks and kitchen staff, guides, and more. We provide a space for local women to do Thai massage (100 percent of the funds go to them), and women also perform traditional Thai dance for our guests and volunteers. Older women from the community are invited to a welcoming ceremony for our volunteers, providing a blessing on their activity. Our own ENP Coffee uses farming partners who empower women as part of a self-sustaining community initiative, which revives the economy in local villages and supports Thailand's reforestation efforts. We also hire villagers to do community work, depending on the need, whether building small schools in remote rural areas, or public washrooms and meeting place facilities. We provide scholarships to students from hill tribe communities, and study supplies for local schools. We support local farmers by consistently purchasing elephant food, as well as food for our guests and volunteers.

Environmental Protection is a very important tenet of Save Elephant Foundation. Elephants and other wildlife have lost their native home due to human encroachment and activity. We work to preserve and protect forests by planting saplings in the rainy season, and we tie saffron sashes around trees in the dry season which helps to protect the forest from being cut down. We also provide education and funds to help manage the local environment more responsibly, including waste management, water usage, and forest fire controls. We protect the forests by promoting farming with ecologically sound methods of shade-grown crops.

I am asked why I rescue the old elephant. The images of suffering should speak for themselves, yet my answer is quite simple. It is about respect. To protect them is a high calling. By doing so, we also protect and strengthen our own hearts. The act of rescuing in many ways rescues ourselves, to preserve a fragile humanity. To see elephants work hard for decades, chained to the human yoke, disconnected from kinship, and finally falling down is a travesty in need of redress. All captive elephants are allotted this fate, while the wild pass before our eyes in the fury of greed and violence. We rescue in order to honor them, to offer a moment of respect in a tragic life. They are too old to carry on. We provide them a chance to live with a measure of freedom and dignity in the time they have left. We want them to have some happiness, to know rest and a gentle hand, and to encounter their own kind with deep meaning. They should not die during work, or shackled, or with torment and abuse hovering above their head.

The rescue of a solitary animal does not solve the overwhelming problems of the elephant and their survival. Those answers await our becoming a more responsible and self-aware species, who regard duty and the care of others as paramount to our own survival. Rescue is but a signpost bringing us back to ourselves. It also means everything to the one being rescued. Our direction is plain; our only agenda to foster awareness of the suffering giants, to provide love and care for them as best as we are able, and to invite others to join us in this march for their freedom.

It is important to dream, and best with eyes wide open. Without a vision, we waste away. To dream is to hope. To hope is to challenge; to challenge is to struggle, and then to achieve. Always follow the first steps to do what is necessary, and more opportunities will present themselves. What seems impossible at first in time becomes inevitable. The elephant has been driven to the edges of life. We must do all that we can to improve this remarkable creature's chances of survival.

Our Partners, the Animals: The Power of Personal Connection

Kathy Stevens, founder of Catskill Animal Sanctuary

Animals have always been in my DNA. I was incredibly privileged to grow up on a Virginia horse farm, where not only horses, but a donkey named Linda, goats Missy and Noodles, Babette the sheep, cows George and Ed, and too many dogs and cats to name punctuated my days—days that often included strolling around the farm with Noodles the goat and kissing horse noses along the way. Because of my upbringing, I've always known that, in the ways that truly matter, we're all the same. We all value our lives. We are all remarkably individual. We all have rich emotional lives, and our basic needs are identical. It's always been patently obvious to me that suffering feels no different to a pig, goat, cow, or chicken than it does to a dog or a person. I don't need to be inside a slaughterhouse to understand that if we animals share the same common emotions, then suffering, too, can be experienced by all of us.

I moved to Boston in my twenties, and after getting my graduate degree at Tufts, spent a decade as a high school English teacher. I absolutely loved the work of helping young people become better writers, speakers, and thinkers, but I secretly hoped that I also encouraged them to become better people: kinder, more courageous, more expansive, and more compassionate. Yet when I was offered the role of principal at a new charter high school, I turned it down, deciding to marry my passion for teaching and learning with my passion for animals.

That was nearly twenty years ago. Today, Catskill Animal Sanctuary, located in New York's beautiful Hudson Valley, has saved over five thousand animals through emergency rescue and exponentially more through innovative signature programming that encourages humanity in its journey to veganism. The animals come from places you'd expect—animal hoarders, the animal agriculture industry, abandonments, and cruelty cases—and those you wouldn't: a chicken found in a mailbox, two pigs tied to a post outside a pet store, boxes of rabbits left in dumpsters, a dying goat, a paper bag filled with rabbits left in our driveway, and so on. To participate in the healing of these broken spirits is a profound privilege. To be able to say each one as they arrive, "You are safe, you are loved, you matter" is the greatest joy of my life. Even better is watching in delight as they learn to trust, and become vital ambassadors for those who aren't as lucky.

Here's what I mean:

The first stop during weekend tours is our pig barn. Here, on my occasional "Break All the Rules" tours (as in, "I made the rules, but on this special tour we pretty much break all of them"), I lie down in the straw with my porcine friends and give my "individuals within any species are truly individuals" talk. I go on to tell stories that illustrate the differences between pigs Moses, Amelia, Mario, and others. There are lots of tears during moments like this, and lots of statements that begin with the words, "I had no idea." Some guests "have no idea" that mother pigs live in cells a couple of inches wider than their bodies; "no idea" that the pigs we eat are babies; and "no idea" that the emotional range of pigs mirrors that of humans! Guests either laugh in delight, or, overcome with emotion, weep as Jasmine the piglet rushes to me, climbs in my lap, and rests her head on my leg when I call her name. As I heard one farmer say, "pigs are people"—sanctuaries help us understand exactly what that means, and then help us sit with the implications.

After our time in the barn, we move outside, where I climb into an industry gestation crate just slightly wider and longer than the pigs who are trapped inside them for months. The crates are made of cold steel, and feces and urine fall through slatted metal floors into a vast pit below. Imagine the stench. It's rare that I need to ask whether our diet justifies this torture—it's obvious on guests' faces that they're asking themselves.

At the turkey barn, Michael and Daisy vie for who gets "lap time" with willing guests—like our pigs and our sheep, our cows and our chickens, turkeys do our work for us: there's little need to talk about how affectionate turkeys are when they clamor to be as close as possible to humans. They *crave* connection. Ditto about cows' emotional lives—we don't need to state the obvious when Tucker and Amos are bathing any willing guest with kisses. Many unsuspecting guests are caught off guard, like a man who rushed up to me after he'd completed a tour, tears streaming down his face, uttering, "I get it now. Please tell me what to do." Thanks to our openhearted and breathtakingly individual animals, sanctuaries are places where the moral imperative of veganism is made real.

It feels ironic that as the number of sanctuaries worldwide explodes, so, too, does criticism of sanctuaries by prominent players within the animal rights movement. This is largely due to the rising influence of a philosophy known as Effective Altruism, which urges people to give generously to charity, but also serves to ensure that their dollars are doing the greatest good. Sanctuaries are "too expensive," the EA folks argue, and they actually speculate about how many "go vegan" leaflets could be distributed for what it costs to care for a cow for life. If Effective Altruism weren't gaining traction, we could dismiss its objections as woefully misinformed and shortsighted, and their conclusions as biased—they admit never having actually evaluated the impact of a sanctuary. But EA is growing—and for sanctuary folks, that's concerning. With a plethora of animal causes vying for financial support and the bulk of that support going to dog and cat organizations, EA is the last thing that farm animal sanctuaries need.

Let's not kid ourselves: the movement to create a vegan world is the largest social change movement in history. It is also the most urgent, with our own survival on the line due to rapidly escalating climate change—a phenomenon driven largely by our consumption of meat and dairy. A brief look at the history of any social movement makes clear that success comes from a variety of approaches. To believe that we can usher in a vegan world without providing people the opportunity to know pigs and cows and chickens is like believing that the LGBTQ movement could have succeeded if none of us knew any gay people, or believing that the ASPCA could raise millions of dollars with their TV campaigns if none of us knew dogs and cats—if they were just an abstract concept. It seems so obvious that since one of the most compelling reasons for adopting veganism is the ethical one—the desire not to contribute to the suffering of other living beings—that the more we can provide people the opportunity to know those living beings, the stronger humanity's resolve will be. Further, let's not say that as we're marching toward our shared and glorious vision of a world free from suffering, that it's okay to sacrifice *those we could save* in order to produce more leaflets. Substitute puppies, kittens, or kids here, and see how this sits with you. Individual lives matter. Period.

Effective Altruism is right about one thing: it is expensive to care for a cow. But what if that cow meets ten thousand visitors each season? When people sit in the grass with our gentle giant Tucker, (2,500 pounds of love and a dairy industry survivor), stroking his neck and accepting kisses from his scratchy tongue, hearts open and epiphanies occur: *so this is who they are.* In that same visit, guests learn from engaging guides about the horrors of the dairy industry, sample vegan food at taste testings, and, with their understanding deepened and their hearts wide open, they can sign up to work with a vegan mentor for free. I don't know of another animal rights initiative that's so . . . complete.

Some sanctuaries rescue and care for animals and are closed to the public. Others offer tours but no other programming. With the breadth and depth of Catskill's educational offerings—a free mentor program currently used by aspiring vegans from thirty countries around the world, a wide variety of tours, a children's leadership camp, school presentations, a robust cooking program, and *All Beings Considered,* a weekly podcast, we are a model for supporting tens of thousands of people or more annually in their vegan journey—and for keeping them vegan once they make that commitment.

Sanctuaries will carry on with the animals as our partners. After all, we've got a vegan world to make and precious little time to make it. At Catskill Animal Sanctuary, post-tour surveys indicate that 93 percent of our non-vegan visitors "intend to reduce or eliminate animal products from their diet." Follow-up surveys done six months after their tour indicate that 92 percent of that group succeeds in eliminating or reducing animal products. As passionate and informed as our tour guides are, it's the animals themselves who are the vegan-makers. In our shared quest to usher in the beautiful vegan world we dream about, let's remember that.

Nonstop Loving:
An Ode to Activists

Sean Hill, award-winning multidisciplinary
artist and humanitarian

Everybody
wants to change the world
but nobody
wants to change

Tolstoy told us that

The definition of activist
consists of a single person's efforts
to promote, impede, direct, or intervene
in social, political, economic
or environmental reform
in order to change
the norms
of society

Whether or not you call yourself activist
thank you for being someone
who is
willing
to
change

to jump inside yourself
rearrange beliefs
like a living room set

I bet it isn't easy
to be so overwhelmed
with compassion and empathy
willing to sacrifice
peace of mind
and your own freedom
to help our fellow animals
see what free feels like
so we can coexist beautifully

Look at all you do:
factory farm and slaughterhouse rescues
cubes of truth to protests to demos
holding signs and chanting
marches of
silence
bearing witness
cow, chicken, and pig vigils
handing out pamphlets like candles
helping people handle the light
so awareness can shine
on their fears inside

When we see our past struggles
in another's eyes
it keeps our patience compassionately alive
to handle the criticism
we confront
for simply living
a lifestyle
where we respect life
so much

that we still connect to it
when it's someone
dead on a plate
not meat, but the body
of a fellow earthling
being tortured
right here and now
not in a galaxy far, far away
but on our tables

As activists
we do our best to check
our egos
to never laugh
at people's ignorance
their banishment of knowledge
or abandonment of perspective

It's hard to travel
with excess baggage
feeling
the weight
of the world daily
knowing
that if
humans
killed each other
at the same rate
we kill
other animals
we would be extinct
in
seventeen
days

We forget
we are all
the thirty septillion atoms
composing
the same heart
no more forgetting
we're letting
our hearts beat for each other
right
NOW

Beliefs
don't makes us
better people
actions do

You put yourself on the line
so many times
maybe no one
has put themselves out
for you
who are so phenomenal at existing
deserving a fiery, friendly reminder
to treat yourself
as good as a friend would

This is a proclamation of gratitude
for all of you

THIS is for
YOU

who chooses
compassion
over convenience

every single day
you never knew
you'd take in the hardest truths
of our identical connection to animals
then reflect those truths to others

It seems an impossible task
to bring awareness
and love to a world
which thinks it already has it
empathy awakens
when we believe in each other
and listen like a key
to an unlocked door

Take a breath
feel the ease seeping in
from history
of what we have accomplished so far

Ever since Jainism, Taoism
Hinduism, Buddhism, and Animism
a thousand years ago plus
before Socrates and Pythagoras
up to Coretta Scott King
and our current understanding
of speciesism
we have been uprooting
for so long

As alone as you may feel sometimes
you are never alone
we are all in this together
the vision to transform the world,
elevate everyone's innate potential
by teaching sacred respect for all life forms

We are committed
to making this world free
of exploitation
a world filled
with compassion
an everlasting persistence
to pursue justice
and heighten
our collective empathy
to live in harmony
with every animal
and our Earth
who just
doesn't stop giving
to us
so why would we
ever stop giving
to her . . . ?

Thank you
to every
nonstop loving
activist
who believes
in themselves
believes
in each other
and believes
in changing
yourselves
to change
the world

CLOSING

Since I started this anthology in June 2018, there have been many victories for animals, proving that the animal rights movement is gaining significant traction. Unfortunately for the trillions of suffering animals, the tragedies still outweigh the victories, yet with respect to the myriad forms of activism, we are moving closer toward the tipping point.

There are hardly enough words to describe the impact that animal rights activism has had on me. It is such an integral part of the core of my being—the essence of who I am. Being an activist has enriched my life in immeasurable ways, some of which are clearly defined and some of which are in the process of being revealed. It is an evolving, unfolding journey as I learn how to become a more effective activist through integrating different ideas and approaches, learning from challenges that arise, and opening myself to new experiences.

In the spring of 2019, I went on my first middle-of-the-night investigation with two fellow activists at a calf farm. This type of farm is where baby cows are raised before being sent to slaughter for veal (if they are male) or transferred to dairy farms (if they are female). Our goal for this clandestine venture was to document the conditions of the animals in order to gather evidence to expose a dairy company and its affiliates.

It was surreal to leave the farm and drive back into reality—passing fast-food restaurants and grocery stores that sell dairy—after having witnessed firsthand the true picture of dairy. The next day I felt empty as I went about my routine, my mind fixed on the many rows of agitated babies who I had seen, as well as the pile of calves who had died during their entrapment on the farm before they could be sent off for their intended purposes. The fact that babies are taken from their mothers and isolated in hutches so small they can't turn around in order to produce cheese and ice cream is disturbing beyond words. When I see someone excited over pizza or ice cream, I think of the calves stuck in those hutches, peering out with wide eyes, and the long low moaning reverberating across the farm. It is visuals like these that haunt me and anger me, yet also ignite my activism to greater heights.

Putting this book together has been inspiring, challenging, and incredibly rewarding. I am ever grateful to my contributors, who worked diligently on their pieces, were open to my feedback for revision, and trusted my editing. I am deeply moved by their powerful narratives. Each contributor has brought something unique and individual to the pages of this book, driven by various backgrounds, perspectives, and approaches, while existing as part of the shared vision of a world free of exploitation for all beings. Until the voices of nonhumans are heard, we will raise ours—through education, outreach, campaigns, demonstrations, protests, marches, civil disobedience actions, bearing witness, rescue, and so on, with the goals of dismantling speciesism and achieving liberation.

This collection encompasses many experiences and perspectives, yet it only scratches the surface of the spectrum of stories within the animal rights movement—there is certainly a vast array of narratives out there, from all corners of the globe. My hope is that the words within these pages will open hearts and minds toward a world that does not view animals as products or commodities, but a world that views them as individuals who are worthy of respect and justice. I see that world on the horizon, every day, as I witness the dedication in the movement, the bold actions taking place, and the risks that activists are willing to face. I see that world emerging in the conversations I have

VOICES

FOR

ANIMAL

LIBERATION

INSPIRATIONAL
ACCOUNTS BY ANIMAL
RIGHTS ACTIVISTS

BRITTANY MICHELSON
FOREWORD BY INGRID NEWKIRK

Skyhorse Publishing

Skyhorse Publishing books may be purchased in bulk at special discounts for
sales promotion, corporate gifts, fund-raising, or educational purposes. Special
editions can also be created to specifications. For details, contact the Special Sales
Department, Skyhorse Publishing, 307 West 36th Street, 11th Floor, New York,
NY 10018 or info@skyhorsepublishing.com.

Skyhorse® and Skyhorse Publishing® are registered trademarks of Skyhorse
Publishing, Inc.®, a Delaware corporation.

Visit our website at www.skyhorsepublishing.com.

10 9 8 7 6 5 4 3 2 1

Library of Congress Cataloging-in-Publication Data is available on file.

Cover design by Daniel Brount
Cover illustrations by Corey J. Rowland

Print ISBN: 978-1-5107-5126-2
Ebook ISBN: 978-1-5107-5128-6

Printed in China

*This book is dedicated to all of the exploited animals,
whose liberation is my greatest dream, and to the humans
who are working hard to make this dream a reality.*

TABLE OF CONTENTS

Foreword
Ingrid Newkirk, founder and president of PETA
xi

Introduction
xv

I. Seasoned Warriors: Inspiring & Transforming
1

How I Became a "Poultry" Rights Activist Who Started
an Organization Some Said Would Never Fly
Karen Davis, founder of United Poultry Concerns
3

Documenting Invisible Animals: Photography
as a Tool for Change
Jo-Anne McArthur, photographer and founder of We Animals Media
12

The Spectrum of Life: Not the Same but Equal
Shaun Monson, documentary filmmaker
18

Ending Bear Bile Farming: A Clarion Call
Jill Robinson, founder and CEO of Animals Asia
26

Liberating Animals and Ourselves
Will Tuttle, visionary author and speaker
32

II. Connecting the Dots: Perspectives on Animal Rights
41

Copy-and-Paste Activism Does Not Work: Perspectives from a POC
Gwenna Hunter, event coordinator for Vegan Outreach
and founder of Vegans of LA
43

Living in Alignment with My Values: My Path
to Animal Rights Activism
Brittany Michelson, teacher and writer
51

How I Made the Connection: Gay Rights,
Feminism, and Animal Liberation
Dani Rukin, citizen journalist for *JaneUnchained News*
62

The Girl I Finally Let In: How Personal Narrative Sets the
Stage for Powerful Animal Rights Activism
Jasmin Singer, cofounder of Our Hen House and Senior
Features Editor for *VegNews*
71

The Evolution: From Animal-Loving Child to Intersectional
Vegan Activist
Gillian Meghan Walters, founder of *Animal Voices Vancouver*
79

III. Overcoming Personal Challenge: Opening the Door to Activism
89

Through Empathic Eyes: A Survivor's Story
Jasmine Afshar, army veteran
91

From Addiction to Healing to Activism: An Olympic
Medalist's Journey
Dotsie Bausch, Olympic medalist and founder of Switch4Good
100

Giving My Struggle Purpose:
Overcoming Depression through Animal Advocacy
Matthew Braun, former investigator of farms and slaughterhouses
106

Activism as a Fast Track to Growth: My Spiritual Awakening
Zafir Molina, truth seeker and movement artist
114

How Veganism Transformed My Relationship with Food
Alexandra Paul, actress and cohost of *Switch4Good*
120

IV. Campaigns & Outreach: Anchors of Change
127

How to Speak about Animal Rights: What I Learned
from Working in Corporate Sales
Alex Bez, founder and director of Amazing Vegan Outreach
129

Lost Souls: Fighting the Harms of Animal
Experimentation and beyond
Cory Mac a'Ghobhainn, organizer with Progress for Science
139

The Least We Can Do: Communicating the Animal Rights Message
Natasha & Luca, "That Vegan Couple," social media influencers
150

Saving Joe and Legal Wins for Captive Animals
Brittany Peet, Director of Captive Animal Law Enforcement for PETA
157

V. Bearing Witness, Civil Disobedience &
Open Rescue: A Movement Rising
167

The Power of Protest: Learning from Nonviolent
Social Justice Movements
Chase Avior, actor and filmmaker
169

Bearing Witness to Babies before and after Motherhood
Amy Jean Davis, founder of Los Angeles Animal Save
178

Turning Repression into Liberation
Wayne Hsiung, cofounder of Direct Action Everywhere (DxE)
182

The Power and Duty of Bearing Witness
Anita Krajnc, founder of the Save Movement
187

The Urgency of Animal Liberation: A Teenage Activist's Perspective
Zoe Rosenberg, founder of Happy Hen Animal Sanctuary
198

VI. The Sanctuary Life: To Heaven from Hell
209

Farm Sanctuaries: Healing Animals, the Planet, and Ourselves
Gene Baur, founder of Farm Sanctuary
211

In the Steps of Giants: Saving Elephants in Southeast Asia
Saengduean Lek Chailert, founder of Save Elephant Foundation
217

Our Partners, the Animals: The Power of Personal Connection
Kathy Stevens, founder of Catskill Animal Sanctuary
222

Nonstop Loving: An Ode to Activists
Sean Hill, award-winning multidisciplinary artist and humanitarian
227

Closing
235

About the Author
239

About the Contributors
241

Acknowledgments
253

Resources
255

Index
261

©Jo-Anne McArthur

FOREWORD

If you are wondering whether to read this book, it must mean you are curious about animal liberation: You aren't exactly sure what it means, perhaps, or you are moved by the plight of animals and wish to explore further. I'm certain you will find a lot in here that will impact and motivate you, such as the reasons why those of us who advocate for animals' rights see the link to other movements as absolute and undeniable. For anyone who is already an activist or who has decided to become one, you are sure to find inspiration, thoughts that might not have occurred to you before, ideas that you can adopt or adapt, and words to cherish.

Brittany Michelson has collected a splendid set of narratives from people who, for myriad reasons, found themselves, often unexpectedly, embracing the idea of animal liberation. It dawned on each of them at some point in their lives that the concept of injustice couldn't rightly, logically, or reasonably be limited to the human animal. They realized that injustice occurs when we fail to connect the dots between ourselves and those who were not born in exactly the same physical form as ours.

The writers' ethical evolutions often began with a question. Alexandra Paul found herself wondering at the "absurdity" of ranking kittens over hamsters, and hamsters over frogs, and asked herself why this was any different from assigning degrees of value to human beings who are often considered "lower on the societal rung."

Brittany Peet loved "Smokey," a bear she often visited at a roadside zoo as a child. Later, she pondered how, back then, she could have been so oblivious to his loneliness and the desolation of his confinement to a barren cage. Jasmine Afshar questioned how people could empathize with the torment she experienced when she was sexually violated, yet dismiss the torment inherent in the routine assault of female animals whose bodies are exploited for meat and milk. Dani Rukin "came out" for animals, casting aside her leather jacket, long after coming out as a lesbian because, after initially mocking vegans, she began to wonder how diversity could rightly be limited to a single species.

Sometimes the animals themselves asked the questions, simply by being present or with an expression. Karen Davis's beloved parrot, Jasmin Singer's waifish cat, the monkey spotted by Jo-Anne McArthur chained to a windowsill high in the Andes—all seemed to nudge them in the direction of animal liberation. Was it recognizing the universal look of despair or hope or sadness in the face of a desperately thirsty pig, seen through the metal slats of a truck in the blistering heat, that changed Anita Krajnc's life? Or was that suffering pig, one among many, who was about to pass through the slaughterhouse gates, someone—and I mean some*one*—she already understood? After all, she was trying to live, and teach her students to live, as Tolstoy advised: "When the suffering of another creature causes you to feel pain, do not submit to the initial desire to flee from the suffering one, but on the contrary, come closer, as close as you can to he who suffers, and try to help him." Anita was charged with criminal mischief for rushing to that pig and offering water, but from her compassionate action, many others came to see that animal liberation is something to work for.

Some writers, like Kathy Stevens and Gene Baur, started sanctuaries, taking in animals with nowhere else to find safety and comfort. Wayne Hsiung left his legal career to start a group that challenges the lack of legal protections for other-than-human beings. Shaun Monson became a filmmaker, whose epic film *Earthlings* has opened more eyes and minds and hearts to the reality of animal exploitation than perhaps any other.

At the end of this book, the individual writers' experiences seem to be summed up in a verse from Sean Hill's poem:

> As alone as you may feel sometimes
> you are never alone
> we are all in this together
> the vision to transform the world,
> elevate everyone's innate potential
> by teaching sacred respect for all life forms

Please read this book. Pass it on to others. And take its lessons to heart, because the Golden Rule requires each of us to do unto others as we would have them do unto us. And that is the message of animal liberation.

Ingrid Newkirk
founder and president of PETA

INTRODUCTION

Animal rights: the rights of animals, claimed on ethical grounds, to the same humane treatment and protection from exploitation and abuse that are accorded to humans

Activism: the use of direct and noticeable action to achieve a result, usually a political or social one

> "Animal rights are not a gift we give to animals. They are a birthright we have taken from them."
>
> —Ryan Phillips

> "Animals have qualities we find important to the legal rights of humans—like self-awareness, the need for sovereignty, and the capacity for suffering, love, and empathy. We will never fully dismantle the injustices humans suffer without deconstructing the same problems that lead to animal suffering."
>
> —Marc Bekoff

As an animal rights activist, it is common to hear remarks such as:

"What about human rights?"
"Don't you care about humans?"
"There are so many human problems in the world; let's solve those first."

There's a widespread view that our own issues should be solved before animal issues are addressed, as if we need to demonstrate loyalty to our own species before advocating on behalf of others. This promotes the ideology of human superiority and reinforces a disconnect between humans and nonhumans. What we should be acknowledging is our interconnectedness: the fact that all beings have the capacity for love, joy, pain, and fear. Animal rights and human rights are inextricably connected. For example, there are multiple human and environmental issues that stem from animal issues. If we want to create a peaceful world, we must pay close attention to the ways in which human and nonhuman issues are related and honor the interdependence between our species and others.

Societal conditioning has taught us that certain animals are to love and other animals are to eat, wear, and use. Speciesism is the assumption of human superiority and involves the designation of values or special consideration solely on the basis of species classification. Speciesism is what underlies the notion that a dog is a beloved member of the family, while the purpose of a chicken is to be eaten. Civil rights, women's rights, gay rights, and other social justice causes have people who fight for their own rights, the rights of their loved ones, and those of their fellow citizens. Human rights movements operate from the ability of humans to use words and actions to stand up for their cause. The animal rights movement is the sole exception: nonhuman beings do not have the benefit of being able to speak for themselves or organize a protest, although they do resist being harmed, as is evident by their struggle, their vocalizations, and their attempts at escape. These are their forms of protest. Yet animals are disregarded because of their inability to communicate in our language, with my young students who are curious about the activism I do and my passion for animal rights.

Let us create a planet where individuals are not assigned value according to whether they have fur, feathers, shells, or scales; whether they bark, moo, chirp, or hiss; or whether they run, fly, hop, or slither— but a planet where all living beings are valued regardless of appearance or behavior. May each individual be acknowledged for the ability to feel fear and joy, the capacity to suffer, and the capability to love. In this we all are the same.

ABOUT THE AUTHOR

Brittany Michelson was born in San Diego, California, and moved to Arizona when she was thirteen. She attended Northern Arizona University and studied abroad for a semester in Costa Rica, completing a bachelor's degree in secondary English education with a Spanish minor. After college, Brittany taught high school English for two years in Arizona and English as a Second Language in Ecuador for six months. While there, she volunteered as a dog walker at a no-kill shelter that took in street dogs and cats. After teaching abroad, she moved to Los Angeles, where she completed a master of fine arts program in creative writing with a focus in creative nonfiction.

©Natalie Ford Photography

Brittany's writing has been published in *PoemMemoirStory* magazine, *Bartleby Snopes* literary magazine, Role Reboot, *Tahoe Blues: Short Lit on Life at the Lake*, *Split Lip* magazine, *The Recovering Self: A Journal of Hope & Healing*, Jaded Ibis Press, and others. Her awareness-raising pieces on animal issues are published in *Elephant Journal*.

Brittany's teaching experience is varied, including previous private homeschool teaching and tutoring work. She currently teaches writing and activism-related classes at The REALM Creative Academy, a private K–8 program, and summer writing classes at Marlborough School in Los Angeles.

In early 2016, Brittany volunteered as a Cove Monitor with Dolphin Project, documenting the dolphin hunts in Taiji, Japan. From there, she volunteered at Elephant

Volunteering at Elephant Nature Park sanctuary

Nature Park (ENP), a sanctuary in Thailand that rescues elephants and other animals. She returned to volunteer at ENP in August 2018, the second week spent in a jungle program called Journey to Freedom.

Brittany's passions include animal rights activism, teaching, international travel, being in nature and hiking, literature, writing, and spending time with animals. She has a rescue dog and three rescue tortoises and plans to adopt more animals, as she dreams of having an animal sanctuary one day. She lives in the Los Angeles area of Topanga Canyon.

ABOUT THE CONTRIBUTORS

Jasmine Afshar served in the army and developed multiple illnesses from her grueling time in service, allowing her to reexperience the world through empathic eyes. She began visiting sites of exploitation to document moments of raw emo-

tion expressed by sentient beings. Since then she has devoted herself to her community in Phoenix, Arizona, engaging in various actions for animals.

Chase Avior found his calling in animal rights activism and dedicates the vast majority of his time to it. His work includes creating motivating animal rights videos, organizing protests and outreach events, making music, writing speeches, and training activists. He is currently based in Berkeley, California.

"Protesting draws attention to the issue, communicates the severity of the problem, and empowers people to take collective action."
- Chase Avior

Gene Baur has been hailed as "the conscience of the food movement" by *Time* magazine and has campaigned to end factory farming abuses since 1985. His undercover images have aired internationally, and his rescue work inspired a global farm sanctuary movement. Gene led efforts to pass the first US laws banning factory farm cruelties and continues advocating for food system reforms. He is the author of two bestselling books and was named one of Oprah Winfrey's SuperSoul 100 Givers.

Dotsie Bausch is an Olympic medalist, speaker, and founder of Switch4Good, a health- and performance-focused nonprofit that encourages a dairy-free lifestyle. She had a fourteen-year professional cycling career concluding with a silver medal at the 2012 Olympics. She stars in the 2018 film *The Game Changers*, is featured in the Netflix documentary *Personal Gold*, and gave a TEDx Talk.

Alex Bez is the founder and director of the nonprofit organization Amazing Vegan Outreach. He leverages his background in corporate sales, coaching, public speaking, and adult learning in order to train activists to be highly effective advocates for nonhuman animals. Alex lives in Toronto, Canada, and travels widely to present AVO workshops and engage in other forms of activism.

Matthew Braun is a former investigator of farms and slaughterhouses and has been vegan since 2006, but regretfully didn't call himself an activist until 2013. Since then he has made it a point to try every type of activism at least once, even if it is outside of his comfort zone. He's originally from Schenectady, New York and currently resides in Los Angeles, California.

Saengduean Lek Chailert, founder of Save Elephant Foundation in Thailand, is internationally recognized for her elephant conservation and rescue work and has been featured in documentaries produced by National Geographic, Discovery, Animal Planet, and the BBC. In 2010, she was honored as one of six Women Heroes of Global Conservation by Hillary Rodham Clinton, and, in 2005, she was named one of *Time* magazine's Heroes of Asia. The documentary *Vanishing Giants*, which highlights Lek's work, was recognized by The Humane Society of the United States's Genesis Award in 2003. In 2001, she received the Ford Foundation's "Hero of the Planet."

Amy Jean Davis came to Los Angeles in 2008 as a top-24 Finalist on American Idol. She's cofounder of the animal sanctuary Love Always. In 2016, she started Los Angeles Animal Save, part of the global Save Movement. She also works for Nation Earth, the production company behind the documentaries *Earthlings* and *Unity*, with filmmaker and partner Shaun Monson.

Karen Davis is the president and founder of United Poultry Concerns, a nonprofit organization that promotes the compassionate and respectful treatment of domestic fowl, including a sanctuary for chickens in Virginia. Inducted into the National Animal Rights Hall of Fame for Outstanding Contributions to Animal Liberation, she is the author of *Prisoned Chickens, Poisoned Eggs: An Inside Look at the Modern Poultry Industry*; *More Than a Meal: The*

Turkey in History, Myth, Ritual, and Reality; *The Holocaust and the Henmaid's Tale*; and *For the Birds: From Exploitation to Liberation*.

Sean Hill is an award-winning multidisciplinary artist and humanitarian with the focus of supporting universal inner and outer peace in a realistic and passionate way. He helped build two gender-equal schools in Malawi and Nepal. As a SAG actor, host, speaker, and workshop facilitator, he has shared stages with Oscar winners, Grammy winners, and youth home children.

Wayne Hsiung is cofounder of the animal rights network Direct Action Everywhere (DxE). Prior to founding DxE, Wayne was an attorney and visiting assistant professor at the Northwestern University School of Law and a National Science Foundation Graduate Fellow at MIT. His father did work involving vivisection for several years, which had a lasting impact on Wayne and motivated him to become an animal rights activist.

Gwenna Hunter was raised in Cleveland, Ohio, and now resides in Los Angeles, California. As the event coordinator for Vegan Outreach and the founder of Vegans of LA, Gwenna enjoys bringing people together for social functions designed for networking and mingling and creating a space for people to experience new and delicious vegan foods.

Anita Krajnc is the founder of the Save Movement, which started in late 2010 with Toronto Pig Save. She holds a PhD in political science and applies Tolstoyan and Gandhian strategies of bearing witness, nonviolent direct action, and love-based community organizing to animal rights and climate actions.

Cory Mac a'Ghobhainn is an artist and a former ESL teacher, author, and editor, who has lived in various cities in the United States, as well as Germany and Iran as a child and Mexico as an adult. She is an organizer with several activist groups, but works primarily with Progress for Science, an anti-vivisection organization. She currently lives in Los Angeles, California.

Jo-Anne McArthur, photographer and the founder of We Animals Media, has been documenting our complex relationship with animals in almost sixty countries for over fifteen years. She was the subject of the acclaimed documentary *The Ghosts in Our Machine* and is the author of two books, *We Animals*

and *Captive*, as well as the cofounder of The Unbound Project, which celebrates women animal advocates worldwide. Her work has been used by hundreds of organizations, media, and academics. Toronto, Canada, is her home.

Zafir Molina was born in La Paz, Bolivia, and moved to California at the age of four. Drawn to psychology, justice, the arts, and working with youth, she started a dance organization in 2015 that focuses on raising awareness through the art of movement. She is dedicated to continuously seeking personal growth in order to help bring peace to humanity, animals, and the Earth.

Shaun Monson is the writer/ director of the documentaries *Earthlings* (2005), and *Unity* (2015) and coproducer of *Dominion* (2018). His first film, narrated by Academy Award Nominee Joaquin Phoenix, is available in over forty languages. His follow-up film, *Unity,* features a cast of one hundred celebrity narrators, including twelve Oscar winners, and is available in more than two hundred countries and a dozen languages. Produced under his production company, Nation Earth, Shaun's films carry a similar theme, "Not the same but equal."

Ingrid E. Newkirk is the president and founder of People for the Ethical Treatment of Animals (PETA)—the largest animal rights organization in the world, with more than 6.5 million members and supporters worldwide. Newkirk—who was recently profiled by the *Los Angeles Times* and is the subject of the HBO documentary *I Am an Animal*—founded PETA in 1980, when no one knew what a vegan was. She started a movement that has changed society's attitudes toward animals and has won a tidal wave of landmark victories, including the end of car-crash tests on animals, the closure of Ringling Bros.

and Barnum & Bailey Circus after 146 years, fur-free policies enacted by almost every major designer, and bans on animal testing by nearly four thousand personal-care product companies.

Natasha & Luca, "That Vegan Couple" are social media influencers from Australia who have over twenty-five million views on their YouTube channel and millions more across social media. They create educational and entertaining video content to help people transition to veganism and empower vegans to become activists. They also host a podcast show

that covers a variety of vegan topics, organize international activism tours (including workshops and events), and have been invited as speakers at international animal rights events and conferences.

Alexandra Paul is an actress who has appeared in more than one hundred films and TV shows. She is best known for starring as Lt. Stephanie Holden on the television series *Baywatch*. She is a certified health coach and cohosts the *Switch4Good* podcast about plant-based living. She resides in Los Angeles.

Brittany Peet is the Director of Captive Animal Law Enforcement for the PETA Foundation. She works on behalf of animals who are held captive in roadside zoos, traveling shows, and the film and television industries through legal and regulatory actions, and public advocacy campaigns. She also negotiates and coordinates wild and exotic animal rescues.

Jill Robinson is founder and CEO of Animals Asia. She divides her time between mainland China, Vietnam, and Hong Kong, and travels frequently around the world to give presentations at conferences and fundraising events. Born in the UK, Jill is the recipient of an MBE from Queen Elizabeth II of Great Britain, the Reader's Digest "Hero for Today" award, The Humane Society of the United States's Genesis Award, and an honorary doctorate from the University of Zurich, Switzerland.

Zoe Rosenberg, a dedicated teenage animal rights activist, founded Happy Hen Animal Sanctuary at age eleven, which has now saved more than eight hundred lives. Zoe is the social media coordinator for Direct Action Everywhere, and she travels the country speaking on the importance of taking action for animals.

Dani Rukin is an active member of the Save Movement and Anonymous for the Voiceless, an organizer for Direct Action Everywhere in Portland, Oregon, and founding coorganizer of Compassionate PDX, a grassroots fur ban campaign. She's also a citizen journalist for digital media outlet *JaneUnChained News*.

Jasmin Singer is the author of the memoir *Always Too Much and Never Enough* (Berkley, 2016), cohost of the *Our Hen House* podcast, Senior Features Editor for *VegNews*, and Media Director for Switch4Good. She presented the

TEDx Talk "Compassion Unlocks Identity" and is featured in the documentaries *Vegucated* and *Ghosts in Our Machine*. Her new book about going vegan will be released by Da Capo in 2020.

Kathy Stevens is the founder of Catskill Animal Sanctuary, one of the world's leading sanctuaries for farmed animals. She is the author of *Where the Blind Horse Sings* and *Animal Camp*, a former *Huffington Post* blogger, and the host of *All Beings Considered*, a weekly podcast featuring prominent thought leaders and everyday people working to change the world for animals.

Dr. Will Tuttle, visionary author of the acclaimed bestseller *The World Peace Diet*, published in sixteen languages, is a recipient of the Courage of Conscience Award and the Empty Cages Prize. He is also the author of several other books on spirituality, intuition, and social justice, as well as the creator of online wellness and advocacy programs. A vegan since 1980 and former Zen monk, he is featured in a number of documentaries and is a frequent radio, television, and online presenter.

Gillian Meghan Walters is a registered clinical counselor with an MA degree in Counseling Psychology. She is the founder of radio show *Animal Voices Vancouver*, cofounder of *BC Vegan Magazine*, and the author and illustrator of two children's books: *King Zoom and the Great Seal Pup Rescue* (2015), and *King Zoom the Vegan Kid: Animals Used for Food* (2018). She writes about the intersections between animal and human oppression and the psychology of veganism. In 2019, she launched *MummyMOO*, a photography blog.